HARCOURT

Math

NORTH CAROLINA EDITION

Orlando   Austin   Chicago   New York   Toronto   London   San Diego

Visit *The Learning Site!*
www.harcourtschool.com

For permission to reprint copyrighted material, grateful acknowledgment is made to the following sources:

Candlewick Press Inc., Cambridge, MA: Cover illustration by Nick Sharratt from *Isn't It Time?* by Judy Hindley. Illustration copyright © 1994 by Nick Sharratt. Cover illustration by Cynthia Jabar from *How Many, How Many, How Many* by Rick Walton. Illustration copyright © 1993 by Cynthia Jabar.

Harcourt, Inc.: Cover illustration from *The Great Kapok Tree: A Tale of the Amazon Rain Forest* by Lynne Cherry. Copyright © 1990 by Lynne Cherry. Cover illustration from *Pancakes for Breakfast* by Tomie dePaola. Copyright © 1978 by Tomie dePaola. Cover illustration from *Fish Eyes* by Lois Ehlert. Copyright © 1990 by Lois Ehlert. Cover illustration by Pamela Lofts from *Koala Lou* by Mem Fox. Illustration copyright © 1988 by Pamela Lofts.

Philomel Books, an imprint of Penguin Books for Young Readers, a division of Penguin Putnam Inc.: Cover illustration from *The Very Busy Spider* by Eric Carle. Copyright © 1984 by The Eric Carle Corporation.

Printed in the United States of America

ISBN 0-15-336605-2

1 2 3 4 5 6 7 8 9 10 030 10 09 08 07 06 05 04 03

Senior Author

Evan M. Maletsky
Professor of Mathematics
Montclair State University
Upper Montclair, New Jersey

Authors

Angela Giglio Andrews
Math Teacher, Scott School
Naperville District #203
Naperville, Illinois

Jennie M. Bennett
Instructional Mathematics Supervisor
Houston Independent School District
Houston, Texas

Grace M. Burton
Professor, Watson School of Education
University of North Carolina at
Wilmington
Wilmington, North Carolina

Lynda A. Luckie
Administrator/Math Specialist
Gwinnett County Public Schools
Lawrenceville, Georgia

Joyce C. McLeod
Visiting Professor
Rollins College
Winter Park, Florida

Vicki Newman
Classroom Teacher
McGaugh Elementary School
Los Alamitos Unified School District
Seal Beach, California

Tom Roby
Associate Professor of Mathematics
California State University
Hayward, California

Janet K. Scheer
Executive Director
Create A Vision
Foster City, California

Program Consultants and Specialists

Janet S. Abbott
Mathematics Consultant
California

Elsie Babcock
*Director, Mathematics and
 Science Center
Mathematics Consultant*
Wayne Regional
Educational Service
Agency
Wayne, Michigan

William J. Driscoll
Professor of Mathematics
Department of
Mathematical Sciences
Central Connecticut State
University
New Britain, Connecticut

Lois Harrison-Jones
*Education and
 Management Consultant*
Dallas, Texas

Rebecca Valbuena
*Language Development
 Specialist*
Stanton Elementary School
Glendora, California

ADDITION AND SUBTRACTION CONCEPTS

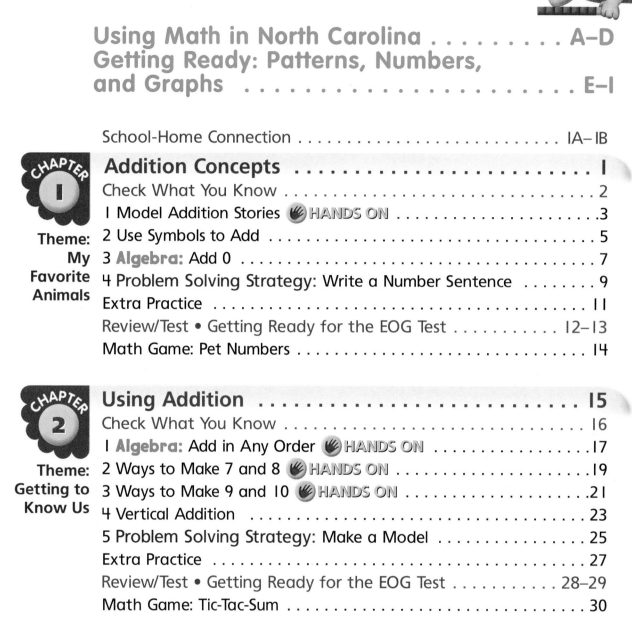

Unit 2

ADDITION AND SUBTRACTION FACTS TO 10

Unit 3

GRAPHS, NUMBERS TO 100, AND FACTS TO 12

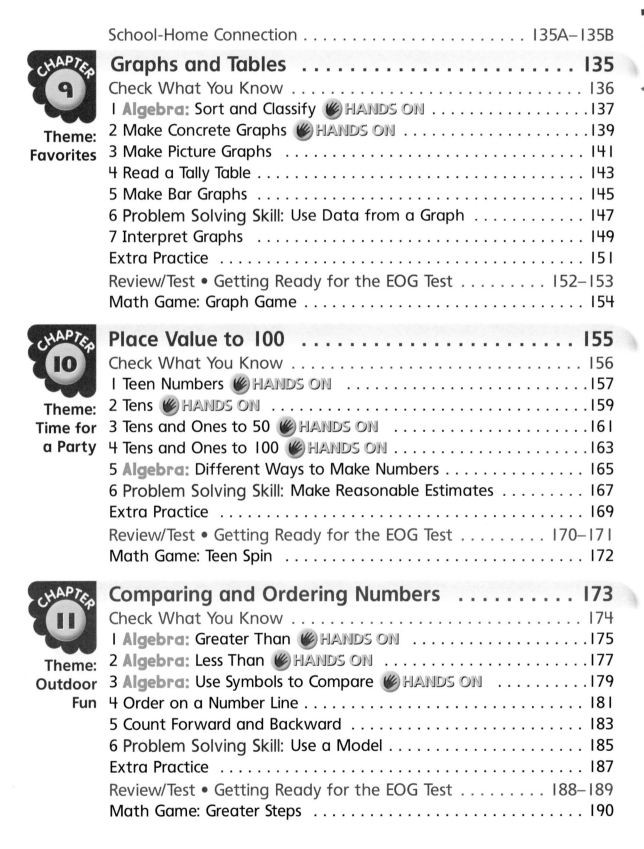

Unit 4

GEOMETRY AND ADDITION AND SUBTRACTION TO 20

Unit 5

MONEY, TIME, AND FRACTIONS

Unit Wrap Up

Unit 6

MEASUREMENT, OPERATIONS, AND DATA

Unit Wrap Up

Using Math in North Carolina

Look at each picture.
Decide what math skill is being used.

Explain It What are some things you do to use math?

Practice What You Learn

IT'S IN THE BAG

PROJECT You will make a math facts vest.

You Will Need

- Large brown bag
- Pattern tracer
- Scissors
- Construction paper
- Glue
- Tape
- Crayons

Directions

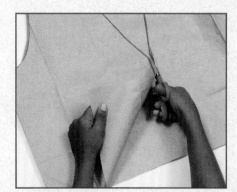

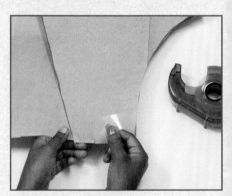

1. Pop out the sides of the bag. Lay the bag flat.

2. Trace the vest pattern 2 times, once on each side of the bag.

3. Trace two arm holes. Cut out two arm holes from two layers of the bag.

4. Cut the vest front from only the top layer of the bag.

5. Tape the front of the bag to the back of the bag. Make pockets. Use construction paper.

C

Test What You Learn

Fill in the checklist to show what you will do when you take a test.

I will:

- listen carefully.
- read carefully.
- follow directions.
- mark answers carefully.
- begin where told.
- begin when told.
- pay attention only to the teacher and the test.
- do the best I can.

_____

Name

1. Color the triangles red.
   Color the squares and rectangles blue.
   Color the circles yellow.

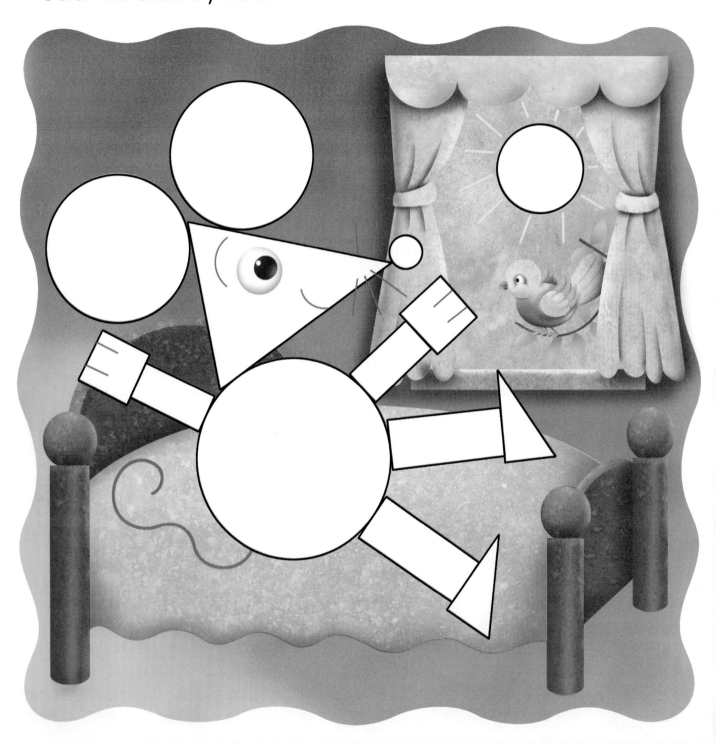

_____

2. Draw what comes next in this pattern.

_____

E

I. Draw 1 sock for each shoe.

Count the objects. Write the numbers.

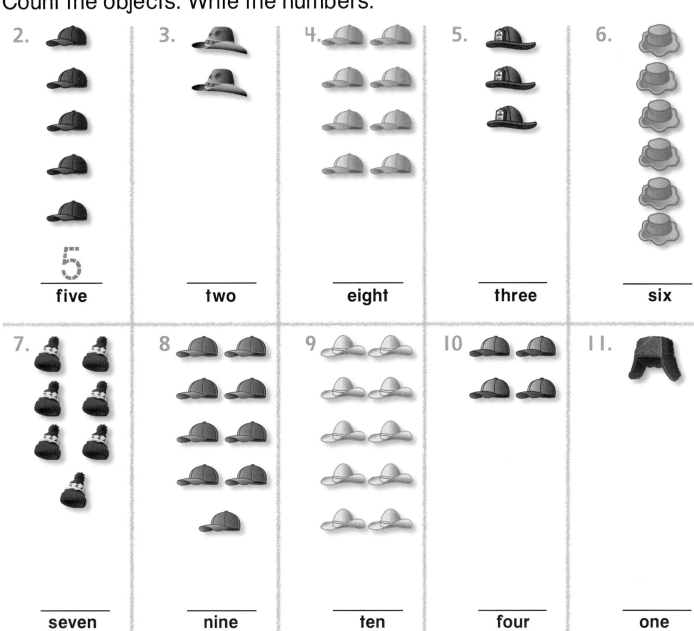

2. _____
five

3. _____
two

4. _____
eight

5. _____
three

6. _____
six

7. _____
seven

8. _____
nine

9. _____
ten

10. _____
four

11. _____
one

1. Circle the row that has more.

2. Circle the row that has fewer.

Write the missing number.

3.

3   4   ____

4.

____   9   10

G

1. Get some 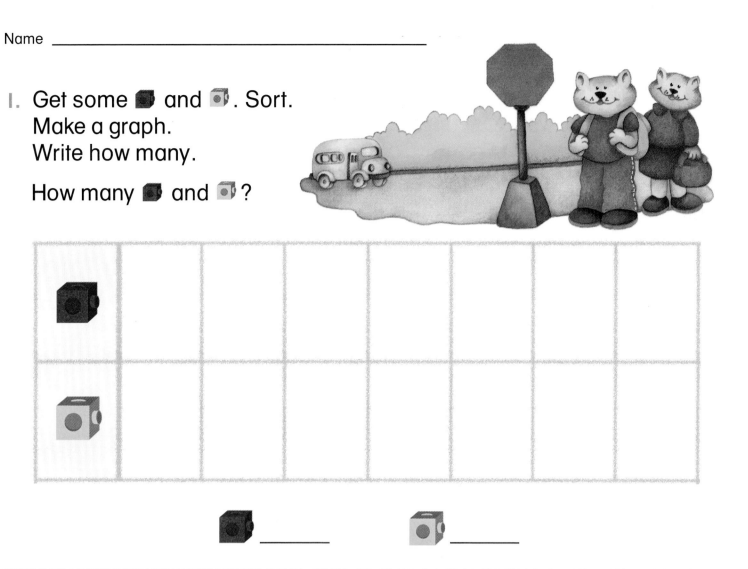 and ▢. Sort.
   Make a graph.
   Write how many.

   How many ▢ and ▢ ?

2. Write how many.

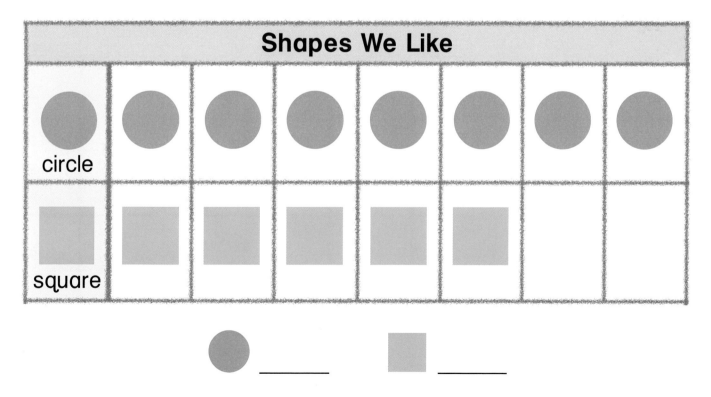

3. Which shape do more children like?
   Circle that shape.

Name _____

1. Write how many.

What We Like to Do	
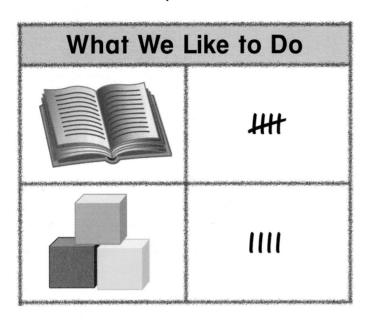	|||||

 _____    _____

2. Which do more children like to do?
Circle that picture.

3. Write how many.

Children Not in School							

 _____    _____

I

Dear Family,

Last year we learned about shapes and numbers to 10. Here is a game for us to play together. This game will give me a chance to share what I already know.

Love,

_____

Directions
1. Put your game piece on START.
2. Use a paper clip and a pencil to make the spinner. Spin.
3. Move your game piece that many spaces.
4. Name the shape your game piece lands on.
5. Say the number your game piece is on.
6. Take turns. The first person to get to END is the winner.

Materials
- 2 game pieces
- pencil
- paper clip

1   **2**   **3**

Number Shapes

4   Go again.   **5**   **7**   **8**   **9**   END

3   **2**   **1**   Go again.   **9**   **8**   **7**

START   **1**   **2**   **3**   Go again.   **5**   **6**

Dear Family,

During the next few weeks, we will learn to add and subtract through 10. Here is important math vocabulary and a list of books to share.

Love,

_____

Vocabulary Power

$$4 + 1 = 5$$

The **sum** tells how many in all.

$4 + 1 = 5$ is an **addition sentence** .

$$3 - 1 = 2$$

The **difference** tells how many are left.

$3 - 1 = 2$ is a **subtraction sentence** .

BOOKS TO SHARE

To read about addition and subtraction with your child, look for these books in your library.

Anno's Counting Book,
by Mitsumasa Anno, HarperCollins, 1992.

**Fish Eyes:
A Book You
Can Count On,**
by Lois Ehlert,
Harcourt, 2001.

**Roll Over! A
Counting Song,**
illustrated by Merle Peek, Clarion, 1999.

Ten Little Mice,
by Joyce Dunbar, Gulliver, 1992.

Visit *The Learning Site* for additional ideas and activities. www.harcourtschool.com

1 Addition Concepts

FUN FACTS

Cats have 4 sets of whiskers.
Look on the chin, cheek, wrist,
and eyebrow.

Theme: My Favorite Animals

Name _____

✓ Check What You Know

Zero

Count the . Write how many .

1. 　　　　　　　　　　_____

2. 　　　　　　　　　　_____

Count and Write the Numbers to 10

Count the ●. Write the number.

3. 　　　　　　　　　　_____

4. 　　　　　　　　　　_____

Model Addition

Use 🎲 to show how many .

Draw the 🎲.
Write the number that tells how many in all.

5.   　　　

　　　　　　4　　　　　　　　1　　　　　　_____

6.    　　　

　　　　　　6　　　　　　　　2　　　　　　_____

2 two　　Use this page to review important skills needed for this chapter.

Model Addition Stories

HANDS ON **Explore**

Use ⬤ to show the story.
Draw the ⬤. Write how many in all.

There are 2 birds in all.

1 big bird   1 little bird   __2__ in all

1.

1 ant   2 ants   _____ in all

2.

3 deer   3 deer come   _____ in all

Explain It ● Daily Reasoning

What happens when more is added to a group?
Explain how you know.

Use ◯ to show the story.
Draw the ◯. Write how many in all.

1.

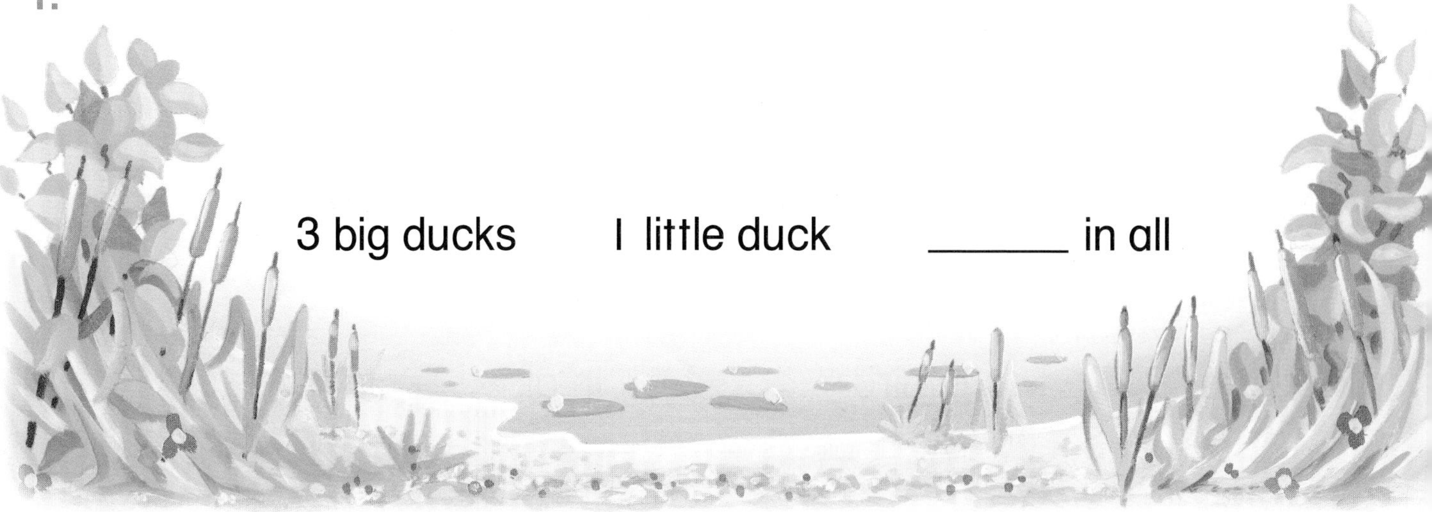

3 big ducks   1 little duck   _____ in all

2.

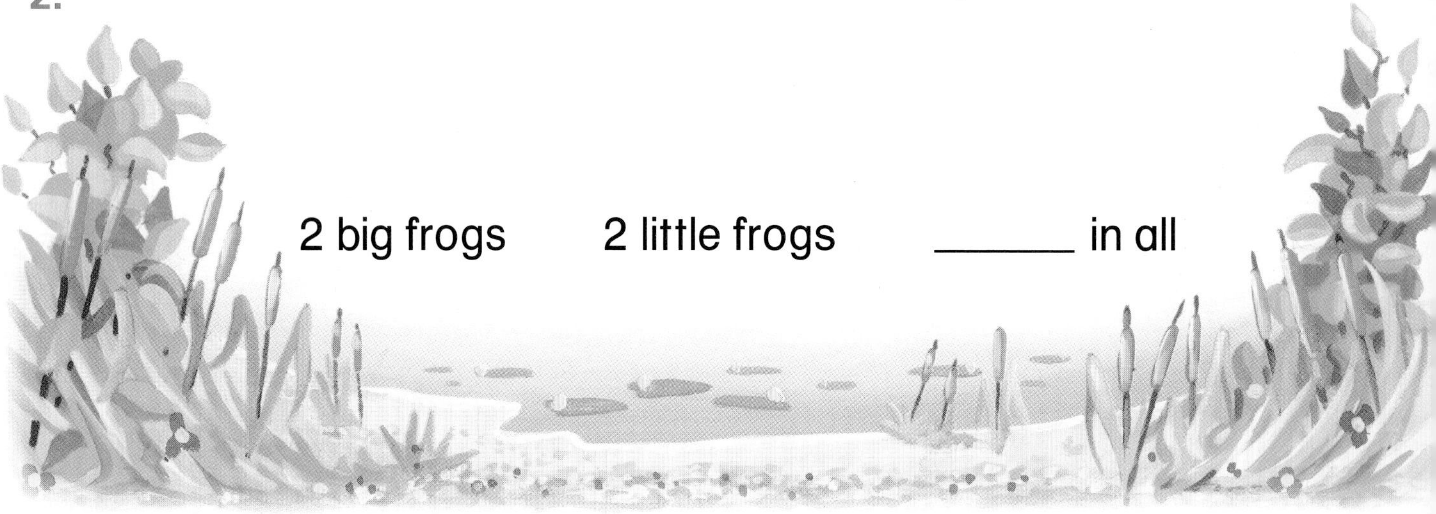

2 big frogs   2 little frogs   _____ in all

3.

1 bee   4 bees come   _____ in all

⬠ **HOME ACTIVITY** • Have your child tell an addition story for each picture.

Name _____

Use Symbols to Add

Vocabulary

plus +
equals =
sum

Learn

$3 \quad + \quad 2 \quad = \quad \underline{5}$

↑ plus ↑ equals ↑ sum

Check

Add. Write the sum.

1.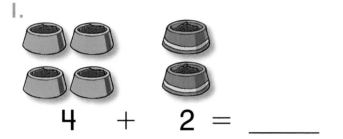

$4 \quad + \quad 2 = \underline{\quad}$

2.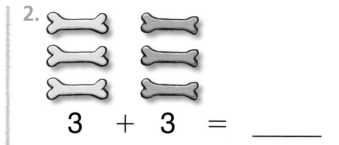

$3 \quad + \quad 3 \quad = \underline{\quad}$

3.

$2 \quad + \quad 2 \quad = \underline{\quad}$

4.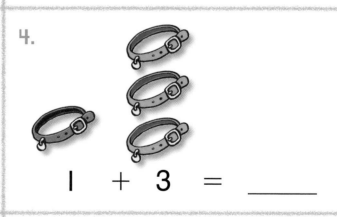

$1 \quad + \quad 3 \quad = \underline{\quad}$

5.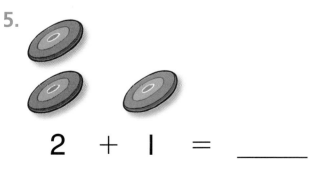

$2 \quad + \quad 1 \quad = \underline{\quad}$

6.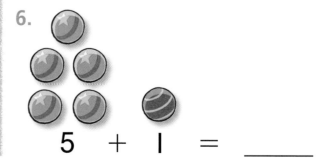

$5 \quad + \quad 1 \quad = \underline{\quad}$

Explain It • Daily Reasoning

How could you find the sum for $1 + 4$ without using pictures?

Add. Write the sum.

1.

3 + 1 = __4__

2.

2 + 3 = _____

3.

4 + 1 = _____

4.

2 + 4 = _____

Problem Solving

Application

Use counters to show the story.
Write the sum.

5. There are 5 black kittens.
There is 1 gray kitten.
How many kittens
are there in all?   _____ kittens

 Write About It • Draw a picture. Show an
addition story about a cat and some dogs.
Write the sum.

🏠 **HOME ACTIVITY** • Ask your child to tell how he or she found each sum. Then have him or her draw
pictures to show 1 + 5 and tell the sum. (6)

Name _____

Algebra: **Add 0**

Learn

Any number plus **0** equals the same number.

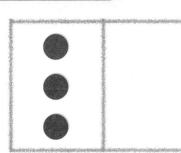

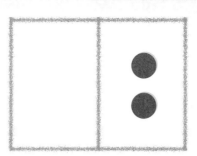

$3 + 0 =$ __3__

$0 + 2 =$ __2__

Check

Write the sum.

1.

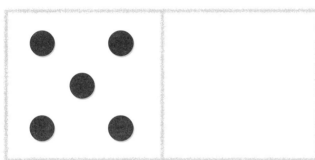

$5 + 0 =$ ____

2.

$0 + 1 =$ ____

3.

$0 + 6 =$ ____

4.

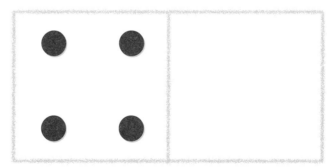

$4 + 0 =$ ____

Explain It • Daily Reasoning

What happens when 0 is added to a number? Why?

Chapter 1 • Addition Concepts

Draw circles to show each number.
Write the sum.

1.

$1 + 0 = \underline{1}$

2.

$1 + 1 = \underline{2}$

3.

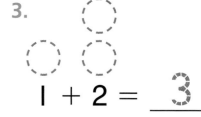

$1 + 2 = \underline{3}$

4.

$0 + 3 = \underline{}$

5.

$0 + 4 = \underline{}$

6.

$0 + 5 = \underline{}$

7.

$2 + 0 = \underline{}$

8.

$2 + 1 = \underline{}$

9.

$2 + 2 = \underline{}$

10.

$0 + 0 = \underline{}$

11.

$0 + 1 = \underline{}$

12.

$0 + 2 = \underline{}$

Problem Solving

Application

13. Circle the problem that you think has the greatest sum. Write the sums to check.

$6 + 1 = \underline{}$ $6 + 2 = \underline{}$ $6 + 0 = \underline{}$

 Write About It • Why does $6 + 0 = 6$?

🏠 HOME ACTIVITY • Ask your child to tell you the sums for $1 + 0$ through $6 + 0$.

Name _____

Problem Solving Strategy
Write a Number Sentence

5 blue fish eat.

1 purple fish joins them.

(How many fish are there in all?)

UNDERSTAND

What do you need to find out?

Circle the question.

PLAN

How do you solve this problem?

Draw a picture.
Then write an addition sentence.

SOLVE

There are ___5___ blue fish.

___1___ purple fish joins them.

___5___ (+) ___1___ (=) ___6___
                                     fish

CHECK

Does your answer make sense?
Explain.

Draw a picture. Then write an
addition sentence to solve.

THINK:
What do I need
to find out?

1. There are 4 fish.
   2 more fish come.
   How many fish are there in all?

                             fish

PROBLEM SOLVING

Problem Solving Practice

Draw a picture.
Then write an addition sentence to solve.

THINK:
What do I need
to find out?

1. 2 green fish swim.
   3 orange fish join them.
   How many fish are there in all?

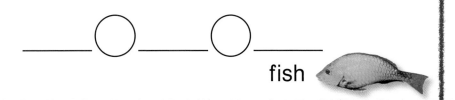

_____ ◯ _____ ◯ _____
                    fish

2. Mike has 1 red fish.
   He gets 2 yellow fish.
   How many fish does he have in all?

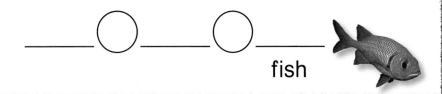

_____ ◯ _____ ◯ _____
                    fish

3. 2 purple fish hide.
   4 blue fish join them.
   How many fish are there in all?

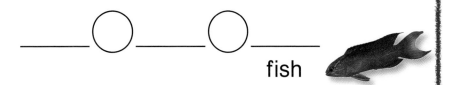

_____ ◯ _____ ◯ _____
                    fish

4. Sue has 1 orange fish.
   She gets 1 blue fish.
   How many fish does she have in all?

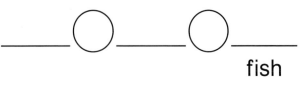

_____ ◯ _____ ◯ _____
                    fish

HOME ACTIVITY • Have your child use small objects to show the addition stories on this page.

Name _____

Extra Practice

Add. Write the sum.

1.

   2 + 1 = ____

2.

   2 + 2 = ____

3.

   3 + 1 = ____

4.

   2 + 4 = ____

Draw circles to show each number.
Write the sum.

5.

   4 + 0 = ____

6.

   4 + 1 = ____

7.

   4 + 2 = ____

Problem Solving

Draw a picture. Then write an
addition sentence to solve.

8. 3 yellow fish swim.
   3 blue fish join them.
   How many fish are there in all?

   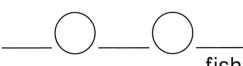 
   ____◯____◯____
            fish

Name _____

✅ Review/Test

Concepts and Skills

Add. Write the sum.

1.

2 + 1 = ____

2.

3 + 2 = ____

3.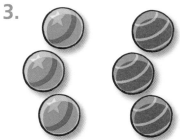

3 + 3 = ____

4.

4 + 2 = ____

Draw circles to show each number.
Write the sum.

5.

5 + 0 = ____

6.

5 + 1 = ____

7.

5 + 2 = ____

Problem Solving

Draw a picture. Then write an addition sentence to solve.

8. There are 3 fish.
2 more fish come.
How many fish are there in all?

____ ____ ____
fish

Getting Ready for the ★EOG Test
Chapter I

Choose the answer for questions 1 – 4.

1. Which addition sentence tells about the picture?

$5 + 2 = 7$	$5 + 1 = 6$	$5 + 0 = 5$	$4 + 2 = 6$
○	○	○	○

2. Which addition sentence tells about the picture?

$4 + 0 = 4$	$4 + 1 = 5$	$3 + 1 = 4$	$4 + 2 = 6$
○	○	○	○

3. What is the sum for $4 + 0$?

0	4	5	40
○	○	○	○

4. Which addition sentence tells how many there are in all?

$1 + 4 = 5$	$3 + 3 = 6$	$3 + 4 = 7$	$3 + 5 = 8$
○	○	○	○

Show What You Know

5. Write an addition sentence about this picture. Explain how you knew which numbers to use.

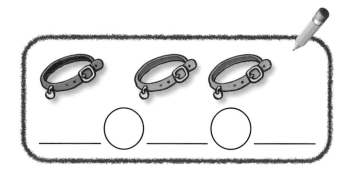

MATH GAME

Pet Numbers

Play with a partner.

You will need

2

1. Put your ♟ at START.
2. Spin the ⊙.
3. Move your ♟ that many spaces.
4. Find the sum.
5. If you are not correct, lose a turn.
6. The first player to get to END wins.

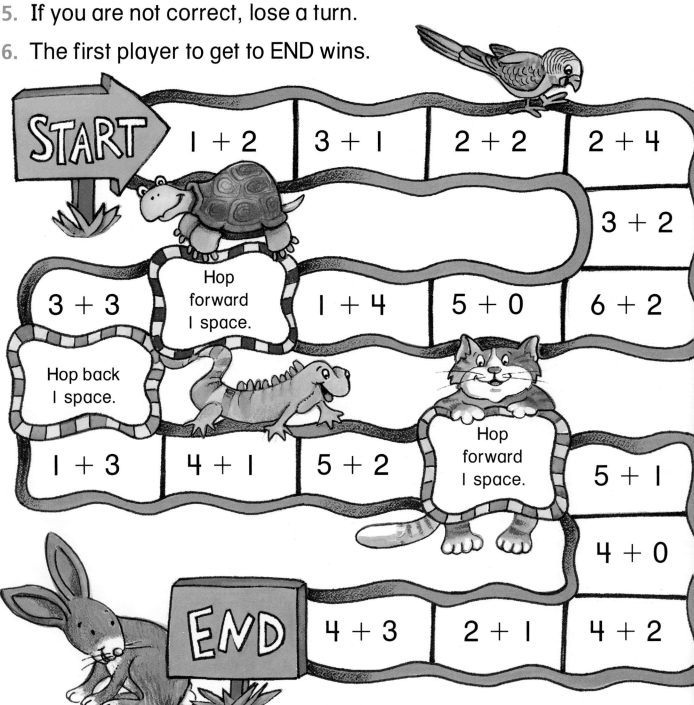

START
1 + 2   3 + 1   2 + 2   2 + 4
3 + 2
3 + 3   Hop forward I space.   1 + 4   5 + 0   6 + 2
Hop back I space.
1 + 3   4 + 1   5 + 2   Hop forward I space.   5 + 1
4 + 0
END   4 + 3   2 + 1   4 + 2

CHAPTER 2

Using Addition

HEALTH

FUN FACTS

Our 4 basic tastes are salt, sweet, bitter, and sour.

✅ Check What You Know

Make a Model: Names for Numbers

Use 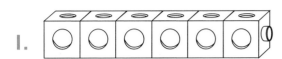 and to make 6.

Color the. Write the numbers.

1.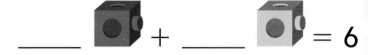

_____ + _____ = 6

Use Pictures to Add

Add. Write the numbers.

2.

_____ + _____ = _____

3.

_____ + _____ = _____

4.

_____ + _____ = _____

5.

_____ + _____ = _____

Use Symbols to Add

Add. Write the sum.

6.

_____ + _____ = _____

7.

_____ + _____ = _____

Name _____

Algebra: **Add in Any Order**

 Explore

You can add in any order and get the same sum.

$2 + 1 = \underline{3}$
sum

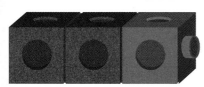

$1 + 2 = \underline{3}$
sum

Connect

Use 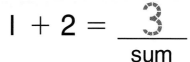 and  to add. Write each sum.
Color to match.

1.

$4 + 1 = \underline{}$

2.
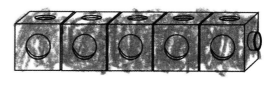

$1 + 4 = \underline{}$

3.
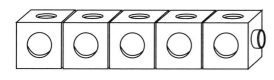

$3 + 2 = \underline{}$

4.
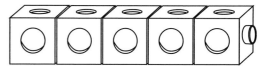

$2 + 3 = \underline{}$

5.
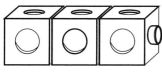

$3 + 0 = \underline{}$

6.
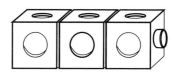

$0 + 3 = \underline{}$

Explain It • Daily Reasoning

What happens to the sum when you change
the order of the numbers you are adding?
Use 🎲 and 🎲 to prove your answer.

Use  and 🔲 to add. Circle the addition sentences in each row that have the same sum.

1. $(3 + 1 = \underline{4})$ 2. $2 + 1 = \underline{3}$ 3. $(1 + 3 = \underline{4})$

4. $4 + 2 = \underline{}$ 5. $2 + 4 = \underline{}$ 6. $1 + 4 = \underline{}$

7. $3 + 3 = \underline{}$ 8. $4 + 0 = \underline{}$ 9. $0 + 4 = \underline{}$

10. $4 + 1 = \underline{}$ 11. $5 + 1 = \underline{}$ 12. $1 + 5 = \underline{}$

13. $2 + 3 = \underline{}$ 14. $2 + 2 = \underline{}$ 15. $3 + 2 = \underline{}$

Problem Solving

Application

Circle your answer.

16. Bob has 1 🔲 and 4 🔲.
    Pat has 4 🔲 and 1 🔲.
    Do they have the same number of cubes?

    Yes   No

    Prove your answer.

 Write About It ● Show two ways to add 1 and 5. Tell why the sums are the same.

⬠ **HOME ACTIVITY** • Have your child use small objects to show 3 + 1 and 1 + 3 and then tell you why the two sums are the same.

18 eighteen

Ways to Make 7 and 8

Vocabulary
plus
equals

HANDS ON Explore

7 ⊕ 0 ⊜ 7
plus   equals

6 ⊕ 1 ⊜ 7

There are many ways to make 7.

Connect

Use 🎲 and 🎲 to make 7.
Color. Write the addition sentence.

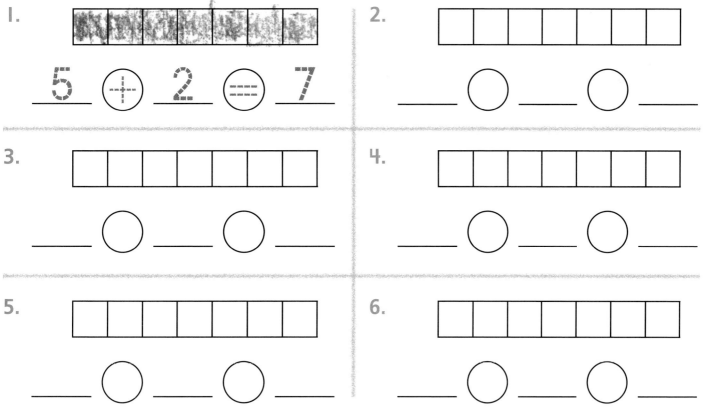

1.
5 ⊕ 2 ⊜ 7

2.
___ ◯ ___ ◯ ___

3.
___ ◯ ___ ◯ ___

4.
___ ◯ ___ ◯ ___

5.
___ ◯ ___ ◯ ___

6.
___ ◯ ___ ◯ ___

Explain It • Daily Reasoning

If you have 3 🎲, how many 🎲 do you need to make 7? Use 🎲 and 🎲 to prove your answer.

This is one way to make 8.

Use and to make 8.
Color. Write the addition sentence.

1.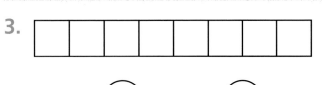

$7 \oplus 1 \ominus 8$

2.

___ ◯ ___ ◯ ___

3.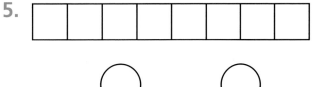

___ ◯ ___ ◯ ___

4.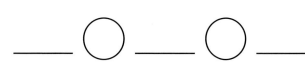

___ ◯ ___ ◯ ___

5.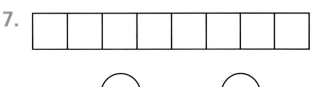

___ ◯ ___ ◯ ___

6.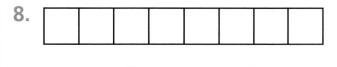

___ ◯ ___ ◯ ___

7.

___ ◯ ___ ◯ ___

8.

___ ◯ ___ ◯ ___

Problem Solving

Visual Thinking

9. Write an addition sentence that tells about the picture.

___ ◯ ___ ◯ ___

 Write About It • How can you show 8 a different way? Draw cars to show how. Write the addition sentence.

🏠 HOME ACTIVITY • Have your child use small objects to show different ways to make 7 and 8.

Name _____

Ways to Make 9 and 10

Explore

$$\underline{5} \;\bigoplus\; \underline{4} \;\bigodot\; \underline{9}$$

This is one way to make 9.

Connect

Use Workmat 7, ●, and ○ to make 9.
Draw and color. Write the addition sentence.

1.
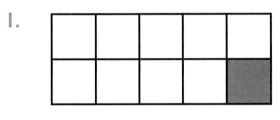

2.
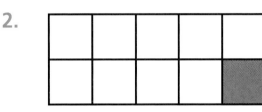

3.
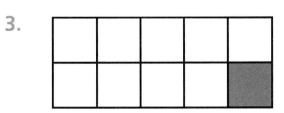

4.
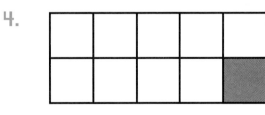

5.
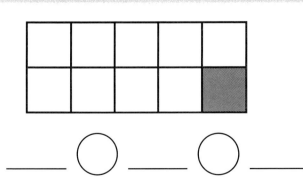

6.
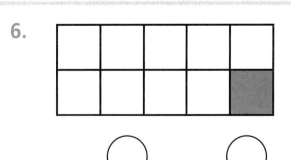

Explain It • Daily Reasoning

How could you use ● and ○ to make 10?

Use Workmat 7, ●, and ○ to make 10.
Draw and color. Write the addition sentence.

1.

 $+$ $=$ 10

2.

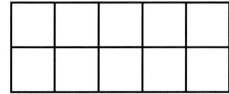

___ ◯ ___ ◯ ___

3.

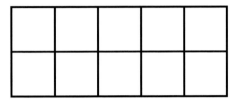

___ ◯ ___ ◯ ___

4.

___ ◯ ___ ◯ ___

5.

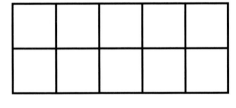

___ ◯ ___ ◯ ___

6.

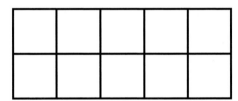

___ ◯ ___ ◯ ___

Problem Solving
Application

7. You have 5 pennies.
   How many more pennies
   do you need to make 10?

   _____ more pennies

 Write About It ● You have 7 pennies. You need
10 pennies. Draw to show how many more pennies
you need. Write the addition sentence.

🏠 HOME ACTIVITY • Have your child use small objects to show different combinations that make 9
and 10.

Name _____

Vertical Addition

Learn

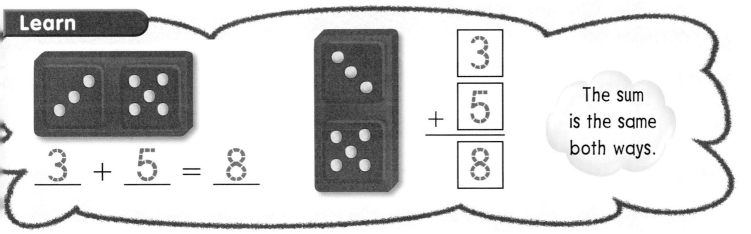

$$\underline{3} + \underline{5} = \underline{8}$$

The sum is the same both ways.

Check

Write the numbers to match the dots.
Write the sum.

 1.

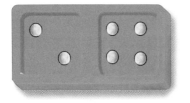

_____ + _____ = _____

2.

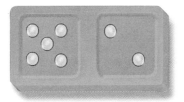

_____ + _____ = _____

 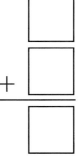

3.

_____ + _____ = _____

Explain It ● Daily Reasoning

How are the problems in each row alike?
How are they different? Explain.

Write the numbers to match the dots.
Write the sum.

1.
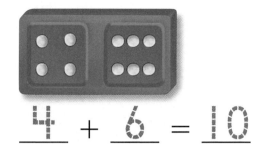

$$\underline{4} + \underline{6} = \underline{10}$$

$$\begin{array}{r} 4 \\ + 6 \\ \hline 10 \end{array}$$

Write the sum.

2.
$$\begin{array}{r} 4 \\ +2 \\ \hline \end{array}$$

3.
$$\begin{array}{r} 6 \\ +2 \\ \hline \end{array}$$

4.
$$\begin{array}{r} 5 \\ +5 \\ \hline \end{array}$$

5.
$$\begin{array}{r} 7 \\ +2 \\ \hline \end{array}$$

6.
$$\begin{array}{r} 0 \\ +5 \\ \hline \end{array}$$

7.
$$\begin{array}{r} 2 \\ +2 \\ \hline \end{array}$$

8.
$$\begin{array}{r} 1 \\ +2 \\ \hline \end{array}$$

9.
$$\begin{array}{r} 5 \\ +4 \\ \hline \end{array}$$

10.
$$\begin{array}{r} 2 \\ +5 \\ \hline \end{array}$$

11.
$$\begin{array}{r} 4 \\ +6 \\ \hline \end{array}$$

12.
$$\begin{array}{r} 8 \\ +1 \\ \hline \end{array}$$

13.
$$\begin{array}{r} 0 \\ +6 \\ \hline \end{array}$$

14.
$$\begin{array}{r} 3 \\ +2 \\ \hline \end{array}$$

15.
$$\begin{array}{r} 2 \\ +3 \\ \hline \end{array}$$

16.
$$\begin{array}{r} 8 \\ +0 \\ \hline \end{array}$$

17.
$$\begin{array}{r} 3 \\ +6 \\ \hline \end{array}$$

18.
$$\begin{array}{r} 7 \\ +3 \\ \hline \end{array}$$

19.
$$\begin{array}{r} 4 \\ +0 \\ \hline \end{array}$$

Problem Solving
Application

20. Each person has 5 red pencils.
They get some blue pencils.
How many pencils does each
person have now?

Pat	Jack	Al
5	5	5
+0	+1	+2
□	□	□

 Write About It ● Look at Exercise
20. What pattern do you see?

HOME ACTIVITY • Write addition problems both across and down for your child to solve.

Name _____

Problem Solving Strategy
Make a Model

How much
do these cost
altogether?

5¢

1¢

UNDERSTAND

What do you know?

Marbles cost ___5___ ¢.   A giraffe costs ___1___ ¢.

PLAN

How do you solve this problem?

Make a model.

SOLVE

Show 5 pennies.
Then show 1 penny.
Count the pennies.

___6___ ¢

CHECK

Explain why you think your answer is right.

Use 🪙 to show each price.

Draw the 🪙. Write how
many there are in all.

THINK:
What do I know?

1. How much do you spend
   for both?

6¢

2¢

___ ¢

Use 🪙 to show each price.

Draw the 🪙. Write how many there are in all.

Keep in Mind!

Understand
Plan
Solve
Check

1. How much will you spend if you buy both?

THINK:
What do I need
to find out?

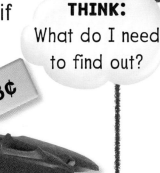

_____ ¢

2. How much do these cost altogether?

_____ ¢

3. How much will you spend for both?

_____ ¢

4. How much will you spend if you buy both?

_____ ¢

⬟ **HOME ACTIVITY** • Choose two objects from pages 25 and 26. Have your child use pennies to show the total.

Name _____

Extra Practice

Add. Circle the addition sentences that have the same sum.

1. $3 + 2 =$ _____   2. $2 + 1 =$ _____   3. $2 + 3 =$ _____

Write two ways to make 7.

4. ____ ◯ ____ ◯ ____   5. ____ ◯ ____ ◯ ____

Write two ways to make 9.

6. ____ ◯ ____ ◯ ____   7. ____ ◯ ____ ◯ ____

Write the numbers to match the dots.
Write the sum.

8.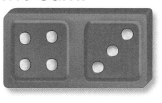

____ + ____ = ____

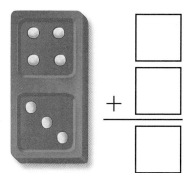

Problem Solving

Use 🪙 to show each price. Draw the 🪙.
Write how many there are in all.

9. How much will you spend
   for both?

 5¢    4¢

_____¢

Name _____

✓ Review/Test

Concepts and Skills

Add. Circle the addition sentences
that have the same sum.

1. $4 + 2 =$ _____   2. $2 + 4 =$ _____   3. $2 + 3 =$ _____

Write two ways to make 8.

4. ___ ◯ ___ ◯ ___   5. ___ ◯ ___ ◯ ___

Write two ways to make 10.

6. ___ ◯ ___ ◯ ___   7. ___ ◯ ___ ◯ ___

Write the numbers to match the dots.
Write the sum.

8.

____ + ____ = ____

 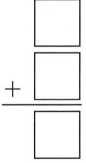

Problem Solving

Use to show each price. Draw the ⬤.
Write how many there are in all.

9. How much would you
   spend for both?

   _____ ¢

Name _____

Getting Ready for the ⭐EOG Test
Chapters 1–2

Choose the answer for questions 1 – 4.

1. Which is a way to make 8?

5 + 1	4 + 4	6 + 4	3 + 2
○	○	○	○

2. Which is another way to write 8 + 2 = 10?

2 +6 ─ 8	6 +2 ─ 8	9 +1 ─ 10	8 +2 ─ 10
○	○	○	○

3. How much do these cost altogether?

3¢	6¢	8¢	9¢
○	○	○	○

4. What is the sum for 7 + 0?

0	4	7	8
○	○	○	○

Show What You Know

5. Write an addition sentence to show the sum of 6. Color some of the cubes red.

Color the rest blue to explain your answer. Write another addition sentence that has the same sum.

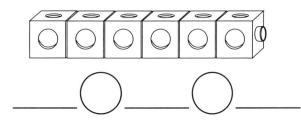

MATH GAME

Tic-Tac-Sum

Play with a partner.

You will need

2 🎲

5 ⚫   5 ⚪

1. One player uses ⚫.
   The other player uses ⚪.

2. Toss two 🎲.

3. Find the sum.
   Cover that number with a counter.

4. Your turn is over if that number is
   already covered.

5. The first player to get 4 counters
   in a row wins.

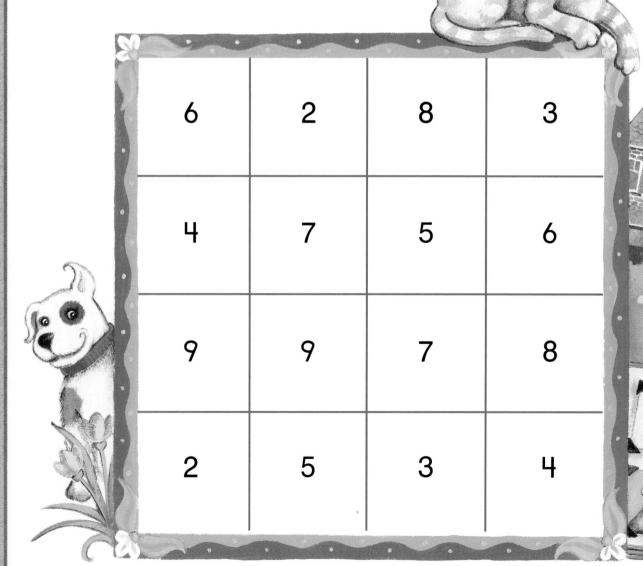

6	2	8	3
4	7	5	6
9	9	7	8
2	5	3	4

Subtraction Concepts

FUN FACTS

Leatherback turtles are as long as 8 of your math books.

Theme: At the Beach

✅ Check What You Know

Zero

Count the . Write how many are in each picture.

1. _____

2. _____

Model Subtraction

Use 🎲 to show the story.

Draw the 🎲. Mark an X on the 🎲 you subtract.
Write how many are left.

3.

         3   1   _____

4.

         4   2   _____

5.

         3   2   _____

Model Subtraction Stories

HANDS ON

Explore

Use ● to show the story. Draw the ●.
Cross out how many go away.
Write how many are left.

2 kites are left.

4 kites   2 fly away   __2__ are left

1.

3 boats   2 sail away   _____ is left

2.

5 birds   3 fly away   _____ are left

Explain It • Daily Reasoning

When you take objects away from a group,
are there **more** or **fewer** objects left? Why?

Use ● to show the story. Draw the ● .
Cross out how many go away. Write how
many are left.

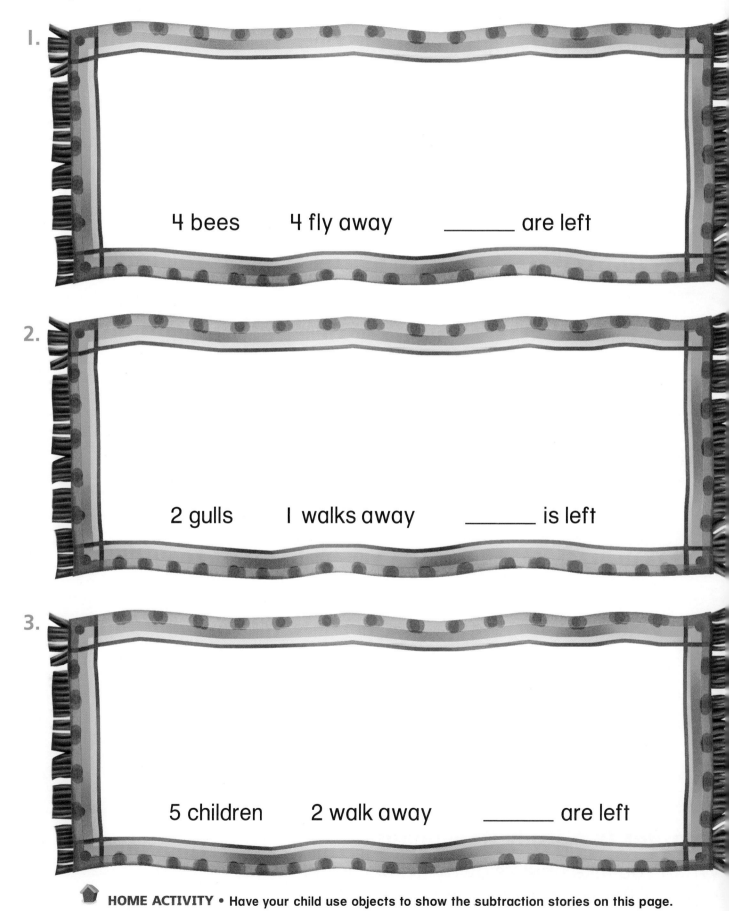

1.

4 bees   4 fly away   _____ are left

2.

2 gulls   1 walks away   _____ is left

3.

5 children   2 walk away   _____ are left

Use Symbols to Subtract

Learn

$$5 - 3 = 2$$

minus ——— equals ——— difference

Check

Cross out pictures to subtract.
Write the difference.

1.

$4 - 2 = $ _____

2.
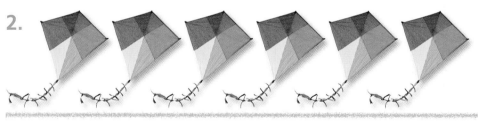

$6 - 3 = $ _____

3.

$5 - 2 = $ _____

4.

$3 - 1 = $ _____

Explain It • Daily Reasoning

What does the minus sign mean?
What does the equal sign mean? Explain.

Cross out pictures to subtract.
Write the difference.

1.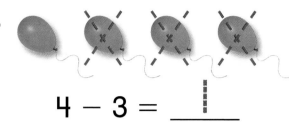

   $4 - 3 = \underline{\ 1\ }$

2.

   $6 - 2 = \underline{\quad}$

3.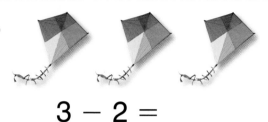

   $3 - 2 = \underline{\quad}$

4.

   $4 - 1 = \underline{\quad}$

5.

   $6 - 5 = \underline{\quad}$

6.

   $6 - 4 = \underline{\quad}$

7.

   $5 - 4 = \underline{\quad}$

8.

   $2 - 1 = \underline{\quad}$

Problem Solving

Logical Reasoning

Solve the riddle. Write the number.

9. I am greater than 4. I am less than 6. What number am I?

   _____

10. I am less than 3. I am greater than 1. What number am I?

    _____

 Write About It ● Write a riddle about the number 4.

🏠 **HOME ACTIVITY** • Have your child draw pictures to show a subtraction problem. Then ask him or her to tell the difference.

Algebra: **Write Subtraction Sentences**

Vocabulary
subtraction sentence

Learn

$$\underline{6} \ominus \underline{2} = \underline{4}$$

$6 - 2 = 4$ is a subtraction sentence.

Check

Write the subtraction sentence.

1.

_____ ◯ _____ ◯ _____

2.
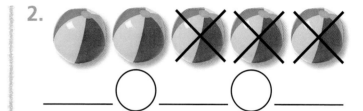
_____ ◯ _____ ◯ _____

3.
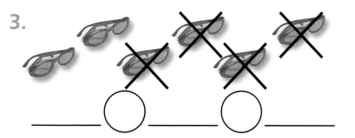
_____ ◯ _____ ◯ _____

4.
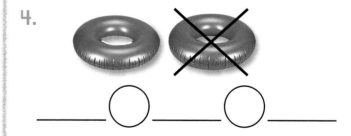
_____ ◯ _____ ◯ _____

5.
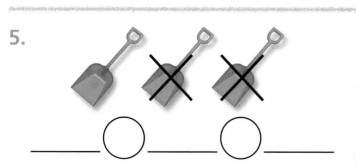
_____ ◯ _____ ◯ _____

6.
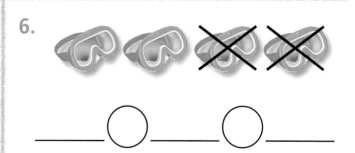
_____ ◯ _____ ◯ _____

Explain It • Daily Reasoning

How can you use these numbers to write two
different subtraction sentences? Explain.

Write the subtraction sentence.

1.

6 ⃝ 1 ⃝ 5

2.

_____ ⃝ _____ ⃝ _____

3.

_____ ⃝ _____ ⃝ _____

4.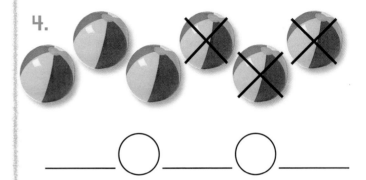

_____ ⃝ _____ ⃝ _____

5.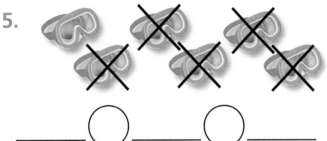

_____ ⃝ _____ ⃝ _____

6.

_____ ⃝ _____ ⃝ _____

Problem Solving
Visual Thinking

Circle the picture that shows the subtraction sentence.

7. 4 − 3 = 1

8. 3 − 1 = 2

 Write About It • Look at Exercises 7 and 8.
Explain why you circled the pictures you did.

🏠 HOME ACTIVITY • Have your child use objects to show subtraction stories. Then ask him or her to write the subtraction sentences.

Name _____

Problem Solving Strategy
Make a Model

3 butterflies are in the tree.

I flies away.

(How many are left?)

UNDERSTAND

What do you need to find out?

Circle the question.
What do you know?

There are ___3___ butterflies.

___I___ flies away.

PLAN

How do you solve this problem?

Use counters. Draw 3 counters. Cross out I.

SOLVE

There are ___2___ butterflies left.   ◯ ◯ ⊗

CHECK

Does your answer make sense?

Explain.

Use ● to subtract.
Draw the ●.
Write the difference.

I. Kathy finds 4 shells.
She gives 2 away.
How many shells
does she have left?

THINK:
What do I need
to find out?

_____ shells

PROBLEM SOLVING

Use  to subtract.
Draw the ●.
Write the difference.

THINK:
How can I solve
the problem?

I. Steve sees 6 pelicans.
   2 fly away.
   How many pelicans
   are left?

_____ pelicans

2. Lisa sees 5 fish.
   3 swim away.
   How many fish
   are left?

_____ fish

3. Tim finds 3 shells.
   He gives 1 to Joe.
   How many shells
   does he have left?

_____ shells

4. Ann sees 2 sand castles.
   1 gets washed away.
   How many sand castles
   are left?

_____ sand castle

HOME ACTIVITY • Make up story problems like the ones in this lesson. Have your child use objects or draw pictures to solve the problems.

Name _____

Algebra: **Subtract All or Zero**

Vocabulary
zero 0

Learn

6 − 0 = __6__

When you subtract zero, you have the same number left.

6 − 6 = __0__

When you subtract all, you have zero left.

Check

Write the difference.

1.

3 − 0 = _____

2.

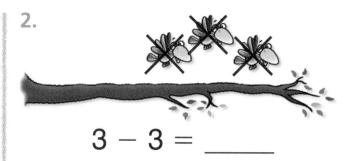

3 − 3 = _____

3.

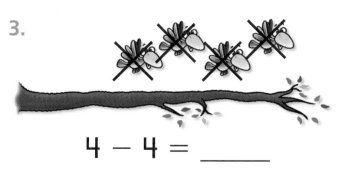

4 − 4 = _____

4.

4 − 0 = _____

5.

2 − 0 = _____

6.

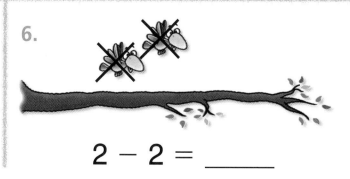

2 − 2 = _____

Explain It • Daily Reasoning

What happens when you subtract all of a group? Why?
What happens when you subtract 0 from a group? Why?

Practice and Problem Solving

Write the difference.

1.

$5 - 5 = \underline{0}$

2.

$6 - 0 = \underline{6}$

3.

$4 - 4 = \underline{}$

4.

$2 - 0 = \underline{}$

5.

$2 - 2 = \underline{}$

6.

$1 - 1 = \underline{}$

7.

$5 - 0 = \underline{}$

8.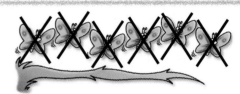

$6 - 6 = \underline{}$

Problem Solving
Application

Write the subtraction sentence.

9. Maria sees 3 butterflies.
   All 3 fly away.
   How many are left?

 Write About It • Look at Exercise 9. Draw pictures to show your subtraction sentence. Explain if you subtracted all or zero.

HOME ACTIVITY • Have your child draw pictures to show 3 − 3 and 3 − 0. Ask your child to tell you how to find each difference.

Name _____

Extra Practice

Cross out pictures to subtract.
Write the difference.

1.

$4 - 3 =$ _____

2.
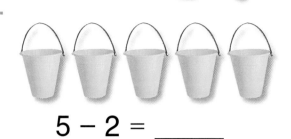

$5 - 2 =$ _____

Write the subtraction sentence.

3.
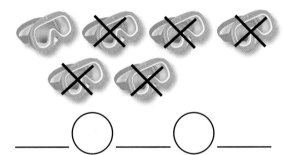

____ ◯ ____ ◯ ____

4.
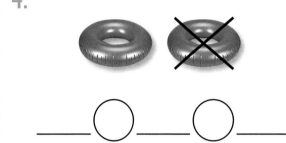

____ ◯ ____ ◯ ____

Write the difference.

5.

$4 - 0 =$ _____

6.

$6 - 6 =$ _____

Problem Solving

Use ⬤ to subtract.
Draw the ⬤.
Write the difference.

7. Joe sees 6 fish.
2 swim away.
How many fish are left?

 _____ fish

✔ Review/Test

Concepts and Skills

Cross out pictures to subtract.
Write the difference.

1.

   6 − 3 = _____

2.

   5 − 4 = _____

Write the subtraction sentence.

3.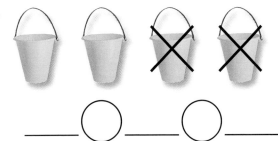

   ____ ◯ ____ ◯ ____

4.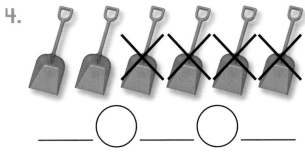

   ____ ◯ ____ ◯ ____

Write the difference.

5.

   5 − 0 = _____

6.

   6 − 6 = _____

Problem Solving

Use ● to subtract.
Draw the ●.
Write the difference.

7. 5 ants are on a log.
   3 ants crawl away.
   How many ants are left?

   _____ ants

Name _____

Choose the answer for questions 1 – 4.

1. Which subtraction sentence tells about the picture?

$6 - 6 = 0$	$6 - 3 = 3$	$6 - 4 = 2$	$6 - 1 = 5$
○	○	○	○

2. What is the difference?

$$8 - 3 = \underline{\hphantom{000}}$$

5	6	8	11
○	○	○	○

3. What is the difference for $4 - 0$?

4	3	2	1
○	○	○	○

4. There are 3 bees. 2 fly away. How many are left?

0	1	3	5
○	○	○	○

Show What You Know

5. Write an addition sentence to show the sum of 8. Use  and to explain your answer. Draw the and you use.

MATH GAME

Numbers in the Sand

Play with a partner.

1. Put your ♟ at START.
2. Toss the 🎲.
3. Move your ♟ that many spaces.
4. Find the difference.
5. If you are not correct, lose a turn.
6. The first player to get to END wins.

You will need

2 ♟   🎲

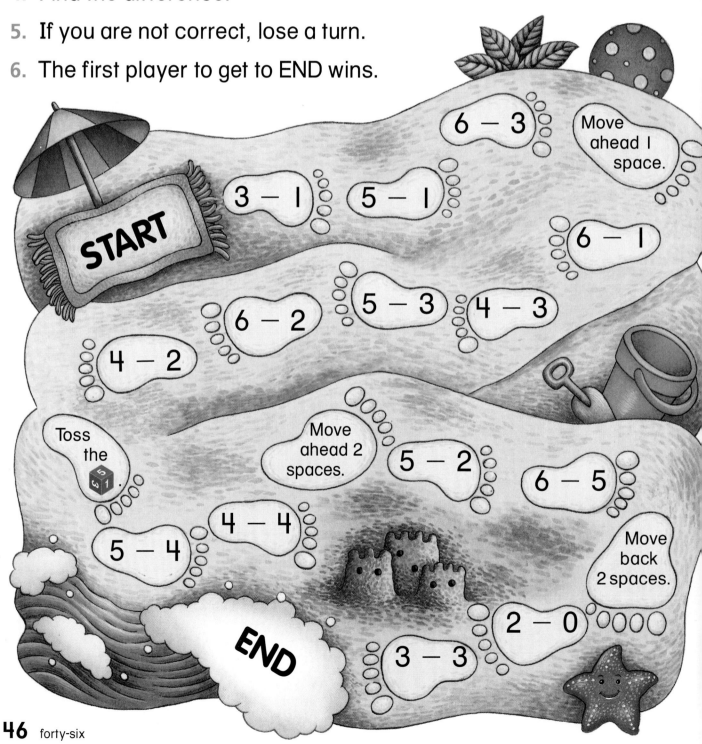

CHAPTER 3 · MATH GAME

Using Subtraction

FUN FACTS

There are three primary colors: red, yellow, and blue.

Name _____

✅ Check What You Know

Use Pictures to Subtract

Subtract. Write the numbers.

1.

_____ − _____ = _____

2.

_____ − _____ = _____

3.

_____ − _____ = _____

4.

_____ − _____ = _____

Use Symbols to Subtract

Cross out pictures to subtract.
Write the difference.

5.

$3 - 1 =$ _____

6.

$6 - 1 =$ _____

7.

$5 - 3 =$ _____

8.

$4 - 3 =$ _____

Use this page to review important skills needed for this chapter.

Take Apart 7 and 8

Explore

HANDS ON

I started with 7 cubes and then took one away.

$$7 - 1 = 6$$

subtraction sentence

Connect

Use  to show all the ways to subtract from 7.
Complete the subtraction sentences.

1. $7 - \underline{0} = \underline{7}$

2. $7 - \underline{} = \underline{}$

3. $7 - \underline{} = \underline{}$

4. $7 - \underline{} = \underline{}$

5. $7 - \underline{} = \underline{}$

6. $7 - \underline{} = \underline{}$

7. $7 - \underline{} = \underline{}$

8. $7 - \underline{} = \underline{}$

Explain It • Daily Reasoning

Continue the pattern.
What comes next?
Explain how you know.

$$7 - 0 = 7$$
$$7 - 1 = 6$$
$$7 - 2 = 5$$

Remember to always start with 8 cubes.

Use to show all the ways to subtract from 8.
Complete the subtraction sentences.

1.

8 – _0_ = _8_

2.

8 – ___ = ___

3.

8 – ___ = ___

4.

8 – ___ = ___

5.

8 – ___ = ___

6.

8 – ___ = ___

7.

8 – ___ = ___

8.

8 – ___ = ___

9.

8 – ___ = ___

Problem Solving
Visual Thinking

Cross out some of the pictures.
Write the subtraction sentence.

10.

___ ◯ ___ ◯ ___

11.

___ ◯ ___ ◯ ___

 Write About It • Explain what happens if you cross out all of the pictures in a group.

 HOME ACTIVITY • Have your child use small objects to show different ways to subtract from 8.

Name _____

Take Apart 9 and 10

Explore

There are many ways to take apart 9.

 $9 - 0 = 9$

 $9 - 1 = 8$

 $9 - 2 = 7$

Remember to look for a pattern.

Connect

Use ⬛ to show all the ways to subtract from 9.
Complete the subtraction sentences.

1. $9 - \underline{0} = \underline{9}$

2. $9 - \underline{} = \underline{}$

3. $9 - \underline{} = \underline{}$

4. $9 - \underline{} = \underline{}$

5. $9 - \underline{} = \underline{}$

6. $9 - \underline{} = \underline{}$

7. $9 - \underline{} = \underline{}$

8. $9 - \underline{} = \underline{}$

9. $9 - \underline{} = \underline{}$

10. $9 - \underline{} = \underline{}$

Explain It • Daily Reasoning

How did using a pattern help you find the answers?

What are the different ways you can subtract from 10?

Use to show all the ways to subtract from 10.
Complete the subtraction sentences.

1.
$$10 - \underline{0} = \underline{10}$$

2.
$$10 - \underline{} = \underline{}$$

3.
$$10 - \underline{} = \underline{}$$

4.
$$10 - \underline{} = \underline{}$$

5.
$$10 - \underline{} = \underline{}$$

6.
$$10 - \underline{} = \underline{}$$

7.
$$10 - \underline{} = \underline{}$$

8.
$$10 - \underline{} = \underline{}$$

9.
$$10 - \underline{} = \underline{}$$

10.
$$10 - \underline{} = \underline{}$$

11.
$$10 - \underline{} = \underline{}$$

Problem Solving
Algebra

Solve. Use to help you.

12. $7 - \blacksquare = 3$

13. $8 - \blacksquare = 6$

14. $7 - \blacksquare = 5$

$\blacksquare = \underline{}$

$\blacksquare = \underline{}$

$\blacksquare = \underline{}$

 Write About It • Look at Exercise 14.
Draw pictures to check your answer.

 HOME ACTIVITY • Have your child use small objects to show ways to subtract from 10.

Vertical Subtraction

Learn

You can subtract across.   You can subtract down.

$5 - 1 = \underline{4}$

Check

Subtract across and down.

1.

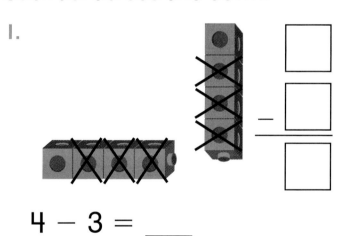

$4 - 3 = \underline{}$

2.

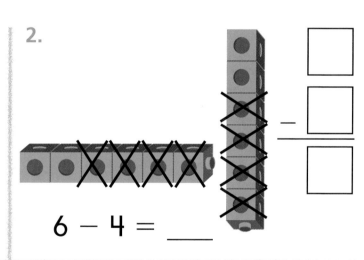

$6 - 4 = \underline{}$

3.

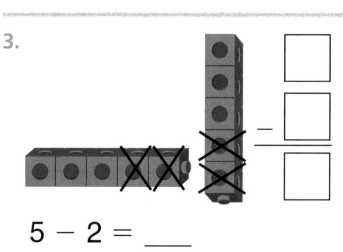

$5 - 2 = \underline{}$

4.

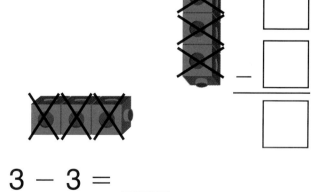

$3 - 3 = \underline{}$

Explain It • Daily Reasoning

Why is the answer the same for both
ways of subtracting?

Write the difference.

1.

$7 - 4 = \underline{3}$

2.

$$\begin{array}{r} 7 \\ -4 \\ \hline 3 \end{array}$$

| 3. $\begin{array}{r} 10 \\ -\ 0 \\ \hline \end{array}$ | 4. $\begin{array}{r} 6 \\ -3 \\ \hline \end{array}$ | 5. $\begin{array}{r} 4 \\ -2 \\ \hline \end{array}$ | 6. $\begin{array}{r} 8 \\ -4 \\ \hline \end{array}$ | 7. $\begin{array}{r} 9 \\ -2 \\ \hline \end{array}$ | 8. $\begin{array}{r} 5 \\ -0 \\ \hline \end{array}$ |

| 9. $\begin{array}{r} 3 \\ -2 \\ \hline \end{array}$ | 10. $\begin{array}{r} 8 \\ -6 \\ \hline \end{array}$ | 11. $\begin{array}{r} 9 \\ -0 \\ \hline \end{array}$ | 12. $\begin{array}{r} 7 \\ -2 \\ \hline \end{array}$ | 13. $\begin{array}{r} 5 \\ -4 \\ \hline \end{array}$ | 14. $\begin{array}{r} 6 \\ -6 \\ \hline \end{array}$ |

| 15. $\begin{array}{r} 10 \\ -\ 5 \\ \hline \end{array}$ | 16. $\begin{array}{r} 4 \\ -0 \\ \hline \end{array}$ | 17. $\begin{array}{r} 7 \\ -7 \\ \hline \end{array}$ | 18. $\begin{array}{r} 9 \\ -4 \\ \hline \end{array}$ | 19. $\begin{array}{r} 8 \\ -0 \\ \hline \end{array}$ | 20. $\begin{array}{r} 7 \\ -6 \\ \hline \end{array}$ |

Problem Solving

Logical Reasoning

Solve. Write the number.

21. I am greater than 8.
I am less than 10.
What number am I?

_____

22. I am less than 5.
I am greater than 3.
What number am I?

_____

 Write About It • Explain how you solve this riddle. I am greater than 0. I am less than 2. What number am I?

HOME ACTIVITY • Write subtraction sentences that go across, and have your child find the difference for each. Then ask your child to write the same problems going down.

Subtract to Compare

Learn

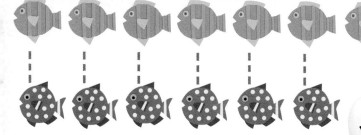

$$10 - 6 = \underline{4}$$

There are more 🐟 than 🐟. You can subtract to find how many more.

Check

Draw lines to match.
Subtract to find how many more.

1.

$$4 - 2 = \underline{}$$

_____ more

2.

$$8 - 5 = \underline{}$$

_____ more

3.

$$7 - 3 = \underline{}$$

_____ more ⚽

4.

$$5 - 4 = \underline{}$$

_____ more

Explain It • Daily Reasoning

Why do you subtract to find how many more ⚪ than ⚫ there are?

Draw lines to match.
Subtract to find how many more.

1.

$6 - 3 = \underline{3}$

$\underline{3}$ more

2.

$4 - 1 = \underline{}$

$\underline{}$ more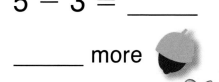

3.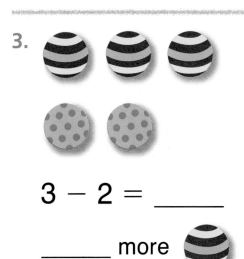

$3 - 2 = \underline{}$

$\underline{}$ more

4.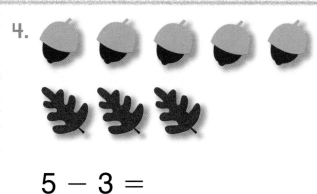

$5 - 3 = \underline{}$

$\underline{}$ more

Problem Solving
Application

Solve.

5. John had 7 stamps.
   Sue had 3 stamps.
   How many more stamps
   did John have?

   $\underline{}$ stamps

6. Jane had 5 pennies.
   Mark had 2 pennies.
   How many more pennies
   did Jane have?

   $\underline{}$ pennies

 Write About It • Look at Exercise 6.
Draw the pennies. Then compare to check
your answer.

🏠 HOME ACTIVITY • Have your child make up subtraction stories for you to solve.

Name _____

Problem Solving Strategy
Draw a Picture

Kathy had a box of 8 crayons.
She gave some crayons away.
She has 5 left.
How many crayons did Kathy give away?

UNDERSTAND

What do you want to find out?

Draw a line under the question.

PLAN

**You can draw a picture
to solve the problem.**

SOLVE

_3__ crayons

What number do I
add to 5 to get 8?
8 − ■ = 5
5 + _3_ = 8

CHECK

Does your answer make sense?

Explain.

Draw a picture to solve the problem.
Write how many were given away.

What number
do I add to 3
to make 10?

I. I had 10 pencils.
I gave some away.
I have 3 left. How many
pencils did I give away?

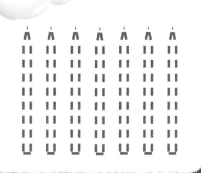

_____ pencils

PROBLEM SOLVING

Draw a picture to solve the problem.
Write how many were given away.

1. Pat had 9 markers.
   She gave some away.
   She has 4 left.
   How many markers
   did Pat give away?

   What number do I add to 4 to make 9?

   __5__ markers

2. Dave had 8 stickers.
   He gave some to Joe.
   He has 6 left.
   How many stickers did
   Dave give to Joe?

   What number do I add to 6 to make 8?

   _____ stickers

3. Ed had 3 erasers.
   He gave some away.
   He has 1 left.
   How many erasers did
   Ed give away?

   What number do I add to 1 to make 3?

   _____ erasers

HOME ACTIVITY • Tell a math story like those in the problems on this page. Ask your child to draw a picture to solve the problem and then explain the drawing to you.

Name _____

Extra Practice

Complete the subtraction sentences.
Show ways to subtract from 7.

1. 7 − _____ = _____

2. 7 − _____ = _____

Show ways to subtract from 9.

3. 9 − _____ = _____

4. 9 − _____ = _____

Write the difference.

5.
$$\begin{array}{r} 5 \\ -0 \\ \hline \end{array}$$

6.
$$\begin{array}{r} 8 \\ -8 \\ \hline \end{array}$$

7.
$$\begin{array}{r} 7 \\ -2 \\ \hline \end{array}$$

8.
$$\begin{array}{r} 10 \\ -7 \\ \hline \end{array}$$

9.
$$\begin{array}{r} 9 \\ -5 \\ \hline \end{array}$$

Draw lines to match.
Subtract to find how many more.

10.

4 − 3 = _____

_____ more

11.

6 − 2 = _____

_____ more

Problem Solving

Draw a picture to solve the problem.

12. Elise had 10 pencils. She gave some away. She has 6 left. How many pencils did Elise give away?

What number do I add to 6 to make 10?

_____ pencils

✔ Review/Test

Concepts and Skills

Complete the subtraction sentences.
Show ways to subtract from 8.

1. $8 - \underline{\hspace{1.5cm}} = \underline{\hspace{1.5cm}}$

2. $8 - \underline{\hspace{1.5cm}} = \underline{\hspace{1.5cm}}$

Show ways to subtract from 10.

3. $10 - \underline{\hspace{1.5cm}} = \underline{\hspace{1.5cm}}$

4. $10 - \underline{\hspace{1.5cm}} = \underline{\hspace{1.5cm}}$

Write the difference.

5. $\begin{array}{r} 6 \\ -4 \\ \hline \end{array}$ 6. $\begin{array}{r} 9 \\ -6 \\ \hline \end{array}$ 7. $\begin{array}{r} 8 \\ -1 \\ \hline \end{array}$ 8. $\begin{array}{r} 10 \\ -\ 9 \\ \hline \end{array}$ 9. $\begin{array}{r} 3 \\ -3 \\ \hline \end{array}$

Draw lines to match.
Subtract to find how many more.

10.

$6 - 3 = \underline{\hspace{1.5cm}}$

_____ more 🐱

11.

$5 - 2 = \underline{\hspace{1.5cm}}$

_____ more ⚽

Problem Solving

Draw a picture to solve the problem.

12. Fran had 5 erasers. She gave some to a friend. She has 3 left. How many erasers did Fran give to her friend?

_____ erasers

> What number do I add to 3 to make 5?

Name _____

 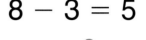
Choose the answer for questions 1– 5.

1. Which subtraction sentence tells how many more cats than pandas there are?

$8 - 2 = 6$ ○ $8 - 3 = 5$ ○

$8 - 4 = 4$ ○ $8 - 6 = 2$ ○

2. Which is another way to write $6 - 2 = 4$?

$$\begin{array}{r} 8 \\ -2 \\ \hline 6 \end{array} \qquad \begin{array}{r} 8 \\ -6 \\ \hline 2 \end{array} \qquad \begin{array}{r} 4 \\ -2 \\ \hline 2 \end{array} \qquad \begin{array}{r} 6 \\ -2 \\ \hline 4 \end{array}$$

○   ○   ○   ○

3. $8 - 2 =$ _____

12 ○   11 ○   6 ○   5 ○

4. $9 - 3 =$ _____

6 ○   7 ○   12 ○   13 ○

5. Ann has 4 flowers. She gives 2 away. How many are left?

1 ○   2 ○   4 ○   6 ○

Show What You Know

6. Write a subtraction sentence that equals 10. Use  to explain your answer. Draw the ⬛ you use.

_____ ◯ _____ ◯ _____

EOG TEST PREP

IT'S IN THE BAG
Cat Pocket-Dots

PROJECT You will make a cat pocket to hold your dot cards to practice your math facts.

You Will Need

- Lunch-size bag
- Blackline patterns
- Crayons
- Glue
- Scissors

Directions

1 Color the cat face. Then cut it out.

2 Lay the bag in front of you. Put the flap at the top facing you. Glue the cat face to the flap.

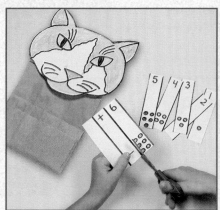

3 Color the dots on the dot cards. Cut the cards apart.

4 Use dot cards 1 to 6 to make number sentences.

My Cat Biff

written by
Cheryl Michaels
illustrated by
Diane Greenseid

This book will help me review addition and subtraction stories.

This book belongs to _____.

Biff had 3 balls.
I gave him one more.

3 + 1 = _____

Biff had 4 balls.
I gave him two more.

4 + 2 = _____

Biff had 6 balls.
He hit one under the chair.

6 – 1 = _____

Name —————————————————————————————

PROBLEM SOLVING IN NORTH CAROLINA

Asheboro, NC

At the Zoological Park

You can see many different kinds of animals at the North Carolina Zoological Park in Asheboro.

In some displays you can see two kinds of animals. Use the pictures to help you write an addition sentence. Find how many animals are in each display.

giraffe

zebra

1 How many in all?

_____ ◯ _____ = _____ animals

elephant

2 How many in all?

_____ ◯ _____ = _____ animals

3 How many in all?

_____ ◯ _____ = _____ animals

CHALLENGE

Equals

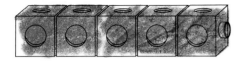 

 __2__ + __3__ = __1__ + __4__

5 = 5

Both sides show 5.
They are equal.

Use different numbers of and .
Show sides that are equal.
Color. Write the numbers.

1.

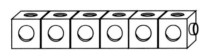 =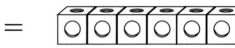

_____ + _____ = _____ + _____

2.

_____ + _____ = _____ + _____

3.

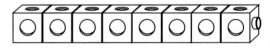

_____ + _____ = _____ + _____

4.

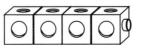

_____ + _____ = _____ + _____

✓ Study Guide and Review

Vocabulary

Add. Circle the **sum**.

Subtract. Circle the **difference**.

1.

5 + 1 = _____

2.

2 − 0 = _____

Skills and Concepts

Draw circles to show each number.
Write the sum.

3.

0 + 5 = _____

4.

2 + 2 = _____

Cross out pictures to subtract. Write the difference

5.

5 − 2 = _____

6.

6 − 5 = _____

Write the subtraction sentence.

7.

_____ ◯ _____ ◯ _____

8.

_____ ◯ _____ ◯ _____

Complete the addition or subtraction sentence.

9. Show a way to subtract from 9.

$$9 - \underline{\quad} = \underline{\quad}$$

10. Show a way to make 10.

$$\underline{\quad} + \underline{\quad} = 10$$

11. Write the numbers to match the dots.
Write the sum.

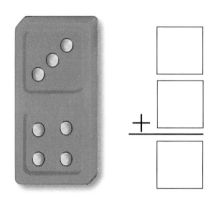

$$\underline{\quad} + \underline{\quad} = \underline{\quad}$$

Draw lines to match.
Subtract to find how many more.

12.

$$6 - 2 = \underline{\quad}$$

$$\underline{\quad} \text{ more}$$

13.

$$5 - 4 = \underline{\quad}$$

$$\underline{\quad} \text{ more}$$

Problem Solving

Draw a picture. Then write an addition sentence to solve.

14. 2 fish swim.
I more fish comes.
How many fish
are there in all?

$$\underline{\quad} \text{ fish}$$

✔️ Performance Assessment

Pick Up Jacks

Ann and Jenny were playing with jacks.

- Jenny placed some jacks in a circle.

- Ann picked up 2 jacks from the circle.

- After Ann picked up the 2 jacks, there were fewer than 4 jacks in the circle.

Write a subtraction number sentence that fits this math story. Draw pictures to help you.

Show your work.

TECHNOLOGY

The Learning Site • Seashell Search

1. Go to **www.harcourtschool.com.**
2. Click on ◖ .
3. Start. ➡
4. Add to play.

Type the sum.
Then click check.   1 + 2 = ☐   Check

Practice and Problem Solving

Write the sum or difference.

| 1. 2 + 4 = _____ | 2. 3 + 1 = _____ | 3. 6 + 4 = _____ |
| 4. 6 − 5 = _____ | 5. 5 − 1 = _____ | 6. 7 − 3 = _____ |

Write two ways to make 7.

7. _____ ◯ _____ ◯ _____   8. _____ ◯ _____ ◯ _____

---

9. Sara has 2 shells.
She finds 4 more.
How many does she
have in all?

_____ shells

10. Jim has 9 pennies.
He gives 2 away.
How many pennies does
he have left?

_____ pennies

Dear Family,

In Unit 1 we learned how to find sums and differences. Here is a game for us to play together. This game will give me a chance to share what I have learned.

Love,

_____

Directions

1. Put a bean on a space.
2. Use pennies to show one way to make that number.
3. Take turns. Your partner uses rocks instead of beans.
4. If you get the same number again, show a new way to make it.
5. The first person to cover 3 spaces in a row wins.

Materials

- 8 beans (or other small objects)
- 8 rocks (or other small objects)
- 10 pennies

3 in a Row

LOOKING FORWARD
SCHOOL HOME CONNECTION

Dear Family,

During the next few weeks, we will learn different ways to memorize addition and subtraction facts. Here is important math vocabulary and a list of books to share.

Love,

_____

Vocabulary Power

count on A way to add by counting on from the greater number.

$$6 + 2 = 8$$

Say 6. Count on 2.
7, 8

count back A way to subtract by counting backward from the greater number.

$$5 - 2 = 3$$

Say 5. Count back 2.
4, 3

A **fact family** includes all the addition and subtraction facts that use the same numbers.

$$5 + 2 = 7 \qquad 7 - 2 = 5$$
$$2 + 5 = 7 \qquad 7 - 5 = 2$$

BOOKS TO SHARE

To read about addition and subtraction with your child, look for these books in your library.

Domino Addition,
by Lynette Long Ph.D.,
Charlesbridge, 1996.

How Many, How Many, How Many,
by Rick Walton,
Candlewick, 1996.

Ten Sly Piranhas,
by William Wise,
Penguin Putnam, 1993.

Seven Little Rabbits,
by John Becker, Walker, 1994.

Visit *The Learning Site* for additional ideas and activities. **www.harcourtschool.com**

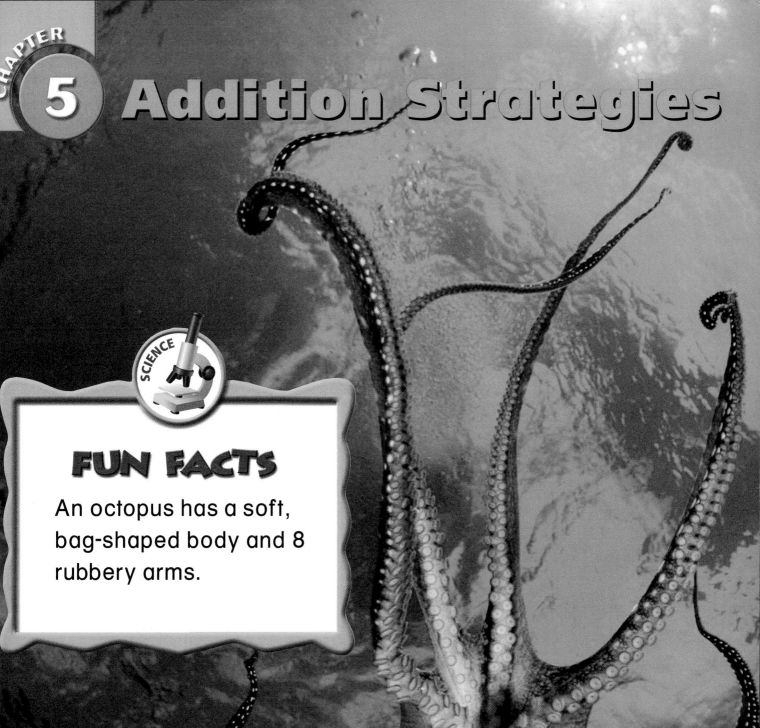

CHAPTER 5 Addition Strategies

SCIENCE

FUN FACTS

An octopus has a soft, bag-shaped body and 8 rubbery arms.

Theme: Sea Life

☑ Check What You Know

Addition Patterns

Count the ⬭. Draw one more.

Write how many in all.

1.

$1 \quad + \quad 1 \quad = \quad \underline{\qquad}$

2.

$2 \quad + \quad 1 \quad = \quad \underline{\qquad}$

3.

$3 \quad + \quad 1 \quad = \quad \underline{\qquad}$

4.

$4 \quad + \quad 1 \quad = \quad \underline{\qquad}$

5.

$5 \quad + \quad 1 \quad = \quad \underline{\qquad}$

6.

$6 \quad + \quad 1 \quad = \quad \underline{\qquad}$

7.

$7 \quad + \quad 1 \quad = \quad \underline{\qquad}$

Use this page to review important skills needed for this chapter.

Count On 1 and 2

Explore

Vocabulary

count on

Say 5. Count on 1.

6

5 + 1 = __6__

Say 6. Count on 2.

7   8

6 + 2 = __8__

Connect

Use ⬤. Count on. Write the sum.

1.

7 + 2 = _____

2.

8 + 1 = _____

3.

4 + 2 = _____

4.

8 + 2 = _____

Explain It • Daily Reasoning

Which number would you start with to find the sum for 2 + 6? Does it matter? Explain.

2 + 6 = ?

Use ⬤. Count on. Write the sum.

1.

5

$4 + 1 =$ __5__

2.

5   6

$4 + 2 =$ ____

3.

$7 + 2 =$ ___

4.

$5 + 1 =$ ___

5.

$5 + 2 =$ ___

6.

$7 + 1 =$ ___

7.

$3 + 2 =$ ___

8.

$8 + 1 =$ ___

9.

$2 + 1 =$ ___

10.

$8 + 2 =$ ___

11.

$3 + 1 =$ ___

Problem Solving
Algebra

Complete the addition sentence.

12.

8 in all

$6 + \blacksquare = 8$

$\blacksquare =$ ____

13.

7 in all

$6 + \blacksquare = 7$

$\blacksquare =$ ____

 Write About It ● Look at Exercise 13.
Explain how you got your answer.

🏠 **HOME ACTIVITY** • Choose numbers from 1 to 7, and have your child count on 1 or 2.

Name _____

Use a Number Line to Count On

You can use a number line to help you count on.

$$4 + 3 = \underline{7}$$

Start on 4.
Then move 3 spaces to
the right. **5, 6, 7**

Check

Use the number line.
Count on to find the sum.

1.

   $$7 + 3 = \underline{}$$

2. ![number line 5 to 10, dot on 6]

    $$6 + 2 = \underline{}$$

3. ![number line 5 to 10, dot on 5]

    $$5 + 2 = \underline{}$$

4. ![number line 5 to 10, dot on 8]

    $$8 + 1 = \underline{}$$

5. ![number line 5 to 10, dot on 9]

    $$9 + 1 = \underline{}$$

6. ![number line 5 to 10, dot on 6]

    $$6 + 3 = \underline{}$$

Explain It ● Daily Reasoning

What is the least sum you can get when you
count on 3? Why?

Use the number line.
Count on to find the sum.

Start on 5.
Count on 3.
6, 7, 8

$$\begin{array}{r} 5 \\ +3 \\ \hline 8 \end{array}$$

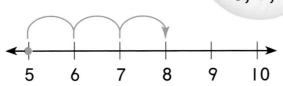

5   6   7   8   9   10

Number line: 0 1 2 3 4 5 6 7 8 9 10

1. $\begin{array}{r} 7 \\ +3 \\ \hline \end{array}$
2. $\begin{array}{r} 8 \\ +2 \\ \hline \end{array}$
3. $\begin{array}{r} 1 \\ +2 \\ \hline \end{array}$
4. $\begin{array}{r} 4 \\ +3 \\ \hline \end{array}$
5. $\begin{array}{r} 3 \\ +1 \\ \hline \end{array}$
6. $\begin{array}{r} 5 \\ +1 \\ \hline \end{array}$

7. $\begin{array}{r} 6 \\ +2 \\ \hline \end{array}$
8. $\begin{array}{r} 4 \\ +1 \\ \hline \end{array}$
9. $\begin{array}{r} 7 \\ +2 \\ \hline \end{array}$
10. $\begin{array}{r} 9 \\ +1 \\ \hline \end{array}$
11. $\begin{array}{r} 6 \\ +3 \\ \hline \end{array}$
12. $\begin{array}{r} 8 \\ +1 \\ \hline \end{array}$

13. $\begin{array}{r} 5 \\ +2 \\ \hline \end{array}$
14. $\begin{array}{r} 4 \\ +2 \\ \hline \end{array}$
15. $\begin{array}{r} 2 \\ +1 \\ \hline \end{array}$
16. $\begin{array}{r} 7 \\ +1 \\ \hline \end{array}$
17. $\begin{array}{r} 3 \\ +2 \\ \hline \end{array}$
18. $\begin{array}{r} 5 \\ +3 \\ \hline \end{array}$

Problem Solving

Mental Math

Solve.

19. Maria is 6 years old.
    Ted is 1 year older than Maria.
    Ann is 2 years older than Ted.
    How old is Ann? _____ years old

Write About It • Look at Exercise 19.
Explain how you got your answer.

HOME ACTIVITY • Have your child count a group of from 1 to 7 objects, tell you the number, and then count on to add 3.

Name _____

Use Doubles

Explore

When you add two numbers that are the same, the sentence is a doubles fact.

3 (+) 3 (=) 6

Connect

Use 🔲 .
Write the addition sentence.

1.

_____ ◯ _____ ◯ _____

2.

_____ ◯ _____ ◯ _____

3.

_____ ◯ _____ ◯ _____

4.

_____ ◯ _____ ◯ _____

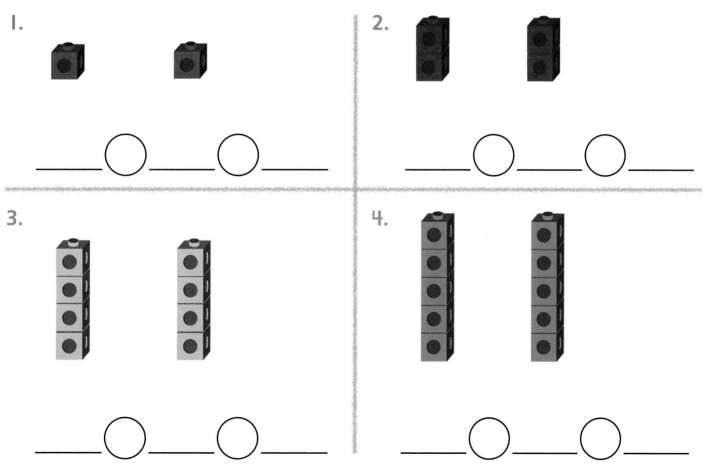

Explain It ● Daily Reasoning

Which of these numbers could not be the sum for a doubles fact? Why?

2, 4, 5, 6, 8, 10

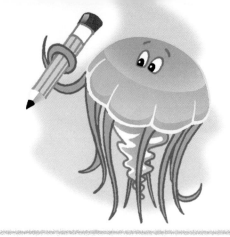

$$\begin{array}{r} 5 \\ +5 \\ \hline 10 \end{array}$$

Add. Then circle the doubles facts.

1. $\begin{array}{r} 5 \\ +3 \\ \hline \end{array}$ 2. $\begin{array}{r} 1 \\ +1 \\ \hline \end{array}$ 3. $\begin{array}{r} 2 \\ +2 \\ \hline \end{array}$ 4. $\begin{array}{r} 4 \\ +2 \\ \hline \end{array}$ 5. $\begin{array}{r} 3 \\ +2 \\ \hline \end{array}$ 6. $\begin{array}{r} 0 \\ +0 \\ \hline \end{array}$

7. $\begin{array}{r} 4 \\ +4 \\ \hline \end{array}$ 8. $\begin{array}{r} 6 \\ +1 \\ \hline \end{array}$ 9. $\begin{array}{r} 5 \\ +2 \\ \hline \end{array}$ 10. $\begin{array}{r} 7 \\ +3 \\ \hline \end{array}$ 11. $\begin{array}{r} 8 \\ +1 \\ \hline \end{array}$ 12. $\begin{array}{r} 9 \\ +1 \\ \hline \end{array}$

13. $\begin{array}{r} 5 \\ +5 \\ \hline \end{array}$ 14. $\begin{array}{r} 6 \\ +3 \\ \hline \end{array}$ 15. $\begin{array}{r} 7 \\ +2 \\ \hline \end{array}$ 16. $\begin{array}{r} 3 \\ +3 \\ \hline \end{array}$ 17. $\begin{array}{r} 3 \\ +2 \\ \hline \end{array}$ 18. $\begin{array}{r} 8 \\ +2 \\ \hline \end{array}$

Problem Solving
Visual Thinking

Write a doubles fact for each picture.

19.

___ ◯ ___ ◯ ___

20.

___ ◯ ___ ◯ ___

 Write About It • Look at Exercise 20.
Draw a picture of something else you could
use to show the doubles fact.

 HOME ACTIVITY • Ask your child to choose a number from 1 to 5 and tell you a doubles fact that
uses that number.

Problem Solving Strategy
Draw a Picture

There are 2 plates.

5 crackers are on each plate.

How many crackers are there?

UNDERSTAND

What do you want to find out?

Draw a line under the question.
Circle the information you need.

PLAN

You can draw a picture to solve the problem.

SOLVE

Draw 2 plates.
Draw 5 crackers on each plate.

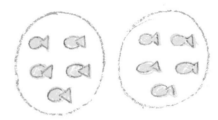

CHECK

Does your answer make sense?

Write an addition sentence to check.

5 ⊕ 5 ⊜ 10 crackers

PROBLEM SOLVING

Draw a picture to solve.
Write an addition sentence
to check.

What numbers
do I need to solve
the problem?

1. There are 4 blue fish.
   There are 4 red fish.
   How many fish
   are there?

____ ◯ ____ ◯ ____ fish

Draw a picture to solve. Write an addition sentence to check.

What numbers will help me solve the problem?

1. 4 crabs walk in the sand. 5 more join them. How many crabs are there?

4 ⊕ 5 ⊜ 9 crabs

2. There are 3 whales. 4 more come. How many whales are there?

___ ◯ ___ ◯ ___ whales

3. There are 2 nests. There are 3 turtles in each nest. How many turtles are there?

___ ◯ ___ ◯ ___ turtles

4. There are 6 big shells. There are 3 little shells. How many shells are there?

___ ◯ ___ ◯ ___ shells

HOME ACTIVITY • Tell your child an addition story. Have him or her draw a picture to solve and then tell you the addition sentence.

Name _____

Extra Practice

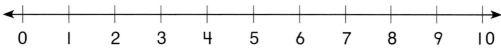

Use the number line.
Count on to find the sum.

```
←—+——+——+——+——+——+——+——+——+——+——+—→
   0   1   2   3   4   5   6   7   8   9  10
```

1. 6 + 2 = _____

2. 9 + 1 = _____

3. 5
    +2

4. 8
    +1

5. 4
    +3

6. 7
    +1

7. 4
    +2

8. 5
    +3

Add. Then circle the doubles facts.

9. 5
    +5

10. 6
    +3

11. 4
    +4

12. 6
    +1

13. 3
    +2

14. 2
    +2

Problem Solving

Draw a picture to solve.
Write an addition sentence to check.

15. There are 4 blue fish.
    There are 3 red fish.
    How many fish are there?

    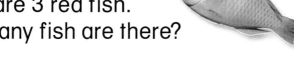

    ___ ◯ ___ ◯ ____ fish

16. There are 2 pails.
    There are 5 shells in each.
    How many shells are there?

    ___ ◯ ___ ◯ ____ shells

Name _____

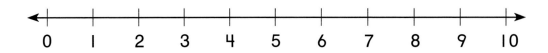✓Review/Test

Concepts and Skills

Use the number line.
Count on to find the sum.

```
←——+——+——+——+——+——+——+——+——+——+——→
   0   1   2   3   4   5   6   7   8   9  10
```

1. $8 + 1 =$ _____

2. $7 + 3 =$ _____

3. $\begin{array}{r} 7 \\ +2 \\ \hline \end{array}$
4. $\begin{array}{r} 8 \\ +2 \\ \hline \end{array}$
5. $\begin{array}{r} 6 \\ +3 \\ \hline \end{array}$
6. $\begin{array}{r} 6 \\ +2 \\ \hline \end{array}$
7. $\begin{array}{r} 9 \\ +1 \\ \hline \end{array}$
8. $\begin{array}{r} 5 \\ +3 \\ \hline \end{array}$

Add. Then circle the doubles facts.

9. $\begin{array}{r} 3 \\ +3 \\ \hline \end{array}$
10. $\begin{array}{r} 4 \\ +3 \\ \hline \end{array}$
11. $\begin{array}{r} 5 \\ +5 \\ \hline \end{array}$
12. $\begin{array}{r} 4 \\ +4 \\ \hline \end{array}$
13. $\begin{array}{r} 2 \\ +2 \\ \hline \end{array}$
14. $\begin{array}{r} 3 \\ +2 \\ \hline \end{array}$

Problem Solving

Draw a picture to solve.
Write an addition sentence to check.

15. There are 7 big sand dollars.
There are 2 little sand dollars.
How many sand dollars are there?

___ ◯ ___ ◯ ___ sand dollars

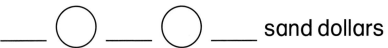

16. There are 2 buckets.
There are 4 starfish in each.
How many starfish are there?

___ ◯ ___ ◯ ___ starfish

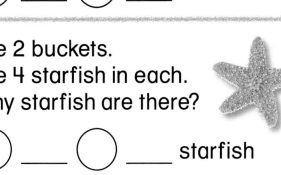

Name _____

Choose the answer for questions 1–3.

1. Which is the sum for 3 + 2?

4	5	6	7
○	○	○	○

2. Which does the number line show?

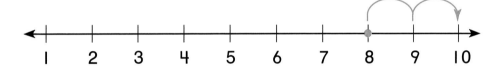

8 + 1	8 + 2	10 − 1	10 − 2
○	○	○	○

3. Which is a way to make 7?

4 + 1	4 + 3	3 + 3	3 + 2
○	○	○	○

Show What You Know

4. Draw a picture of a doubles fact. Write the number sentence to explain your answer.

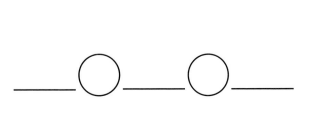

MATH GAME

Doubles Bubbles

Play with a partner.

You will need

2

1. Put your at START.

2. Toss the .

3. Move your that many spaces.

4. If you land on **doubles,** give the doubles fact for the number you tossed.

5. The first player to get to END wins.

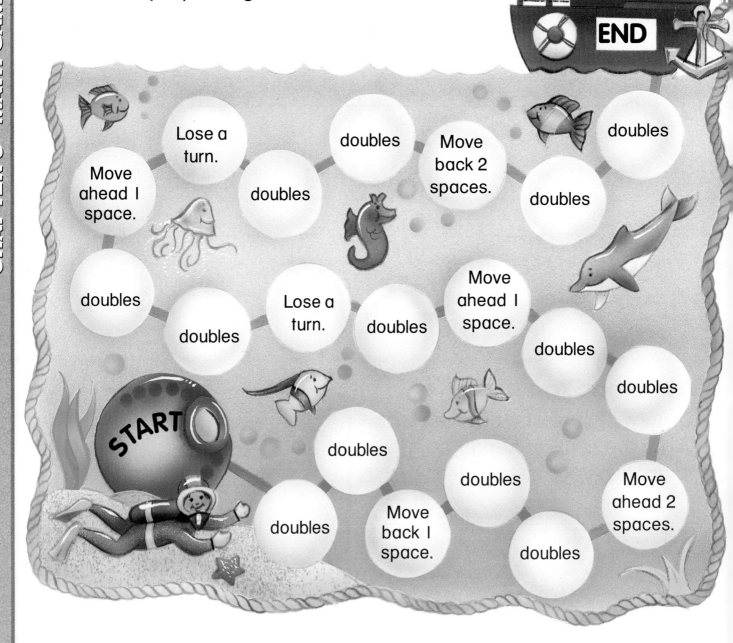

PHYSICAL
EDUCATION

FUN FACTS

Children who
like to exercise
usually stay
active from
year to year.

✔ Check What You Know

Add in Any Order

Add. Circle the addition sentences in each row
that have the same sum.

1. $3 + 1 = $ _____   2. $1 + 3 = $ _____   3. $1 + 2 = $ _____

4. $2 + 5 = $ _____   5. $7 + 1 = $ _____   6. $5 + 2 = $ _____

7. $4 + 2 = $ _____   8. $4 + 1 = $ _____   9. $2 + 4 = $ _____

10. $0 + 3 = $ _____   11. $1 + 3 = $ _____   12. $3 + 0 = $ _____

Use a Number Line to Count On

```
0   1   2   3   4   5   6   7   8   9   10
```

Use the number line. Count on to find the sum.

13. $\begin{array}{r} 4 \\ +2 \\ \hline \end{array}$ 14. $\begin{array}{r} 3 \\ +2 \\ \hline \end{array}$ 15. $\begin{array}{r} 5 \\ +1 \\ \hline \end{array}$ 16. $\begin{array}{r} 7 \\ +2 \\ \hline \end{array}$ 17. $\begin{array}{r} 6 \\ +2 \\ \hline \end{array}$

18. $\begin{array}{r} 8 \\ +2 \\ \hline \end{array}$ 19. $\begin{array}{r} 4 \\ +3 \\ \hline \end{array}$ 20. $\begin{array}{r} 6 \\ +3 \\ \hline \end{array}$ 21. $\begin{array}{r} 2 \\ +1 \\ \hline \end{array}$ 22. $\begin{array}{r} 3 \\ +1 \\ \hline \end{array}$

Use the Strategies

Learn

What helps you remember these facts?

$$1 + 0 = 0$$
$$1 + 1 = 2$$
$$1 + 2 = 3$$
$$1 + 3 = 4$$

I use add 0, doubles, or count on.

Check

Add. Write the sums.

1.

Count On 1
$5 + 1 = $ ___
$6 + 1 = $ ___
$7 + 1 = $ ___
$8 + 1 = $ ___
$9 + 1 = $ ___

2.

Count On 2
$4 + 2 = $ ___
$5 + 2 = $ ___
$6 + 2 = $ ___
$7 + 2 = $ ___
$8 + 2 = $ ___

3.

Count On 3
$4 + 3 = $ ___
$5 + 3 = $ ___
$6 + 3 = $ ___
$7 + 3 = $ ___

4.

Add 0
$6 + 0 = $ ___
$7 + 0 = $ ___
$8 + 0 = $ ___
$9 + 0 = $ ___
$10 + 0 = $ ___

5.

Use Doubles
$1 + 1 = $ ___
$2 + 2 = $ ___
$3 + 3 = $ ___
$4 + 4 = $ ___
$5 + 5 = $ ___

Explain It • Daily Reasoning

Why is $3 + 3 = 6$ a doubles fact?

$$\begin{array}{r} 4 \\ +3 \\ \hline 7 \end{array}$$

Add. Write the sum.

1. $\begin{array}{r} 4 \\ +3 \\ \hline 7 \end{array}$
2. $\begin{array}{r} 7 \\ +3 \\ \hline \end{array}$
3. $\begin{array}{r} 5 \\ +2 \\ \hline \end{array}$
4. $\begin{array}{r} 8 \\ +1 \\ \hline \end{array}$
5. $\begin{array}{r} 2 \\ +2 \\ \hline \end{array}$

6. $\begin{array}{r} 5 \\ +3 \\ \hline \end{array}$
7. $\begin{array}{r} 5 \\ +1 \\ \hline \end{array}$
8. $\begin{array}{r} 6 \\ +1 \\ \hline \end{array}$
9. $\begin{array}{r} 4 \\ +4 \\ \hline \end{array}$
10. $\begin{array}{r} 9 \\ +1 \\ \hline \end{array}$

11. $\begin{array}{r} 4 \\ +2 \\ \hline \end{array}$
12. $\begin{array}{r} 4 \\ +5 \\ \hline \end{array}$
13. $\begin{array}{r} 3 \\ +3 \\ \hline \end{array}$
14. $\begin{array}{r} 1 \\ +1 \\ \hline \end{array}$
15. $\begin{array}{r} 3 \\ +2 \\ \hline \end{array}$

16. $\begin{array}{r} 6 \\ +3 \\ \hline \end{array}$
17. $\begin{array}{r} 5 \\ +5 \\ \hline \end{array}$
18. $\begin{array}{r} 9 \\ +0 \\ \hline \end{array}$
19. $\begin{array}{r} 6 \\ +2 \\ \hline \end{array}$
20. $\begin{array}{r} 8 \\ +2 \\ \hline \end{array}$

Problem Solving

21. There are 9 children in all.
    2 are outside the playhouse,
    and the rest are inside.
    How many children are inside?

    _____ children are inside.

 Write About It • Look at Exercise
21. Draw pictures to show how you got
your answer.

HOME ACTIVITY • On each day of the week, choose a different number and work with your child to practice the facts that have that sum. For example, on Monday, practice all the facts that have a sum of 5.

Name _____

Sums to 8

You can change the order of the numbers you add. The sum is the same.

$$5 \\ +3 \\ \hline 8$$

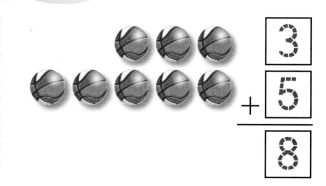

$$3 \\ +5 \\ \hline 8$$

Check

Add. Change the order.
Write the new fact.

1.
$$\begin{array}{r} 5 \\ +2 \\ \hline \end{array}$$
$$\begin{array}{r} \Box \\ +\Box \\ \hline \Box \end{array}$$

2.
$$\begin{array}{r} 4 \\ +3 \\ \hline \end{array}$$
$$\begin{array}{r} \Box \\ +\Box \\ \hline \Box \end{array}$$

3.
$$\begin{array}{r} 1 \\ +7 \\ \hline \end{array}$$
$$\begin{array}{r} \Box \\ +\Box \\ \hline \Box \end{array}$$

4.
$$\begin{array}{r} 6 \\ +2 \\ \hline \end{array}$$
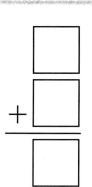

5.
$$\begin{array}{r} 7 \\ +0 \\ \hline \end{array}$$
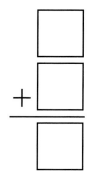

6.
$$\begin{array}{r} 5 \\ +1 \\ \hline \end{array}$$
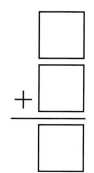

Explain It • Daily Reasoning

Does the sum change when you change the
order of the numbers you are adding? Explain.

1. Add. Use the key. Color each space by the sum. What patterns do you see?

2 +3 **5**	5 +2	0 +5	3 +4	4 +1
3 +3	2 +6	6 +0	3 +5	2 +4
7 +0	1 +4	1 +6	3 +2	2 +5
6 +2	1 +5	7 +1	4 +2	0 +8

Problem Solving
Mental Math

Solve. Draw a picture to check.

2. Eric has 8 flowers in two pots.
He has the same number in each pot.
How many flowers are in each pot?

_____ flowers

Write About It • Write a math story about this number sentence. Draw a picture to show your story.

$3 + 3 = 6$

HOME ACTIVITY • Ask your child to see how many addition facts with a sum of 8 he or she can write.

Sums to 10

Learn

The order of the numbers changed. The sum is the same.

```
  5     4
+ 4   + 5
  9     9
```

```
  6     4
+ 4   + 6
 10    10
```

Check

Add. Write the sums.

1.
```
  9     0
+ 0   + 9
```

2.
```
  9     1
+ 1   + 9
```

3.
```
  7     2
+ 2   + 7
```

4.
```
  7     3
+ 3   + 7
```

5.
```
  5     4
+ 4   + 5
```

6.
```
  4     3
+ 3   + 4
```

7.
```
 10     0
+  0  + 10
```

8.
```
  8     1
+ 1   + 8
```

9.
```
  6     2
+ 2   + 6
```

10.
```
  6     3
+ 3   + 6
```

11.
```
  3     5
+ 5   + 3
```

12.
```
  5     2
+ 2   + 5
```

13.
```
  8     2
+ 2   + 8
```

14.
```
  4     2
+ 2   + 4
```

15.
```
  1     7
+ 7   + 1
```

Explain It • Daily Reasoning

When is the sum the same as one of the two numbers you are adding?

Add across. Add down.
Write the sums.

1.

2	4	6
5	3	8
7	7	

2.

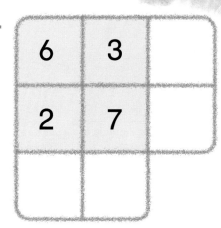

6	3	
2	7	

3.

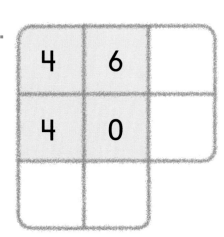

4	6	
4	0	

4.

8	2	
1	2	

Problem Solving
Mental Math

Circle two ways to name the same number.

5. 6 + 2   4 + 4   5 + 1   3 + 2

6. 0 + 9   7 + 3   6 + 3   5 + 2

 Write About It • Look at Exercise 6.
Write another way to name the same
number.

 HOME ACTIVITY • Say a number from 1 to 10, and ask your child to tell you an addition fact that
has that number as its sum. Repeat the activity for a new sum.

Algebra: **Follow the Rule**

Vocabulary

rule

Learn

Add 5	
0	5
1	6
2	7

The rule is Add 5.
I add 5 each time.

Check

Complete the table. Follow the rule.

1.

Add 2	
4	
6	
8	

2.

Add 3	
4	
3	
2	

3.

Add 4	
4	
5	
6	

4.

Add 1	
9	
8	
7	

5.

Add 2	
1	
2	
3	

6.

Add 0	
8	
9	
10	

Explain It ● Daily Reasoning

Does every table on this page have a pattern?
Explain.

Practice and Problem Solving

Complete the table. Follow the rule.

1.

Add 3	
5	8
6	9
7	10

2.

Add 5	
5	
4	
3	

3.

Add 1	
4	
5	
6	

4.

Add 2	
3	
5	
7	

5.

Add 4	
3	
2	
1	

6.

Add 6	
3	
2	
1	

Problem Solving
Logical Reasoning

Write the rule.

7.

Add ____	
2	5
4	7
6	9

8.

Add ____	
4	9
2	7
0	5

9.

Add ____	
7	7
8	8
9	9

 Write About It ● Look at Exercise 9.
Explain how you figured out the rule.

HOME ACTIVITY • Ask your child to write an addition rule. Help your child make a table that follows the rule.

92 ninety-two

Problem Solving Strategy
Write a Number Sentence

<u>6 children play.</u>

<u>3 more come.</u>

How many children are there now?

UNDERSTAND

What information do you know?

Underline it.

PLAN

How can you solve this problem?

Write a number sentence.

SOLVE

__6__ children play

__3__ more come

__6__ $\bigoplus$ __3__ $\bigominus$ __9__
children

CHECK

Does your answer make sense?

Explain.

Solve. Write a number sentence.
Draw a picture to check.

1. 3 boys go down the slide.
   3 girls go down the slide.
   How many children in
   all go down the slide?

   _____ $\bigcirc$ _____ $\bigcirc$ _____
   children

THINK:
How can I
find out how many
children there
are in all?

Problem Solving Practice

Solve. Write a number sentence.
Draw a picture to check.

Keep in Mind!
Understand
Plan
Solve
Check

THINK:
What do I need
to use to solve
the problem?

1. There are 8 bean bags.
Kendra finds 1 more.
How many bean bags
are there in all?

_____ ◯ _____ ◯ _____
bean bags

2. 6 boys run races.
2 girls join them.
How many children run in all?

_____ ◯ _____ ◯ _____
children

3. There are 4 soccer balls in one bag.
There are 6 in another bag. How
many soccer balls are there in all?

_____ ◯ _____ ◯ _____
soccer balls

4. 3 girls jump rope.
4 more girls join them.
How many girls
jump rope?

_____ ◯ _____ ◯ _____
girls

HOME ACTIVITY • Tell your child a math story, and ask him or her to write a number sentence to solve it.
For example: "A boy has 5 toy cars. Then he finds 3 more. How many toy cars does he have now?"
(5 + 3 = 8)

Extra Practice

Complete the table.
Follow the rule.

1.

Add 1	
9	
8	
7	

Add. Change the order.
Write the new fact.

2.
$$9$$
$$+0$$

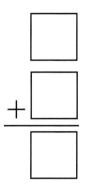

3.
$$6$$
$$+2$$

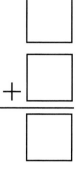

Add. Write the sum.

4.
$$4$$
$$+2$$

5.
$$6$$
$$+3$$

6.
$$1$$
$$+1$$

7.
$$8$$
$$+2$$

8.
$$7$$
$$+2$$

9.
$$5$$
$$+3$$

10.
$$5$$
$$+1$$

11.
$$4$$
$$+4$$

12.
$$4$$
$$+3$$

13.
$$6$$
$$+1$$

14.
$$7$$
$$+3$$

15.
$$2$$
$$+2$$

Problem Solving

Solve. Write a number sentence.
Draw a picture to check.

16. 2 girls are playing catch.
4 more girls join them.
How many girls are there
in all?

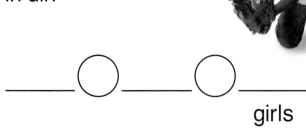

_____ ◯ _____ ◯ _____
girls

✓ Review/Test

Concepts and Skills

Complete the table.
Follow the rule.

1.

Add 3	
4	
5	
6	

Add. Change the order.
Write the new fact.

2.
$$\begin{array}{r} 2 \\ +8 \\ \hline \end{array}$$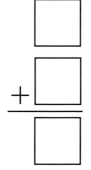

3.
$$\begin{array}{r} 4 \\ +5 \\ \hline \end{array}$$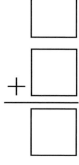

Add. Write the sum.

4.
$$\begin{array}{r} 9 \\ +1 \\ \hline \end{array}$$

5.
$$\begin{array}{r} 5 \\ +2 \\ \hline \end{array}$$

6.
$$\begin{array}{r} 4 \\ +4 \\ \hline \end{array}$$

7.
$$\begin{array}{r} 7 \\ +2 \\ \hline \end{array}$$

8.
$$\begin{array}{r} 6 \\ +3 \\ \hline \end{array}$$

9.
$$\begin{array}{r} 4 \\ +2 \\ \hline \end{array}$$

10.
$$\begin{array}{r} 3 \\ +3 \\ \hline \end{array}$$

11.
$$\begin{array}{r} 7 \\ +1 \\ \hline \end{array}$$

12.
$$\begin{array}{r} 6 \\ +2 \\ \hline \end{array}$$

13.
$$\begin{array}{r} 8 \\ +1 \\ \hline \end{array}$$

14.
$$\begin{array}{r} 5 \\ +5 \\ \hline \end{array}$$

15.
$$\begin{array}{r} 7 \\ +3 \\ \hline \end{array}$$

Problem Solving

Solve. Write a number sentence.
Draw a picture to check.

16. 5 boys play kickball.
    4 more boys join them.
    How many boys are
    playing in all?

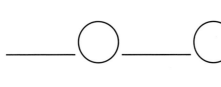

____ ◯ ____ ◯ ____
        boys

Getting Ready for the **EOG** Test
Chapters 1–6

Choose the answer for questions 1– 6.

1.   2 + 3 = _____

| 1 | 5 | 7 | 8 |
| ○ | ○ | ○ | ○ |

2.   7 + 1 = _____

| 6 | 8 | 10 | 13 |
| ○ | ○ | ○ | ○ |

3.   5 + 2 = _____

| 1 | 2 | 7 | 9 |
| ○ | ○ | ○ | ○ |

4.   5 + 5 = _____

| 0 | 6 | 10 | 16 |
| ○ | ○ | ○ | ○ |

5. Which is a way to make 10?

| 7 + 2 | 6 + 1 | 5 + 3 | 8 + 2 |
| ○ | ○ | ○ | ○ |

6. Kathy has 9 goldfish. She buys 1 more.
How many goldfish does she have in all?

| 12 | 10 | 7 | 6 |
| ○ | ○ | ○ | ○ |

Show What You Know

7. Write a rule.
Write numbers in the table that explain the rule.

Add _____	
4	
5	
6	

EOG TEST PREP

MATH GAME

Building Numbers

Play with a partner.
Fill in your chart.

You will need

2 🎲

5 ⚫   5 ⚪

1. One player uses ⚫. The other player uses ⚪.

2. Toss the 🎲 and 🎲.

3. Find an answer in your chart that matches one of the numbers you tossed. Cover that answer with a ⚫.

4. Your turn is over if there is no match.

5. The first player to cover all the answers wins.

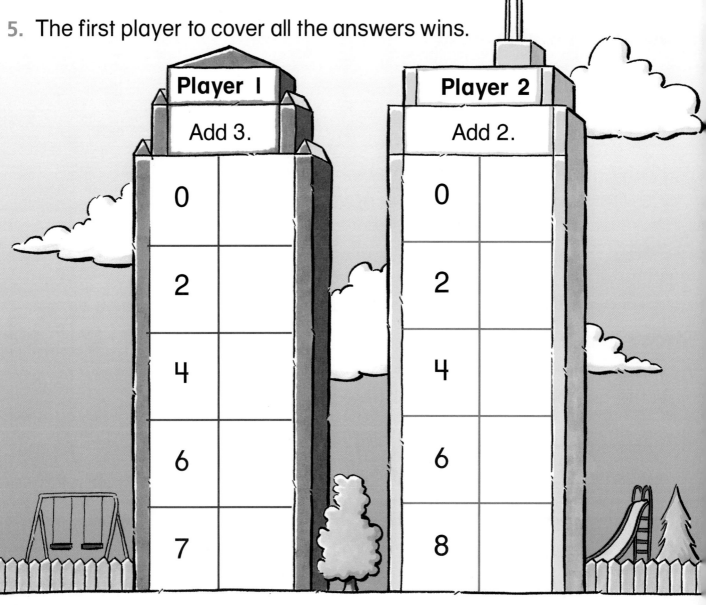

Player 1	
Add 3.	
0	
2	
4	
6	
7	

Player 2	
Add 2.	
0	
2	
4	
6	
8	

Subtraction Strategies

SCIENCE

FUN FACTS

A good mixture for making bubbles is 2 parts dishwashing liquid, 4 parts glycerine, and 1 part light corn syrup.

Theme: Things in the Air

✔ Check What You Know

Count Back on a Number Line

Start at 9.
Count back.
Circle the number you are on.

1. Count back 1.

2. Count back 2.

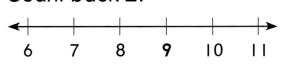

Subtraction Patterns

Count the birds.
Mark an X on the bird that is flying away.
Write how many birds are left.

3.

8 − 1 = _____

4.

7 − 1 = _____

5.

6 − 1 = _____

6.

5 − 1 = _____

Use this page to review important skills needed for this chapter.

Use a Number Line to Count Back 1 and 2

Vocabulary

number line
count back

Learn

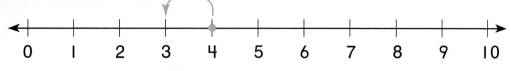

$4 - 1 =$ __3__

Start at 4 on the number line .
Count back 1. You are on 3.

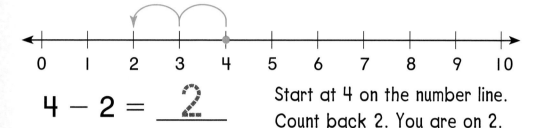

$4 - 2 =$ __2__

Start at 4 on the number line.
Count back 2. You are on 2.

Check

Use the number line.
Count back to subtract.

1.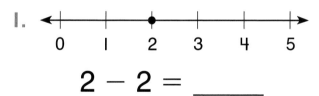

$2 - 2 =$ ____

2.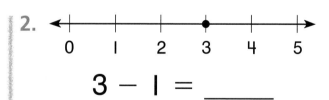

$3 - 1 =$ ____

3.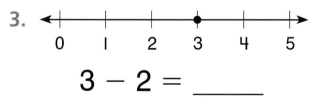

$3 - 2 =$ ____

4.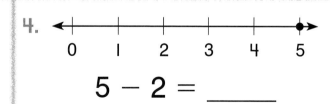

$5 - 2 =$ ____

5.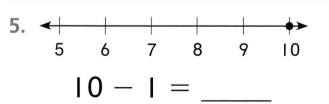

$10 - 1 =$ ____

6.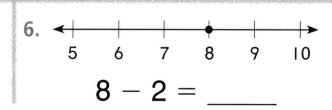

$8 - 2 =$ ____

Explain It • Daily Reasoning

When you use a number line to help you
subtract, why do you move to the left?

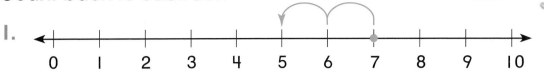

Start at 7.
Count back 2.
You are on 5.

Use the number line.
Count back to subtract.

1.

$$7 - 2 = \underline{5}$$

2.

0 1 2 3 4 5

$$5 - 1 = \underline{\quad}$$

3.

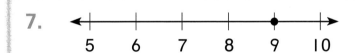

5 6 7 8 9 10

$$9 - 1 = \underline{\quad}$$

4.

5 6 7 8 9 10

$$10 - 2 = \underline{\quad}$$

5.

5 6 7 8 9 10

$$8 - 1 = \underline{\quad}$$

6.

0 1 2 3 4 5

$$1 - 1 = \underline{\quad}$$

7.

5 6 7 8 9 10

$$9 - 2 = \underline{\quad}$$

Problem Solving

Application

Use the number line to solve.
Write the number sentence.

0 1 2 3 4 5 6 7 8

8. There are 6 birds.
2 birds fly away.
How many birds are left?   _____ ◯ _____ ◯ _____ birds

 Write About It • Explain how you used the number line in Exercise 8 to find your answer.

Use a Number Line to Count Back 3

Learn

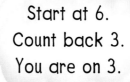

Start at 6.
Count back 3.
You are on 3.

0 1 2 3 4 5 6 7 8 9 10

$$6 - 3 = \underline{3}$$

Check

Use the number line. Count back to subtract.

1.
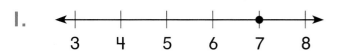
3 4 5 6 7 8

$$7 - 3 = \underline{\hphantom{00}}$$

2.
3 4 5 6 7 8

$$8 - 3 = \underline{\hphantom{00}}$$

3.

5 6 7 8 9 10

$$10 - 3 = \underline{\hphantom{00}}$$

4.
0 1 2 3 4 5

$$4 - 3 = \underline{\hphantom{00}}$$

5.

0 1 2 3 4 5

$$5 - 3 = \underline{\hphantom{00}}$$

6.
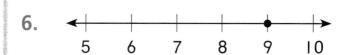
5 6 7 8 9 10

$$9 - 3 = \underline{\hphantom{00}}$$

Explain It • Daily Reasoning

How could you count back to subtract
without using a number line?

Count back to subtract. Use the key.
Color each part by the difference.

5 or less: GREEN
6 or greater: YELLOW

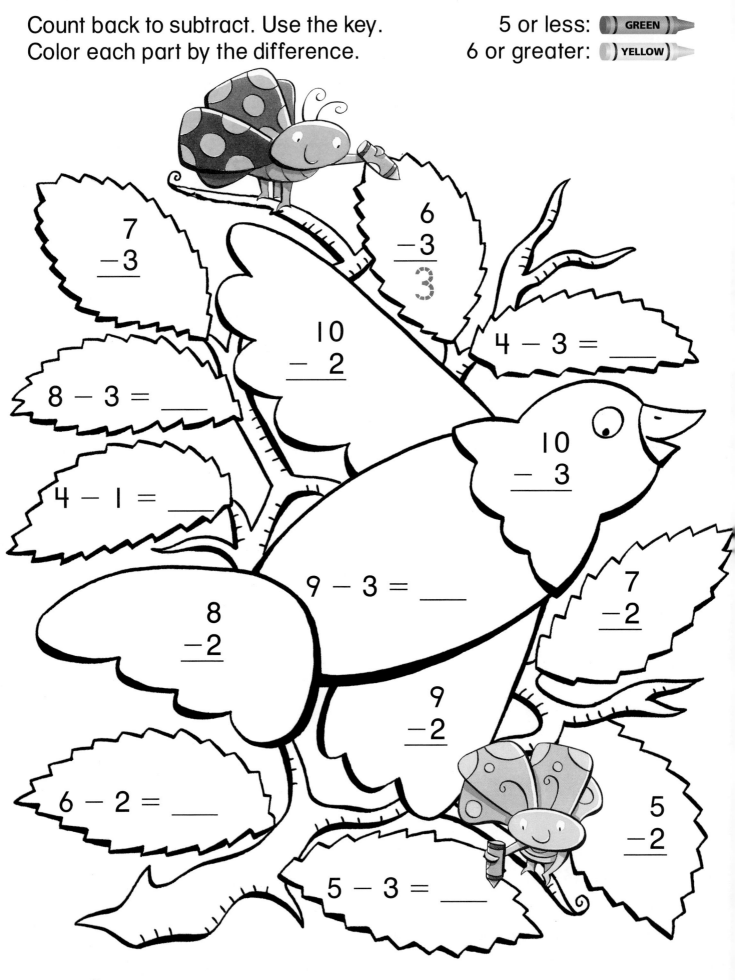

$7 - 3$

$6 - 3 = 3$

$4 - 3 = $ ___

$10 - 2$

$8 - 3 = $ ___

$10 - 3$

$4 - 1 = $ ___

$9 - 3 = $ ___

$8 - 2$

$7 - 2$

$9 - 2$

$6 - 2 = $ ___

$5 - 2$

$5 - 3 = $ ___

🏠 **HOME ACTIVITY** • Have your child explain how to count back to find the difference for $9 - 3$.

Algebra: **Relate Addition and Subtraction**

Vocabulary

related facts

Explore

These addition and subtraction sentences are related facts.

These facts use the same numbers!

$7 + 3 = 10$

$10 - 3 = 7$

Connect

Use 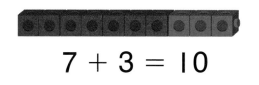 and to add and to subtract.
Complete the chart.

	Use	Add	Write the sum.	Take away	Write the difference.
1.	4	2	$4 + 2 =$ _6_	2	$6 - 2 =$ _4_
2.	5	3	$5 + 3 =$ ___	3	$8 - 3 =$ ___
3.	2	5	$2 + 5 =$ ___	5	$7 - 5 =$ ___
4.	7	2	$7 + 2 =$ ___	2	$9 - 2 =$ ___
5.	8	0	$8 + 0 =$ ___	0	$8 - 0 =$ ___

Explain It • Daily Reasoning

How are $6 + 3 = 9$ and $9 - 3 = 6$ alike? How are they different? Why are they called related facts?

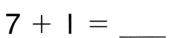

Add. Then subtract.

1.

$5 + 4 = \underline{9}$

$9 - 4 = \underline{5}$

2.

$7 + 1 = \underline{}$

$8 - 1 = \underline{}$

3.

$4 + 3 = \underline{}$

$7 - 3 = \underline{}$

4.
$$\begin{array}{cc} 8 & 9 \\ +1 & -1 \\ \hline \end{array}$$

5.
$$\begin{array}{cc} 4 & 8 \\ +4 & -4 \\ \hline \end{array}$$

6.
$$\begin{array}{cc} 6 & 10 \\ +4 & -\ 4 \\ \hline \end{array}$$

Problem Solving
Application

Solve. Write the addition or subtraction sentence.

7. 5 bugs are on a leaf.
   3 more join them. Now how
   many bugs are there?

   ____ ◯ ____ ◯ ____

8. 8 bugs are on a leaf.
   3 bugs fly away. Now how
   many bugs are there?

   ____ ◯ ____ ◯ ____

 Write About It • Make up a subtraction
story that uses the number 10. Draw to show
your story. Write the number sentence.

Name _____

Problem Solving Strategy
Draw a Picture

6 ladybugs were flying.

Some landed on a leaf.

4 ladybugs are still in the air.

How many ladybugs landed?

UNDERSTAND

What do you want to find out?

Draw a line under the question.

PLAN

You can draw a picture
to solve the problem.

SOLVE

$6 - \boxed{} = 4$

What number do I add to 4 to get 6?

$4 + \underline{2} = 6$

$\underline{2}$ ladybugs landed.

CHECK

Does your answer make sense?
Explain.

Draw a picture to solve the problem.

What number do I add to 5 to make 7?

I. 7 birds were flying.
   Some landed on a tree.
   5 birds are still in the air.
   How many birds landed?

   _____ birds

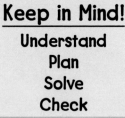

Draw a picture to solve the problem.

1. 9 butterflies were flying. Some butterflies landed on a bush. 6 butterflies are still in the air. How many butterflies landed?

What number do I add to 6 to make 9?

_____ butterflies

2. 8 kites were flying. Some kites came down. 4 kites are still in the air. How many kites came down?

What number do I add to 4 to make 8?

_____ kites

3. 10 bees were flying. Some went into a hive. 7 bees are still in the air. How many bees went into the hive?

What number do I add to 7 to make 10?

_____ bees

HOME ACTIVITY • Tell a math story like these in the problems on this page. Ask your child to draw a picture to solve the problem and then explain his or her drawing to you.

Name _____

Extra Practice

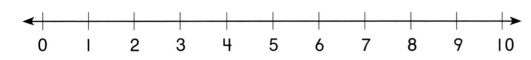

Use the number line.
Count back to subtract.

0 1 2 3 4 5 6 7 8 9 10

1.

$4 - 1 =$ _____

2.

$3 - 2 =$ _____

3.

$7 - 3 =$ _____

4.

$8 - 1 =$ _____

5.

$2 - 2 =$ _____

6.

$10 - 3 =$ _____

7.

$5 - 1 =$ _____

8.

$5 - 2 =$ _____

Add. Then subtract.

9.

$\begin{array}{r} 6 \\ +2 \\ \hline \end{array}$
$\begin{array}{r} 8 \\ -2 \\ \hline \end{array}$

10.

$\begin{array}{r} 5 \\ +1 \\ \hline \end{array}$
$\begin{array}{r} 6 \\ -1 \\ \hline \end{array}$

11.

$\begin{array}{r} 4 \\ +2 \\ \hline \end{array}$
$\begin{array}{r} 6 \\ -2 \\ \hline \end{array}$

Problem Solving

Draw a picture to solve the problem.

12. 5 birds were flying.
Some landed on a tree.
2 are still in the air.
How many birds landed?

What number
do I add to
2 to make 5?

_____ birds

✅ Review/Test

Concepts and Skills

Use the number line.
Count back to subtract.

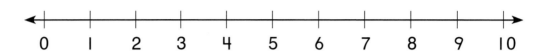

0 1 2 3 4 5 6 7 8 9 10

1.
$7 - 1 =$ _____

2.
$4 - 3 =$ _____

3.
$8 - 2 =$ _____

4.
$10 - 1 =$ _____

5.
$3 - 3 =$ _____

6.
$9 - 2 =$ _____

7.
$6 - 2 =$ _____

8.
$9 - 1 =$ _____

Add. Then subtract.

9.
$\begin{array}{r} 7 \\ +3 \\ \hline \end{array}$
$\begin{array}{r} 10 \\ -\ 3 \\ \hline \end{array}$

10.
$\begin{array}{r} 6 \\ +3 \\ \hline \end{array}$
$\begin{array}{r} 9 \\ -3 \\ \hline \end{array}$

11.
$\begin{array}{r} 2 \\ +7 \\ \hline \end{array}$
$\begin{array}{r} 9 \\ -7 \\ \hline \end{array}$

Problem Solving

Draw a picture to solve the problem.

12. 8 bees were flying. Some went into a hive. 6 bees are still flying. How many bees went into the hive?

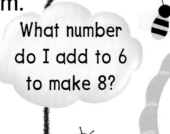

What number do I add to 6 to make 8?

_____ bees

Name _____

Getting Ready for the ★EOG Test
Chapters 1–7

Choose the answer for questions 1– 4.

1. Which does the number line show?

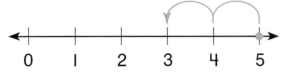

5 − 3 = __	5 − 2 = __	3 + 2 = __	2 + 3 = __
○	○	○	○

2. Which fact is related to 8 + 2 = 10?

6 + 2 = 8	7 + 1 = 8	8 − 2 = 6	10 − 8 = 2
○	○	○	○

3. Which does the number line show?

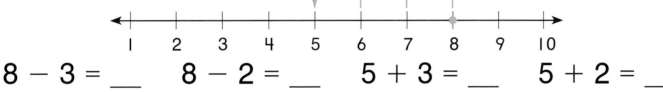

8 − 3 = __	8 − 2 = __	5 + 3 = __	5 + 2 = __
○	○	○	○

4. Which does the number line show?

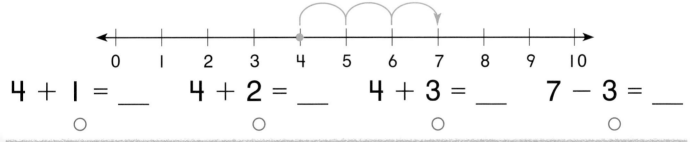

4 + 1 = __	4 + 2 = __	4 + 3 = __	7 − 3 = __
○	○	○	○

Show What You Know

5. Write numbers on the number line.
Draw arrows to show subtraction.
Write the subtraction sentence to explain.

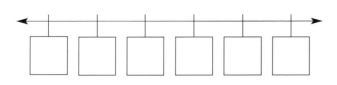

MATH GAME

Up, Up, and Away
Play with a partner.

1. Put your at START.

2. Stack the subtraction cards face down.

3. Take a card, and find the difference.

4. Move your that many spaces.

5. The first player to get to END wins.

You will need
subtraction cards

2

END

Take a card.

Take a card.

Take a card.

Take a card.

START

Subtraction Facts Practice

FUN FACTS

The starfruit is star-shaped when cut. It has 6 points.

✅ Check What You Know

Count Back to Subtract: Facts to 10

Use the number line. Count back to subtract.

1.
```
←+——+——+——+——+——●——+→
  0   1   2   3   4   5
```
$4 - 1 =$ _____

2.
```
←+——+——+——+——●——+——+——+→
  0   1   2   3   4   5
```
$3 - 2 =$ _____

3.
```
←+——+——+——+——+——●→
  0   1   2   3   4   5
```
$5 - 1 =$ _____

4.
```
←+——+——●——+——+——+→
  5   6   7   8   9   10
```
$7 - 2 =$ _____

5.
```
←+——+——+——●——+——+→
  5   6   7   8   9   10
```
$8 - 2 =$ _____

6.
```
←+——+——+——+——+——●→
  5   6   7   8   9   10
```
$10 - 1 =$ _____

Relate Addition and Subtraction

Add. Then subtract.

7.

$6 + 3 =$ _____

$9 - 3 =$ _____

8.

$5 + 2 =$ _____

$7 - 5 =$ _____

9.
```
   3       5
  +2      -3
  ___     ___
```

10.
```
   8      10
  +2     - 8
  ___     ___
```

11.
```
   3       7
  +4      -3
  ___     ___
```

Name _____

Use the Strategies

You can count back,
subtract 0, or subtract all.

10 − 1
10 − 2
10 − 3
10 − 0
10 − 10

Subtract. Write the difference.

1.

Count Back 1

10 − 1 = _9_

9 − 1 = ___

8 − 1 = ___

7 − 1 = ___

2.

Count Back 2

10 − 2 = _8_

9 − 2 = ___

8 − 2 = ___

7 − 2 = ___

3.

Count Back 3

10 − 3 = _7_

9 − 3 = ___

8 − 3 = ___

7 − 3 = ___

4.

Subtract 0

10 − 0 = _10_

9 − 0 = ___

8 − 0 = ___

5.

Subtract All

10 − 10 = _0_

9 − 9 = ___

8 − 8 = ___

Explain It • Daily Reasoning

How can knowing that 10 − 3 = 7 help
you find the difference for 10 − 4?

Practice and Problem Solving

Subtract. Circle the facts for
subtract 0 and for **subtract all**.

1. $\begin{array}{r} 9 \\ -9 \\ \hline 0 \end{array}$ 2. $\begin{array}{r} 8 \\ -0 \\ \hline 8 \end{array}$ 3. $\begin{array}{r} 7 \\ -2 \\ \hline \end{array}$ 4. $\begin{array}{r} 8 \\ -3 \\ \hline \end{array}$ 5. $\begin{array}{r} 6 \\ -3 \\ \hline \end{array}$ 6. $\begin{array}{r} 10 \\ -1 \\ \hline \end{array}$

7. $\begin{array}{r} 7 \\ -3 \\ \hline \end{array}$ 8. $\begin{array}{r} 9 \\ -2 \\ \hline \end{array}$ 9. $\begin{array}{r} 10 \\ -2 \\ \hline \end{array}$ 10. $\begin{array}{r} 4 \\ -0 \\ \hline \end{array}$ 11. $\begin{array}{r} 6 \\ -1 \\ \hline \end{array}$ 12. $\begin{array}{r} 8 \\ -8 \\ \hline \end{array}$

13. $\begin{array}{r} 7 \\ -1 \\ \hline \end{array}$ 14. $\begin{array}{r} 10 \\ -0 \\ \hline \end{array}$ 15. $\begin{array}{r} 9 \\ -3 \\ \hline \end{array}$ 16. $\begin{array}{r} 5 \\ -3 \\ \hline \end{array}$ 17. $\begin{array}{r} 4 \\ -2 \\ \hline \end{array}$ 18. $\begin{array}{r} 10 \\ -10 \\ \hline \end{array}$

19. $\begin{array}{r} 6 \\ -0 \\ \hline \end{array}$ 20. $\begin{array}{r} 8 \\ -1 \\ \hline \end{array}$ 21. $\begin{array}{r} 7 \\ -7 \\ \hline \end{array}$ 22. $\begin{array}{r} 9 \\ -1 \\ \hline \end{array}$ 23. $\begin{array}{r} 8 \\ -2 \\ \hline \end{array}$ 24. $\begin{array}{r} 10 \\ -3 \\ \hline \end{array}$

Problem Solving
Visual Thinking

25. Cross out some of the apples.
Write a subtraction sentence
to tell about the picture.

____ ◯ ____ ◯ ____

 Write About It • Why is 0 the answer
when you subtract all?

HOME ACTIVITY • Make subtraction flash cards with your child. Have your child find all the facts
that have a difference of 1, for example, 4 – 3 = 1.

Subtraction to 10

Learn

These facts use the same numbers.

```
  10          10
-  2        -  8
-----       -----
   8           2
```

$10 - 2 = 8$, so
$10 - 8 = 2$.

Check

Subtract. Circle the pair of facts
if they use the same numbers.

1.
```
   9       9
-  1     - 8
-----    -----
   8       1
```

2.
```
   7       7
-  7     - 0
-----    -----
```

3.
```
  10      10
-  5     - 9
-----    -----
```

4.
```
  10      10
-  6     - 4
-----    -----
```

5.
```
   8       8
-  3     - 7
-----    -----
```

6.
```
   9       9
-  5     - 4
-----    -----
```

7.
```
   8       8
-  5     - 4
-----    -----
```

8.
```
  10      10
-  7     - 3
-----    -----
```

9.
```
   9       9
-  2     - 7
-----    -----
```

10.
```
   9       9
-  6     - 3
-----    -----
```

11.
```
   8       8
-  2     - 6
-----    -----
```

12.
```
   7       7
-  5     - 1
-----    -----
```

Explain It • Daily Reasoning

If you know that $10 - 1 = 9$, what other
subtraction fact do you know? Explain.

$10 - 1 = 9$

Practice and Problem Solving

Subtract across. Subtract down.

1.

5	4	1
3	2	1
2	2	0

2.

6	3	
4	3	

3.

7	1	
6	0	

4.

8	4	
7	4	

Problem Solving

Logical Reasoning

Solve the riddle. Write the number.

5. If you count back 2 from me, the answer is 3. What number am I?

_____

6. If you count back 3 from me, the answer is 4. What number am I?

_____

 Write About It ● Look at Exercise 6. Explain how you got your answer.

⬠ HOME ACTIVITY • Have your child tell you all the subtraction facts from 8 − 0 through 8 − 8.

Name _____

Algebra: **Follow the Rule**

Vocabulary

rule

Learn

Subtract 2	
10	8
8	6
6	4

The rule is subtract 2, so I subtract 2 from each number.

Check

Complete the table. Follow the rule.

1.

Subtract 1	
7	
5	
3	

2.

Subtract 5	
10	
9	
8	

3.

Subtract 3	
5	
6	
7	

4.

Subtract 0	
5	
7	
9	

5.

Subtract 4	
7	
8	
9	

6.

Subtract 2	
2	
4	
6	

Explain It ● Daily Reasoning

What patterns do you see? Explain.

Complete the table. Follow the rule.

1.

Subtract 2	
5	3
4	
3	

2.

Subtract 0	
2	
4	
6	

3.

Subtract 3	
10	
9	
8	

4.

Subtract 1	
10	
8	
6	

5.

Subtract 5	
5	
6	
7	

6.

Subtract 4	
4	
5	
6	

Problem Solving

Logical Reasoning

Write the rule.

7.

Subtract _____	
7	5
5	3
3	1

8.

Subtract _____	
6	5
4	3
2	1

 Write About It • Look at Exercise 8.
Explain how you got your answer.

HOME ACTIVITY • Ask your child to write a subtraction rule and make a table that follows the rule.
Have him or her explain how to use the table.

Name _____

Fact Families to 10

Explore

The numbers in this fact family are 2, 4, and 6.

$4 + 2 = \underline{6}$ $6 - 2 = \underline{4}$

$2 + 4 = \underline{6}$ $6 - 4 = \underline{2}$

Connect

Use and to add or subtract.
Write the numbers in the fact family.

1. $8 + 2 = \underline{\hspace{1cm}}$

$2 + 8 = \underline{\hspace{1cm}}$

$10 - 2 = \underline{\hspace{1cm}}$

$10 - 8 = \underline{\hspace{1cm}}$

2	8	10

2. $4 + 1 = \underline{\hspace{1cm}}$

$1 + 4 = \underline{\hspace{1cm}}$

$5 - 1 = \underline{\hspace{1cm}}$

$5 - 4 = \underline{\hspace{1cm}}$

3. $7 + 2 = \underline{\hspace{1cm}}$

$2 + 7 = \underline{\hspace{1cm}}$

$9 - 2 = \underline{\hspace{1cm}}$

$9 - 7 = \underline{\hspace{1cm}}$

4. $8 + 1 = \underline{\hspace{1cm}}$

$1 + 8 = \underline{\hspace{1cm}}$

$9 - 1 = \underline{\hspace{1cm}}$

$9 - 8 = \underline{\hspace{1cm}}$

Explain It • Daily Reasoning

How many addition and subtraction facts are in the fact family for these numbers?
Use and to prove your answer.

Add or subtract. Write the numbers in the fact family.

1.

$$
\begin{array}{r} 6 \\ +2 \\ \hline 8 \end{array}
\qquad
\begin{array}{r} 2 \\ +6 \\ \hline 8 \end{array}
\qquad
\begin{array}{r} 8 \\ -2 \\ \hline 6 \end{array}
\qquad
\begin{array}{r} 8 \\ -6 \\ \hline 2 \end{array}
$$

| 2 | 6 | 8 |

2.

$$
\begin{array}{r} 4 \\ +3 \\ \hline \end{array}
\qquad
\begin{array}{r} 3 \\ +4 \\ \hline \end{array}
\qquad
\begin{array}{r} 7 \\ -3 \\ \hline \end{array}
\qquad
\begin{array}{r} 7 \\ -4 \\ \hline \end{array}
$$

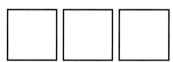

| | | |

3.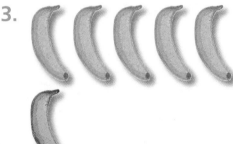

$$
\begin{array}{r} 5 \\ +1 \\ \hline \end{array}
\qquad
\begin{array}{r} 1 \\ +5 \\ \hline \end{array}
\qquad
\begin{array}{r} 6 \\ -1 \\ \hline \end{array}
\qquad
\begin{array}{r} 6 \\ -5 \\ \hline \end{array}
$$

| | | |

Problem Solving
Algebra

4. Write the missing numbers.

$$
\begin{array}{r} 6 \\ +\ \square \\ \hline 9 \end{array}
\qquad
\begin{array}{r} \square \\ +\ 6 \\ \hline 9 \end{array}
\qquad
\begin{array}{r} 9 \\ -\ \square \\ \hline 6 \end{array}
\qquad
\begin{array}{r} 9 \\ -\ 6 \\ \hline \square \end{array}
$$

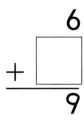 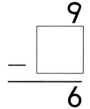 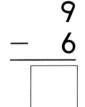

Write About It • Look at Exercise 4.
Explain why the number facts belong in a fact family.

 HOME ACTIVITY • Have your child write the facts in a fact family and then explain to you why those number sentences belong in that family.

Problem Solving Skill
Choose the Operation

Jessie has 6 apples.
She gives 4 away.
How many apples does
she have left?

Some apples are taken away. I need to subtract.

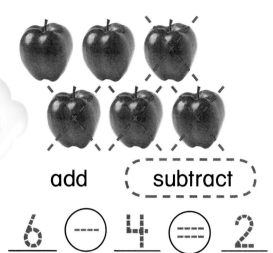

add   (subtract)

_2_ apples

6 (−) 4 (=) 2

There are 3 forks on a table.
Ida brings 2 more.
How many are there now?

More forks are added. I need to add.

(add)   subtract

_5_ forks

3 (+) 2 (=) 5

Circle **add** or **subtract**.
Write the number sentence.

THINK:
Do I add
or subtract?

1. There are 7 pretzels.
   Children eat 4 of them.
   How many are left?

   _____ pretzels

   add   subtract

   __○__○__

2. There are 9 carrots.
   Bunnies eat 5 of them.
   How many carrots
   are left?

   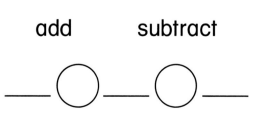

   _____ carrots

   add   subtract

   __○__○__

PROBLEM SOLVING

Problem Solving Practice

Circle **add** or **subtract**.
Write the number sentence.

THINK:
Do I add or subtract?

1. There are 5 muffins.
   Zoe brings 2 more.
   How many are there now?

   _7_ muffins

   (add)   subtract

   5 (+) 2 (=) 7

2. There are 6 apples.
   Children eat 2 of them.
   How many are left?

   _____ apples

   add   subtract

   ___ ◯ ___ ◯ ___

3. There are 7 pears.
   John brings 3 more.
   How many are there now?

   _____ pears

   add   subtract

   ___ ◯ ___ ◯ ___

4. There are 8 sandwiches.
   Children eat 3 of them.
   How many are left?

   _____ sandwiches

   add   subtract

   ___ ◯ ___ ◯ ___

5. There are 8 oranges.
   Children eat 4 of them.
   How many are left?

   _____ oranges

   add   subtract

   ___ ◯ ___ ◯ ___

HOME ACTIVITY • For each problem, ask your child to tell how he or she decided whether to add or subtract.

124 one hundred twenty-four

Name _____

Extra Practice

Subtract. Circle the pair of facts if they use the same numbers.

1.
```
   6      6
  -2     -4
```

2.
```
   7      7
  -5     -3
```

3.
```
   8      8
  -3     -5
```

Add or subtract.
Write the numbers in the fact family.

4.

```
   3      2      5      5
  +2     +3     -3     -2
```

☐ ☐ ☐

Complete the table. Follow the rule.

5.

Subtract 1	
9	
8	
7	

6.

Subtract 0	
5	
4	
3	

7.

Subtract 3	
3	
4	
5	

Problem Solving

Circle **add** or **subtract**.
Write the number sentence.

8. There are 6 acorns under a tree.
   A squirrel eats 3 acorns.
   How many acorns are left?

   _____ acorns

   add   subtract

   ____ ◯ ____ ◯ ____

✔ Review/Test

Concepts and Skills

Subtract. Circle the pair of facts if they use the same numbers.

1.
$$9 \atop -5$$
$$9 \atop -4$$

2.
$$10 \atop -8$$
$$10 \atop -1$$

3.
$$7 \atop -4$$
$$7 \atop -3$$

Add or subtract.
Write the numbers in the fact family.

4.

$$4 \atop +2$$
$$2 \atop +4$$
$$6 \atop -2$$
$$6 \atop -4$$

Complete the table. Follow the rule.

5.

Subtract 3	
10	
9	
8	

6.

Subtract 2	
8	
9	
10	

7.

Subtract 5	
5	
7	
9	

Problem Solving

Circle **add** or **subtract**.
Write the number sentence.

8. There are 10 grapes. Meg eats
   2 of them. How many are left?

   _____ grapes

add   subtract

____○____○____

Getting Ready for the EOG Test
Chapters 1–8

Choose the answer for questions 1 – 6.

1. Which number completes the table?

Count Back 2
8 – 2 = 6
9 – 2 = 7
10 – 2 = ?

4   6   8   10
○   ○   ○   ○

2. Which number completes the table?

Subtract 4	
4	0
5	1
6	?

1   2   9   10
○   ○   ○   ○

3.   10 – 1 = ____

9   10   11   13
○   ○   ○   ○

4.   9 – 2 = ____

6   7   10   11
○   ○   ○   ○

5. Which subtraction fact is related to 4 + 3 = 7?

7 – 5 = 2   8 – 4 = 4   7 – 3 = 4   10 – 3 = 7
○   ○   ○   ○

6. 3 pickles are in a bowl. 2 more are added. Which number sentence tells how many pickles are in the bowl now?

3 – 2 = 1   3 – 3 = 0   3 + 2 = 5   2 + 2 = 4
○   ○   ○   ○

Show What You Know

7. Use 3, 7, and 10. Write the four number sentences that explain the fact family.

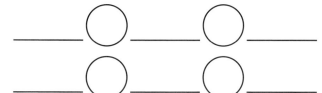 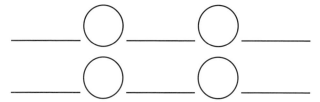

IT'S IN THE BAG
Math Under the Sea

PROJECT Create your own snorkel mask to practice your math facts.

You Will Need

- Blackline patterns
- Crayons
- Scissors

Directions

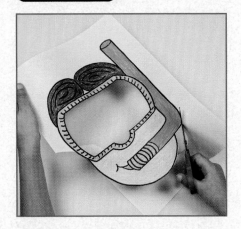

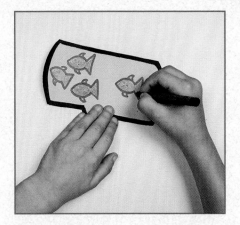

1. Color the snorkel person.
2. Cut out the snorkel person.

3. Draw an addition or subtraction problem. Use turtles, fish, or shells in your problem.

4. Write the addition or subtraction sentence. Then write the answer on a bubble.

5. Draw other problems. Write the number sentences and answers.

UNDER THE Sea

written by Jo Sumara
illustrated by Jui Ishida

This book will help me review addition and subtraction facts.

This book belongs to _____.

1 lobster sits on the
sand in the sea.

2 more come along,

so now there are _____.

6 dolphins jump up,
do a flip, and then dive.

1 swims away,
so now there are ____.

1 sea horse floats by.

He looks like a hero.

Soon he is gone,
and then there are _____.

F

Name _____

PROBLEM SOLVING IN NORTH CAROLINA

Unahwi Ridge, NC

At the Raspberry Festival

Pomme de Terre farm in Unahwi Ridge grows fruits and vegetables. It has a Raspberry Festival each year in July.

How many raspberries were eaten?

Use ● to solve.

Write the number sentence.

raspberry bushes

1

before   after

$\underline{9} \ominus \blacksquare = \underline{5}$

$\underline{4}$ raspberries

2

before   after

_____ $\bigcirc$ $\blacksquare$ = _____

_____ raspberries

3

before   after

_____ $\bigcirc$ $\blacksquare$ = _____

_____ raspberries

4

before   after

_____ $\bigcirc$ $\blacksquare$ = _____

_____ raspberries

Name _____

CHALLENGE

Missing Parts

$6 = \underline{8} - 2$ \qquad $6 = 8 - \underline{2}$

Add or subtract.
Write the missing numbers.

1.

$10 = \underline{\quad} + 4$ \qquad $10 = 6 + \underline{\quad}$

2.

$4 = \underline{\quad} - 3$ \qquad $4 = 7 - \underline{\quad}$

3.

$5 = \underline{\quad} - 4$ \qquad $5 = 9 - \underline{\quad}$

4.

$8 = \underline{\quad} + 3$ \qquad $8 = 5 + \underline{\quad}$

Name _____

✓ Study Guide and Review

Skills and Concepts

Use the number line. Circle the number you use to **count on**. Add.

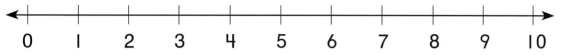

0 1 2 3 4 5 6 7 8 9 10

1. 6 + 2 = _____

2. 7 + 3 = _____

Use the number line. Circle the number you use to **count back**. Subtract.

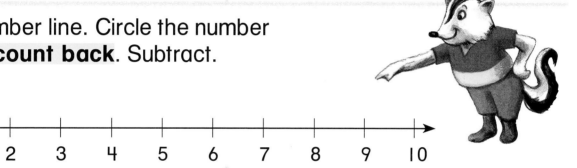

0 1 2 3 4 5 6 7 8 9 10

3. 8 − 2 = _____

4. 9 − 3 = _____

Add. Then circle the doubles facts.

5.
```
  2
+ 2
```

6.
```
  8
+ 2
```

7.
```
  2
+ 5
```

8.
```
  4
+ 4
```

9.
```
  3
+ 3
```

10.
```
  7
+ 2
```

Add. Then subtract.

11.
```
  5      9
+ 4    − 4
```

12.
```
  7     10
+ 3    − 7
```

13.
```
  4      8
+ 4    − 4
```

Add. Change the order. Write the new fact.

14.
$$4$$
$$+\ 2$$
☐
$$+$$ ☐
$$\overline{}$$ ☐

15.
$$1$$
$$+\ 6$$
☐
$$+$$ ☐
$$\overline{}$$ ☐

16.
$$3$$
$$+\ 5$$
☐
$$+$$ ☐
$$\overline{}$$ ☐

Add or subtract.
Write the numbers in the fact family.

17. $4 + 6 =$ _____ $10 - 6 =$ _____

$6 + 4 =$ _____ $10 - 4 =$ _____

☐ ☐ ☐

Complete the table. Follow the rule.

18.
Add 3	
0	
2	
4	

19.
Subtract 2	
6	
5	
4	

20.
Subtract 1	
10	
9	
8	

Problem Solving

Circle add or subtract. Write the number sentence.

21. Max has 8 apples.
He gives 5 apples away.
How many does he have left?

_____ apples

add   subtract

_____ ◯ _____ ◯ _____

Performance Assessment

Little Lambs

Maria went inside the barn.
Little lambs were in two stalls.

- She counted 3 little lambs in one stall.

- She counted some more little lambs in the other stall.

- Maria counted fewer than 7 little lambs in all.

Write a number sentence that fits this math story. Write the other number sentences in that fact family.

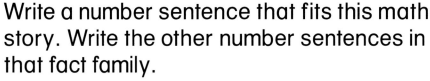

Show your work.

PERFORMANCE ASSESSMENT

TECHNOLOGY

Calculator • Add and Subtract

Use a .
Write the answers.

Press

Press ON/C [2] [+] [3] [=] **5** [−] [1] [=] **4**

Practice and Problem Solving

1. Press ON/C [6] [+] [4] [=] _____ [−] [1] [=] _____

2. Press ON/C [6] [−] [4] [=] _____ [+] [4] [=] _____

3. Press ON/C [3] [+] [0] [=] _____ [+] [7] [=] _____

4. Press ON/C [3] [−] [0] [=] _____ [+] [6] [=] _____

5. Press ON/C [7] [+] [2] [=] _____ [+] [1] [=] _____

6. Press ON/C [7] [−] [2] [=] _____ [+] [1] [=] _____

7. Press ON/C [6] [−] [3] [=] _____

Explain your answer.
Use ⬤ .

Dear Family,

In Unit 2 we learned addition and subtraction facts to 10. Here is a game for us to play together. This game will give me a chance to share what I have learned.

Love,

_____

Directions
1. Put your game piece on START.
2. Use a paper clip and a pencil to make the spinner. Spin. Move that many spaces.
3. Add or subtract the number you spin and the number your game piece is on.
4. Move forward 1 if you added. Move forward 2 if you subtracted.
5. Take turns. The first person to get to END wins.

Materials
- 2 game pieces or beans
- pencil
- paper clip

Spinner: 1 2 3 4 5

Get Those Numbers

START 5 → 6 4 2 5 9 3 7 Go again. 10

Go again. 3 4 5 3 2 5 7 2 4

6 3 1 5 4 8 6 6 END

LOOKING FORWARD
SCHOOL HOME CONNECTION

Dear Family,

During the next few weeks, we will learn about graphs and about numbers to 100. Here is important math vocabulary and a list of books to share.

Love,

_____

Vocabulary Power

picture graph

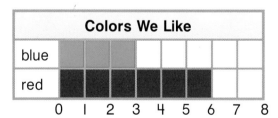

Favorite Fruits

| apples | 🍎 🍎 🍎 🍎 🍎 |
| oranges | 🍊 |

bar graph

Colors We Like

blue								
red								
	0	1	2	3	4	5	6	7	8

26 > 24

26 is greater than 24.

24 < 26

24 is less than 26.

24 = 24

24 is equal to 24.

BOOKS TO SHARE

To read about graphs and about numbers to 100 with your child, look for these books in your library.

Is It Rough? Is It Smooth? Is It Shiny?
by Tana Hoban, Greenwillow, 1990.

Pancakes for Breakfast,
by Tomie dePaola, Harcourt, 1990.

Two of Everything,
by Lily Toy Hong, Albert Whitman, 1993.

Splash,
by Ann Jonas, Greenwillow, 1995.

Visit *The Learning Site* for additional ideas and activities. **www.harcourtschool.com**

CHAPTER 9

Graphs and Tables

FUN FACTS

You see ten fingers when you make handprint paintings.

Name ———————————————

✔ Check What You Know

Read a Tally Table

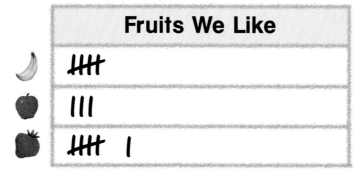

Fruits We Like	
🍌	ＨＨＴ
🍎	|||
🍓	ＨＨＴ	

Write how many.

1. ———

2. ———

3. ———

4. Circle the fruit the most children chose.

Make Picture Graphs

5. Look at the picture.
   Make a graph about pennies and nickels.

Pennies and Nickels

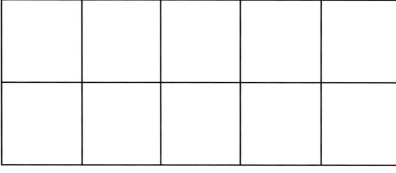

Write how many of each coin.
Circle the number that shows fewer.

6.

 ———

7.

 ———

Name _____

Algebra: **Sort and Classify**

Vocabulary
sort

Explore

You can sort these shapes.

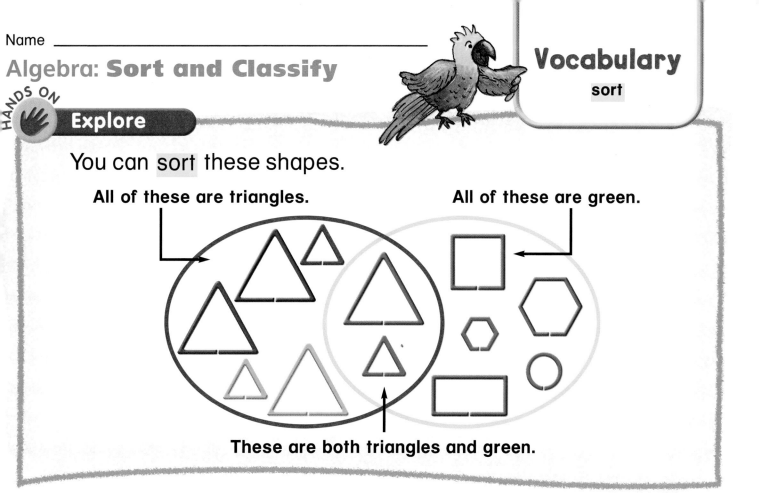

All of these are triangles.

All of these are green.

These are both triangles and green.

Connect

Sort your shapes a different way.
Draw each group. Tell how you sorted.

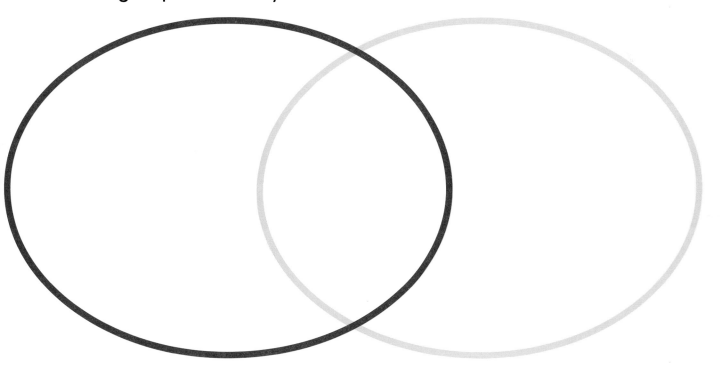

Explain It • Daily Reasoning

How could you sort your shapes into four
different groups? Show one way.

Draw a line from each shape
to the group where it belongs.

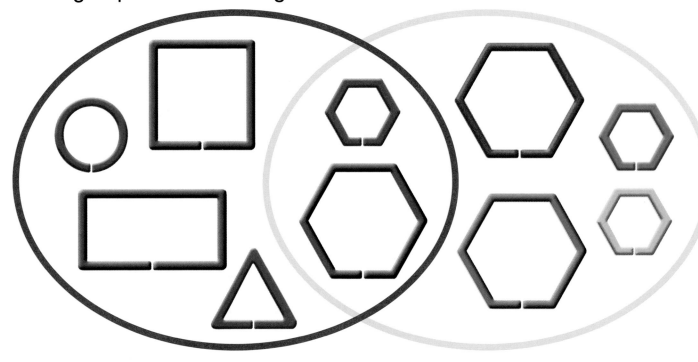

1.

2.

3.

4.

Problem Solving
Application

5. Draw how you could sort
these buttons.

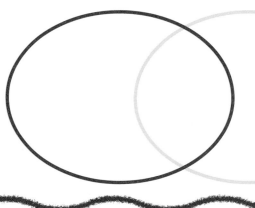

 Write About It ● Draw how
you could sort these buttons.

🏠 **HOME ACTIVITY** • Ask your child to explain how he or she sorted in Exercises 1–4.

Make Concrete Graphs

 Explore

This concrete graph shows how many crayons there are of each color.

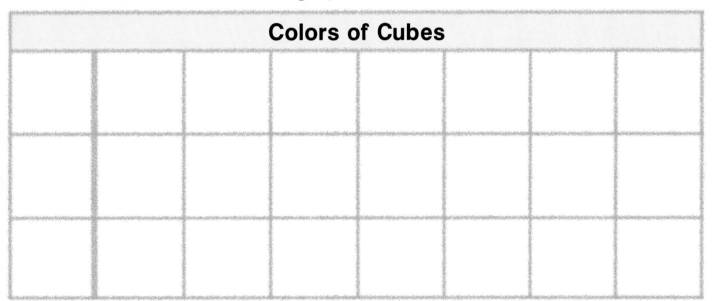

Colors of Crayons

red	red	red	red	red	red	red	red
blue	blue	blue	blue				
green	green	green	green	green	green		

Connect

Sort ⬛, ⬛, and ⬛. Make a graph.

Colors of Cubes

1. How many ⬛ are there? _____

2. How many ⬛ are there? _____

3. How many ⬛ are there? _____

Explain It • Daily Reasoning

Which color cube did you have the most of?
How do you know?

Practice and Problem Solving

Use the graph to answer the questions.

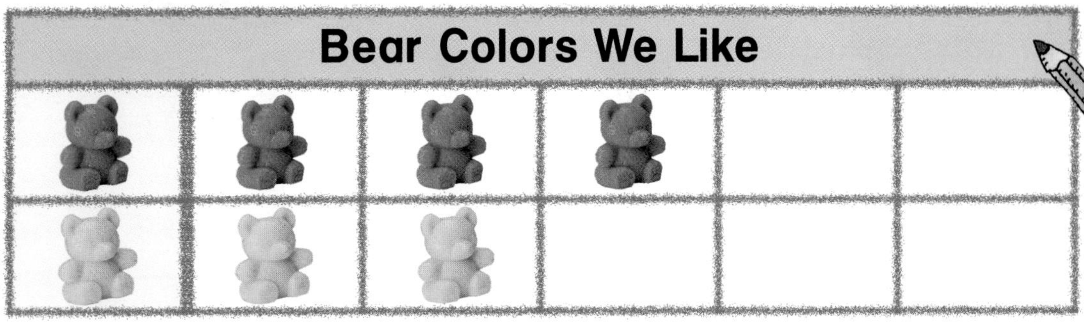

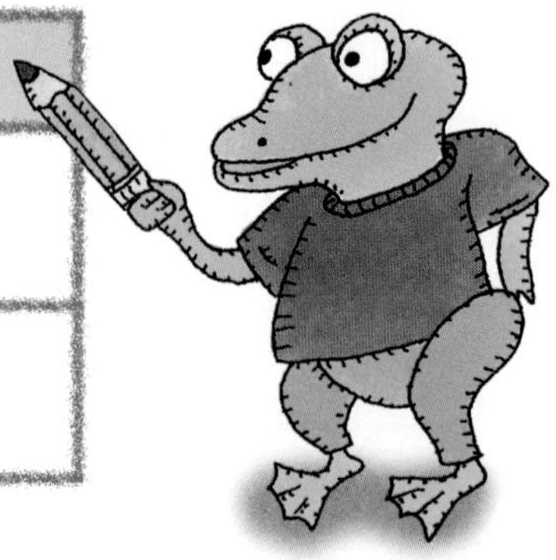

1. How many children chose ? ______
2. How many children chose ? ______
3. Which color did more children choose? ______________
4. Which color did fewer children choose? ______________
5. How many children in all chose colors? ______

Problem Solving

Application

6. Ask six classmates what their favorite bear color is. Use , , , to show each choice.

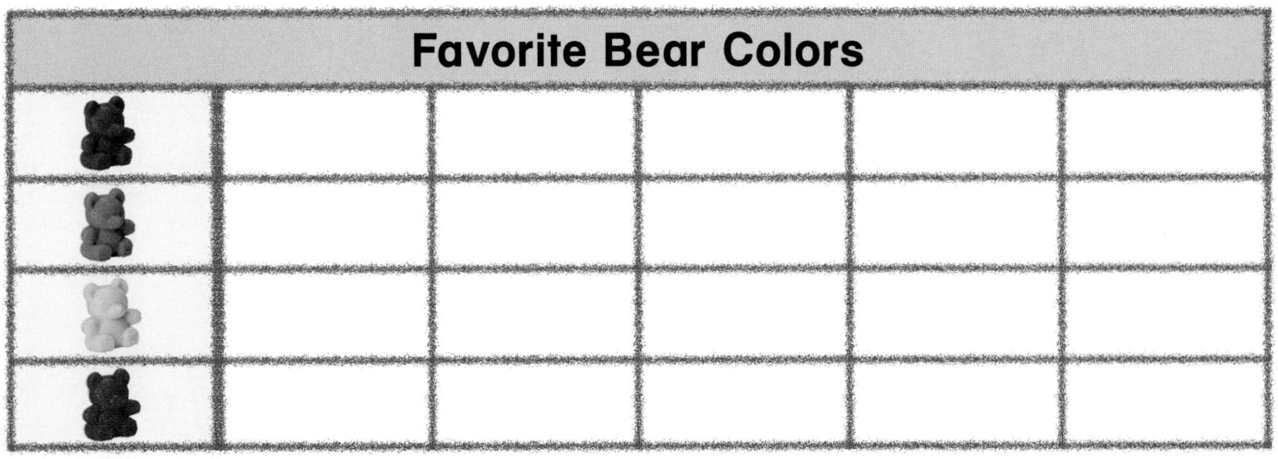

Write About It • Which is the favorite bear color of the most classmates? Explain how you know.

HOME ACTIVITY • Give your child a collection of pots and lids. Have him or her line them up in two rows. Ask how many are in each row, which row has more, and which has fewer.

Name _____

Make Picture Graphs

Learn

This picture graph uses pictures to show
how many children chose each fruit.

Fruits We Like

🍎 apples	🍎	🍎	🍎				
🍊 oranges	🍊	🍊					
🍌 bananas	🍌	🍌	🍌	🍌			

The most
children
chose
bananas.

Check

1. Some children drew pictures of their favorite fruits.
   Sort. Draw to complete the picture graph.

Fruits We Like

🍓 strawberries	🍓					
grapes						
🍒 cherries	🍒					

2. How many children drew ?   _____

3. Which fruit did the most children draw?   _____

4. Which fruit did the fewest children draw?   _____

Explain It • Daily Reasoning

What would you ask to find out
your classmates' favorite fruits?

Vegetables We Like

potatoes									
peas									
carrots									
beans									

Use the picture graph to answer the questions.

1. How many children chose carrots? _____

2. Did more choose beans or peas? _____

3. Did fewer choose potatoes or carrots? _____

4. How many more chose carrots than beans? _____

Problem Solving

Logical Reasoning

5. Complete the graph.

   There are 3 fewer oranges than apples. There are 2 more pears than oranges.

Fruits in the Bowl

Write About It ● Look at Exercise 5. How did you know how many oranges to draw?

HOME ACTIVITY • Have your child collect 10 to 15 stuffed animals or other toys. Have him or her sort them into groups and tell how many are in the group that has the most.

Name _____

Read a Tally Table

Learn

Which snack do you like better?

Snacks We Like		Total
pretzels	ЖHt II	7
carrots	ЖHt IIII	9

This tally table shows how many children chose each snack.

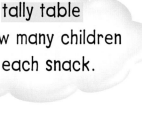

Each tally mark I stands for one child.
ЖHt stands for five children.
More children chose carrots than pretzels.

Check

Choose two kinds of juice from the pictures.
Ask eight children the question.
Then fill in the tally table.

Which juice do you like better?

Juices We Like		Total

orange   grape   apple

Use the tally table to answer these questions.

1. How many children chose _____ ? _____

2. How many children chose _____ ? _____

3. Which juice did more children choose? _____

Explain It • Daily Reasoning

What would happen if you added
more choices of juice?

Choose two bird colors from the pictures.
Ask eight children the question.
Then fill in the tally table.

green   red   blue

Which bird color do you like better?

Bird Colors We Like		Total

HIII
stands for 5.

Use the tally table to answer these questions.

1. How many children chose _____ ? _____

2. How many children chose _____ ? _____

3. Did fewer children choose _____ or _____ ?
   Circle the color word.

4. How many fewer? _____

Problem Solving

Application

5. How many more children chose 🐦 than 🐦 ?
   Use the tally table. Write the number sentence.

   ___ ◯ ___ ◯ ___

   ____ more children

Birds We Like		Total
🐦	HIII III	
🐦	IIII	

 Write About It • Look at Exercise 5.
Explain how you got your answer.

🏠 **HOME ACTIVITY** • Give your child 10 to 12 objects of two kinds, such as forks and spoons. Have him or her make a tally table to show how many there are of each kind.

Make Bar Graphs

Vocabulary
bar graph

Learn

Make a bar graph by coloring one box for each tally mark.

More children ride than walk.

How We Go to School	Total
walk 🚶	IIII	4
ride 🚌	IIII I	6

How We Go to School						
walk 🚶						
ride 🚌						

0 1 2 3 4 5 6

Check

1. Write how many tally marks.

Things We Like to Do		Total
read 📕	IIII III	8
paint 🖌	IIII	
play sports ⚾	IIII	

2. What is the question for this graph?

_____

3. Color the bar graph to match the tally marks.

Things We Like to Do										
read 📕										
paint 🖌										
play sports ⚾										

0 1 2 3 4 5 6 7 8 9 10

Explain It • Daily Reasoning

How does writing how many tally marks help you make a bar graph?

1. Write how many tally marks.

2. Color the bar graph to match.

Our Pets		Total
cat	ЖН II	
dog	ЖН ЖН	
fish	IIII	

Use the graph to answer the questions.

3. How many children have cats? _____

4. How many more children have cats than fish? _____

Kinds of Pets

10
9
8
7
6
5
4
3
2
1
0

cat   dog   fish

Problem Solving

Logical Reasoning

5. Use these clues to make a bar graph.
   More children have bears than cars.
   The fewest children have dolls.

Our Toys											
car											
bear											
doll											

0   1   2   3   4   5   6   7   8   9   10

 Write About It • How is the bar graph in Exercise 5 different from the first bar graph on this page?

🏠 **HOME ACTIVITY** • Cover the tally table. Ask your child how many children have each kind of pet.

Name _____

Problem Solving Skill
Use Data from a Graph

THINK:
Each box equals one child's choice.

Use the bar graph to answer the questions.

Subjects We Like										
math										
reading										
science										
social studies										

0   1   2   3   4   5   6   7   8   9   10

1. How many children chose math or reading?

_____ children

THINK:
You can add to solve a problem.

$7 \oplus 3 \ominus 10$

2. How many more children chose social studies than science?

_____ children

THINK:
You can subtract to solve a problem.

____ ◯ ____ ◯ ____

3. Did more children choose science or reading?

_____
- - - - - - - - - - - - - - - -
_____

4. How many more children chose science than reading?

_____ children chose science.

_____ children chose reading.

_____ more child

____ ◯ ____ ◯ ____

Problem Solving Practice

Use the bar graph to answer the questions.

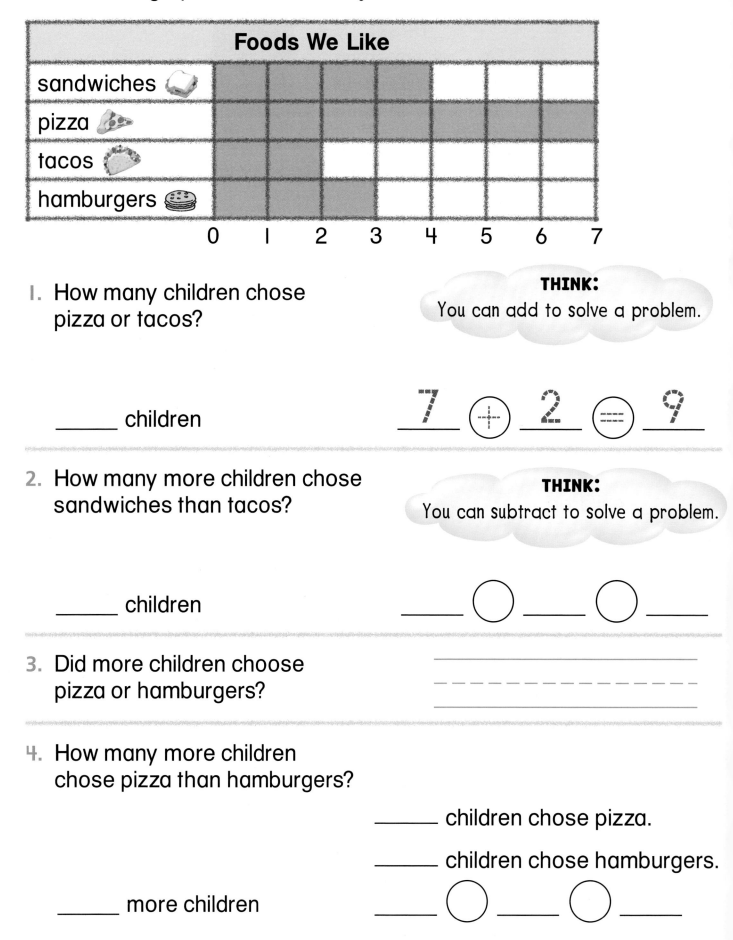

Foods We Like

sandwiches 🥪							
pizza 🍕							
tacos 🌮							
hamburgers 🍔							

0 1 2 3 4 5 6 7

1. How many children chose pizza or tacos?

   THINK:
   You can add to solve a problem.

   _____ children $7 \oplus 2 \ominus 9$

2. How many more children chose sandwiches than tacos?

   THINK:
   You can subtract to solve a problem.

   _____ children   ____ ◯ ____ ◯ ____

3. Did more children choose pizza or hamburgers?

   _____
   - - - - - - - - - - - -
   _____

4. How many more children chose pizza than hamburgers?

   _____ children chose pizza.

   _____ children chose hamburgers.

   _____ more children   ____ ◯ ____ ◯ ____

Interpret Graphs

Learn

These are the numbers of pets some children have.

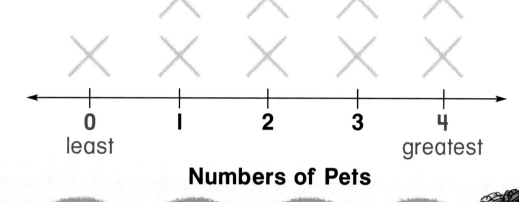

Numbers of Pets

Check

Use the graph to answer the questions.

1. How many pets do the most children have? _____

2. What is the least number of pets children have? _____

3. What is the greatest number of pets children have? _____

4. What is the difference between the greatest number of pets and the least number of pets?

Explain It • Daily Reasoning

How many children were asked about their pets? How do you know?

Use the graph to answer the questions.

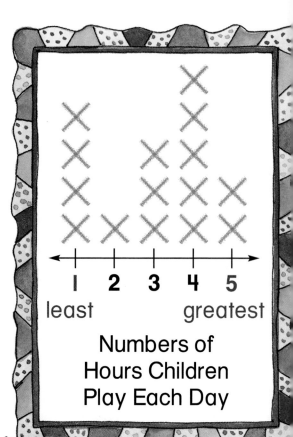

1. How many hours do the most children play? _____

2. What is the greatest number of hours children play? _____

3. What is the least number of hours children play? _____

4. What is the difference between the greatest number of hours and the least number of hours?

_____ ◯ _____ ◯ _____

Problem Solving

Application

Solve.

5. Two more children play 2 hours each day. How many children play 2 hours each day now?

_____ children

6. Two more children play 4 hours each day. How many children play 4 hours each day now?

_____ children

 Write About It • Look at Exercise 6. Draw a picture of how the graph would look.

HOME ACTIVITY • Help your child make a graph like the one on this page to show how many hours family members watch television on weekdays.

Name _____

Extra Practice

Children chose from three sports.

1. Write how many tally marks.

   Which sport do you like the best?

Sports We Like		Total
soccer	卌	
baseball	‖	
basketball	‖‖	

2. Color the bar graph to match the tally table.

Sports We Like					
soccer					
baseball					
basketball					

       0   1   2   3   4   5

Problem Solving

Use the bar graph to answer the questions.

3. How many children chose basketball?

   _____

4. Which game did the most children choose?

   _____

5. How many children chose soccer? _____

 Review/Test

Concepts and Skills

Children chose from three shirt colors.

1. Write how many tally marks.

   Which shirt color do you like the best?

Shirt Colors We Like		Total
red	‖‖‖	
yellow	‖‖‖	
blue	‖‖‖ ‖	

2. Color the bar graph to match the tally table.

Shirt Colors We Like						
red						
yellow						
blue						

   0   1   2   3   4   5   6

Problem Solving

Use the bar graph to answer the questions.

3. How many children chose red?

   _____

4. Which color did the most children choose?

   _____

5. How many children chose blue? _____

Getting Ready for the ★EOG Test
Chapters 1-9

Choose the answer for questions 1- 3.
Use the graph to answer questions 1 and 2.

Our Pets					
dog	🐕	🐕	🐕	🐕	🐕
cat	🐈	🐈	🐈		
rabbit	🐇	🐇			

1. How many children have ?

   2   3   5   7
   ○   ○   ○   ○

2. Which pet do the fewest children have?

             🐇   🐕
   ○   ○   ○

3. Which subtraction fact is related to 4 + 2 = 6?

   4 − 1 = 3   6 − 5= 1   4 − 3 = 1   6 − 2 = 4
   ○   ○   ○   ○

Show What You Know

4. Sort. Fill in the tally table to explain how you sorted. Color the bar graph to match the tally marks.

Fruits We Like		
apple	🍎	
banana	🍌	
strawberry	🍓	

Fruits We Like						
apple	🍎					
banana	🍌					
strawberry	🍓					

0   1   2   3   4   5

5. How many more children chose apples than bananas?

   1   3   4   5
   ○   ○   ○   ○

MATH GAME

Graph Game

Play with a partner.

You will need

1. Spin the .

2. Put 1 cube of that color in your graph.

3. Take turns until one player fills a row.

4. That player tosses the 🎲.

5. The player who has a row with that many cubes wins. If no player has a row with that many, toss again.

Player 1

Player 2

FUN FACTS

A medium size piñata can hold about 100 pieces of hard candy and small toys.

Name _____

✅ Check What You Know

Make Groups of 10
Count. Draw more to make a group of 10.

1.

2.

3.

4.

11 to 20: Using Ten Frames
Count. Circle the number that tells how many.
Write the number.

5.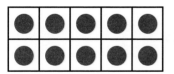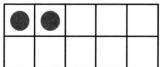

11   12   13   ____

6.

13   14   15   ____

7.

17   18   19   ____

8.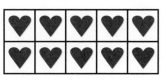

18   19   20   ____

Use this page to review important skills needed for this chapter.

Teen Numbers

Explore

You use 1 ten and ones to show teen numbers.

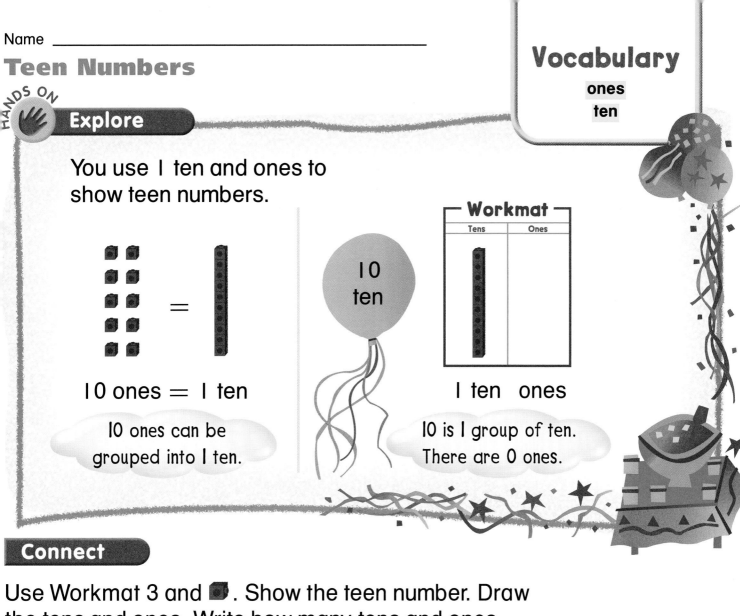

10 ones = 1 ten

10 ones can be grouped into 1 ten.

10 ten

Workmat

Tens	Ones

1 ten   ones

10 is 1 group of ten. There are 0 ones.

Connect

Use Workmat 3 and ⬛. Show the teen number. Draw the tens and ones. Write how many tens and ones.

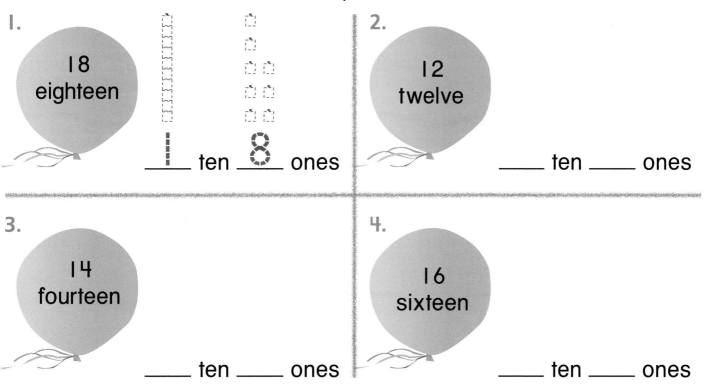

1.

18 eighteen

__1__ ten __8__ ones

2.

12 twelve

____ ten ____ ones

3.

14 fourteen

____ ten ____ ones

4.

16 sixteen

____ ten ____ ones

Explain It • Daily Reasoning

What number comes before the first teen number?

Draw the tens and ones.
Write how many tens and ones.

1.

14
fourteen

_____ ten _____ ones

2.

19
nineteen

_____ ten _____ ones

3.

13
thirteen

_____ ten _____ ones

4.

11
eleven

_____ ten _____ ones

5.

17
seventeen

_____ ten _____ ones

6.

15
fifteen

_____ ten _____ ones

Problem Solving

Logical Reasoning

Write the teen number that solves the riddle.

7. I am less than 19.
   I am more than 17.
   What teen number am I?   _____

 Write About It ● Look at Exercise 7.
Draw the tens and ones to show your answer.

Name _____

Tens

Explore

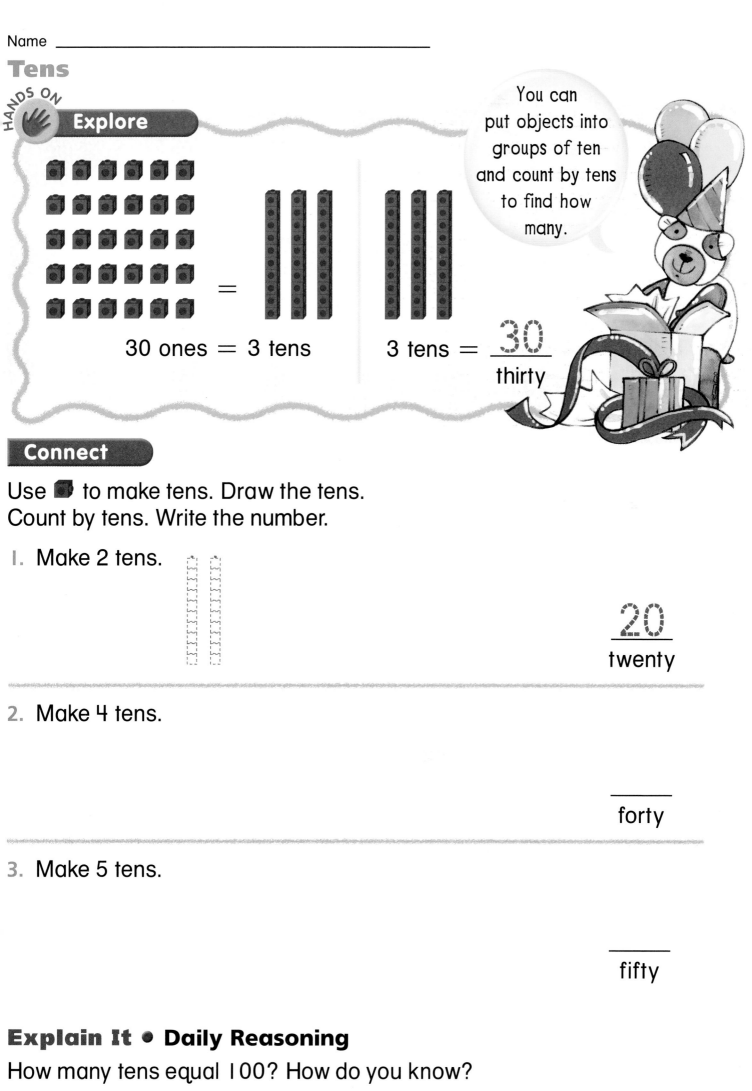

30 ones = 3 tens

3 tens = __30__
thirty

You can put objects into groups of ten and count by tens to find how many.

Connect

Use 🎲 to make tens. Draw the tens.
Count by tens. Write the number.

1. Make 2 tens.

__20__
twenty

2. Make 4 tens.

_____
forty

3. Make 5 tens.

_____
fifty

Explain It • Daily Reasoning

How many tens equal 100? How do you know?

Count by tens. Write the number.

1.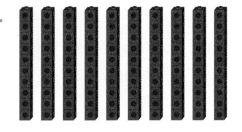

$\underline{10}$ = $\underline{100}$

tens   one hundred

2.

_____ = _____

tens   ninety

3.

_____ = _____

tens   seventy

4.

_____ = _____

tens   eighty

Problem Solving
Application

Draw to show the story. Write the answer.

5. Jon gave 6 friends marbles.
   He gave each friend 10 marbles.
   How many marbles did he give
   his friends?

_____ marbles

Write About It • Look at Exercise 5.
Explain how you got your answer.

 HOME ACTIVITY • Have your child group objects into tens and tell how many there are in all.

Name _____

Tens and Ones to 50

Explore

42 is
4 groups of ten
and 2 ones.

24 is 2 groups of ten and 4 ones.

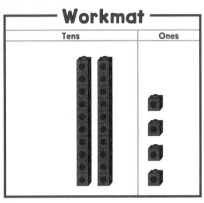

__2__ tens __4__ ones = __24__

__4__

Connect

Use Workmat 3 and .
Show the groups of ten. Show the ones.
Write how many tens and ones. Write the number.

1.

_____ tens _____ one = _____

2.

_____ ten _____ ones = _____

3.

_____ tens _____ ones = _____

4.

_____ tens _____ ones = _____

Explain It • Daily Reasoning

What does the zero mean in the number **30**?
Use to prove your answer.

30

Write how many tens and ones. Write the number.

1.

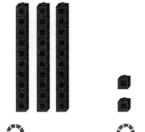

___3___ tens ___2___ ones = ___32___

2.

_____ tens _____ ones = _____

3.

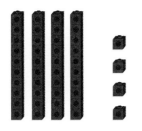

_____ tens _____ ones = _____

4.

_____ tens _____ ones = _____

5.

_____ tens _____ ones = _____

6.

_____ tens _____ ones = _____

Problem Solving
Visual Thinking

7. Show the same number using only tens. Write how many tens and ones.

_____ tens _____ ones | _____ tens _____ ones

 Write About It • Look at Exercise 7. Explain what happens to the tens and ones when you use only tens.

HOME ACTIVITY • Say numbers up to 50. Have your child draw cubes to show them. Ask him or her to write how many tens and ones are shown in each drawing and then to write the number.

Tens and Ones to 100

 Explore

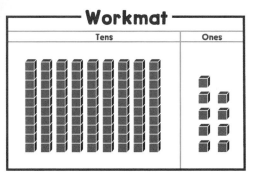

__9__ tens __9__ ones = __99__

99 is 9 groups of ten
and 9 ones.

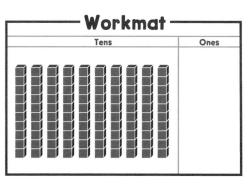

__10__ tens __0__ ones = __100__

100 is 10 groups of ten.
100 is 1 hundred .

Connect

Use Workmat 3 and ▬▬▬▬ ▪ .
Write how many tens and ones.
Write the number.

1.
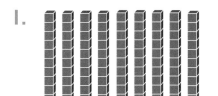
_____ tens _____ ones = _____

2.
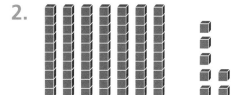
_____ tens _____ ones = _____

3.
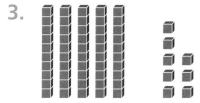
_____ tens _____ ones = _____

4.
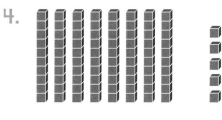
_____ tens _____ ones = _____

Explain It • Daily Reasoning

What number would you write for 9 tens 1 one?
What number would you write for 9 tens 8 ones?

Practice and Problem Solving

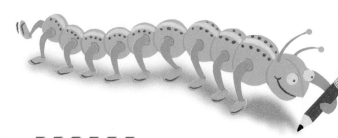

Write how many tens and ones.
Write the number.

1.

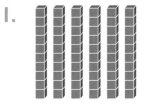

6 tens 1 one = 61

2.

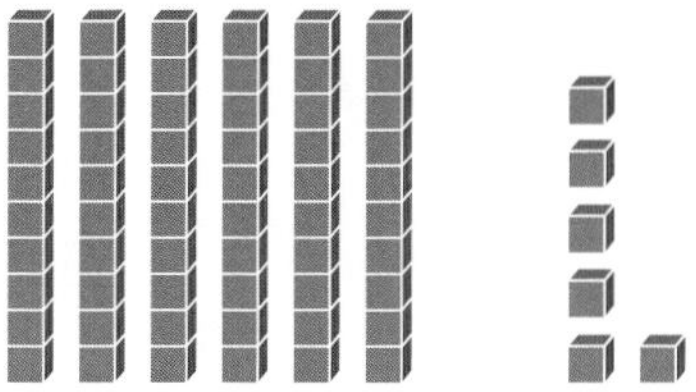

_____ tens _____ ones = _____

3.

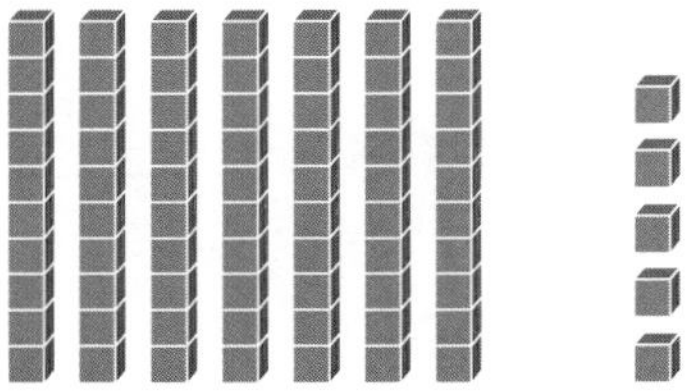

_____ tens _____ ones = _____

4.

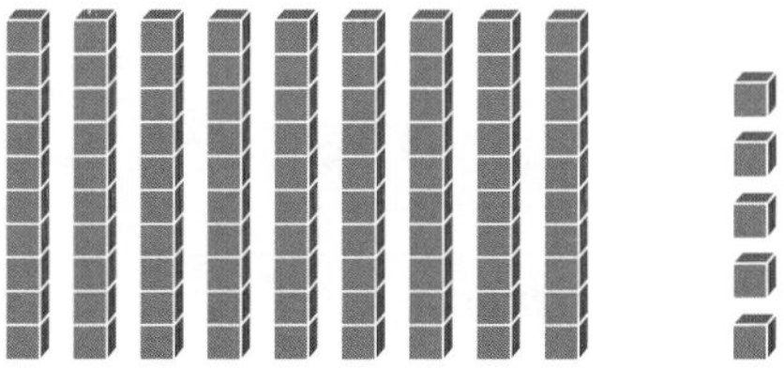

_____ tens _____ ones = _____

5.

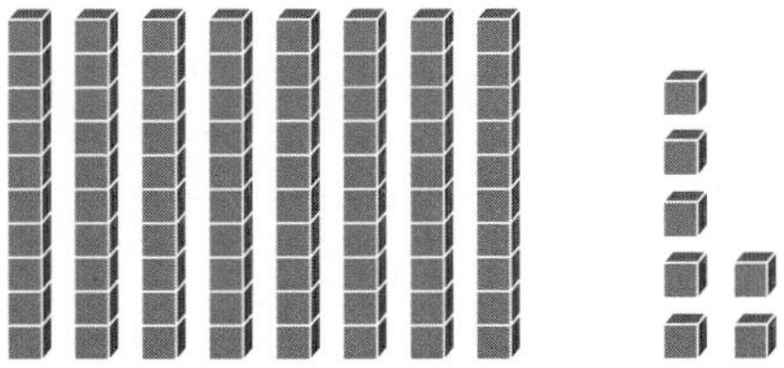

_____ tens _____ ones = _____

6.

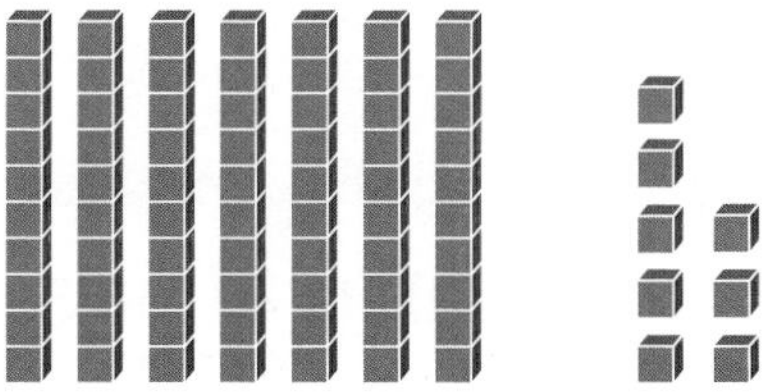

_____ tens _____ ones = _____

Problem Solving

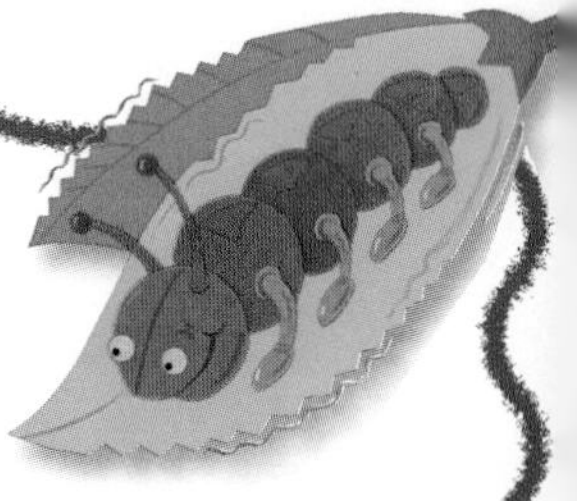

Application

Is the line under tens or ones?
Circle your answer.

7. 2<u>3</u> tens ones

8. <u>2</u>5 tens ones

9. <u>4</u>7 tens ones

10. 3<u>0</u> tens ones

Write About It • What does the **2** in **27** stand for?

HOME ACTIVITY • Say a number between 50 and 100. Have your child draw cubes to show the number, tell how many tens and ones there are, and then write the number.

Name _____

Algebra: **Different Ways to Make Numbers**

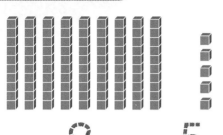

_9_ tens _5_ ones = _95_

_90_ + _5_

Here are some different ways to think about a number.

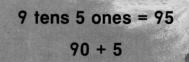

9 tens 5 ones = 95

90 + 5

Check

Write how many tens and ones.
Write the number in a different way.

1.

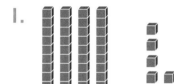

____ tens ____ ones = ____

____ + ____

2.

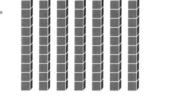

____ tens ____ ones = ____

____ + ____

3.

____ tens ____ ones = ____

____ + ____

4.

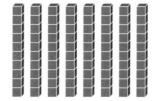

____ tens ____ ones = ____

____ + ____

Explain It • Daily Reasoning

What does the 8 mean in each of these numbers?
Use ▭▭▭▭▭ ▫ to prove your answer.

Write how many tens and ones.
Write the number in a different way.

1.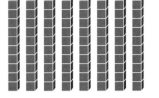

__8__ tens __8__ ones = __88__

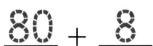

__80__ + __8__

2.

____ tens ____ ones = ____

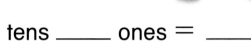

____ + ____

3.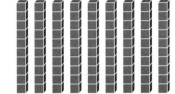

____ tens ____ ones = ____

____ + ____

4.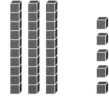

____ tens ____ ones = ____

____ + ____

Problem Solving
Application

Solve.

5. Jesse puts 97 stickers in his book.
Each page holds 10 stickers.
How many pages does he fill?　　　_____ pages

6. How many stickers are left over to
start a new page?　　　_____ stickers

 Write About It • Explain how you
found the answer to Exercise 6.

HOME ACTIVITY • Say a number between 10 and 100. Ask your child to write it first as tens and ones and then as addition. For example, 34 is 3 tens 4 ones and 30 + 4.

Name _____

Problem Solving Skill
Make Reasonable Estimates

About how many books can you carry?

When I don't need to know the exact number, I can estimate.

 about 5

about 50

about 500

50 and 500 are too many. 5 is a good estimate.

PROBLEM SOLVING

Circle the closest estimate.
Tell how you know.

1. About how many would ride on one bus?

   about 3

   about 30

   about 300

2. About how many would fill up one book bag?

   about 5

   about 50

   about 500

3. About how many 👟 are in the classroom?

   about 4

   about 40

   about 400

4. About how many ⊂⊃ would fill two hands?

   about 1

   about 10

   about 100

Circle the closest estimate.

THINK: Which number makes the most sense?

1. About how many are in your classroom?

   about 3

   (about 30 )

   about 300

2. About how many could fill a lunch box?

   about 1

   about 10

   about 100

3. About how many could you hold in one hand?

   about 5

   about 50

   about 500

4. About how many  would fill a cup?

   about 1

   about 10

   about 100

5. About how many sheets of would cover your desk?

   about 4

   about 40

   about 400

6. About how many are in your classroom?

   about 3

   about 30

   about 300

HOME ACTIVITY • Ask your child to choose the closest estimate for the number of pennies he or she can hold in one hand: about 10 pennies or about 100 pennies. Then have him or her check.

Name _____

Extra Practice

Write how many tens. Write the number.

1.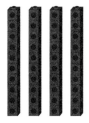

_____ tens = _____

2.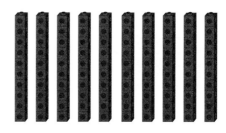

_____ tens = _____

Write how many tens and ones. Write the number.

3.

_____ ten _____ ones = _____

4.

_____ tens _____ ones = _____

Write how many tens and ones. Write the number in a different way.

5.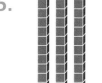

_____ tens _____ ones = _____

_____ + _____

6.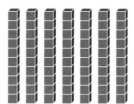

_____ tens _____ ones = _____

_____ + _____

Problem Solving

Circle the closest estimate.

7. About how many 🔲 would fill the bag?

about 2 🔲

about 20 🔲

about 200 🔲

Name _____

✓ Review/Test

Concepts and Skills

Write how many tens. Write the number.

1.

_____ tens = _____

2.

_____ tens = _____

Write how many tens and ones. Write the number.

3.

_____ tens _____ ones = _____

4.

_____ ten _____ ones = _____

Write how many tens and ones. Write the number in a different way.

5.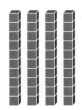

_____ tens _____ one = _____

_____ + _____

6.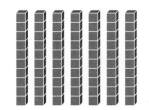

_____ tens _____ ones = _____

_____ + _____

Problem Solving

Circle the closest estimate.

7. About how many  would fill the cup?

about 1

about 10

about 100

Name _____

Choose the answer for questions 1–4.

1. Which is another way to write the number?

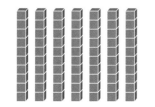

7 tens + 6 ones = 76

60 + 7 ○   70 + 3 ○

70 + 2 ○   70 + 6 ○

2. Which does the picture show?

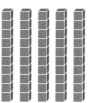

3 tens ○   5 tens ○

7 tens ○   9 tens ○

3. Which is the closest estimate?
About how many are in your classroom?

about 3 ○   about 30 ○   about 300 ○

4. Which fact is related to 5 − 2 = 3?

1 + 4 = 5 ○   5 + 3 = 8 ○   3 + 2 = 5 ○   3 − 2 = 1 ○

Show What You Know

5. Choose a number.
Draw to explain how
many tens and ones.
Write the number two ways.

_____

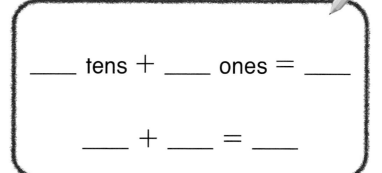

_____ tens + _____ ones = _____

_____ + _____ = _____

MATH GAME

Teen Spin

Play with a partner.

1. Put all the 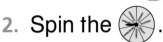 in the penny pile.
2. Spin the 🌀.
3. Read the teen number word.
4. Tell how many more than 10 that number is.
5. Put that many 🪙 in your bank.
6. Take turns until the penny pile is gone.
7. The player with more 🪙 wins.

You will need

50 🪙

Penny Pile

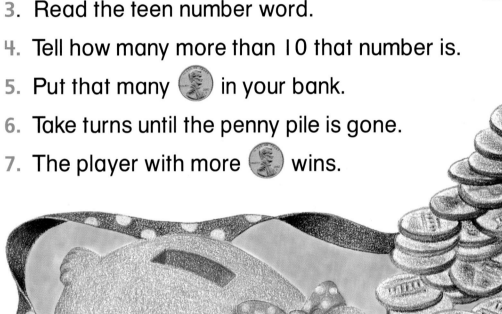

Comparing and Ordering Numbers

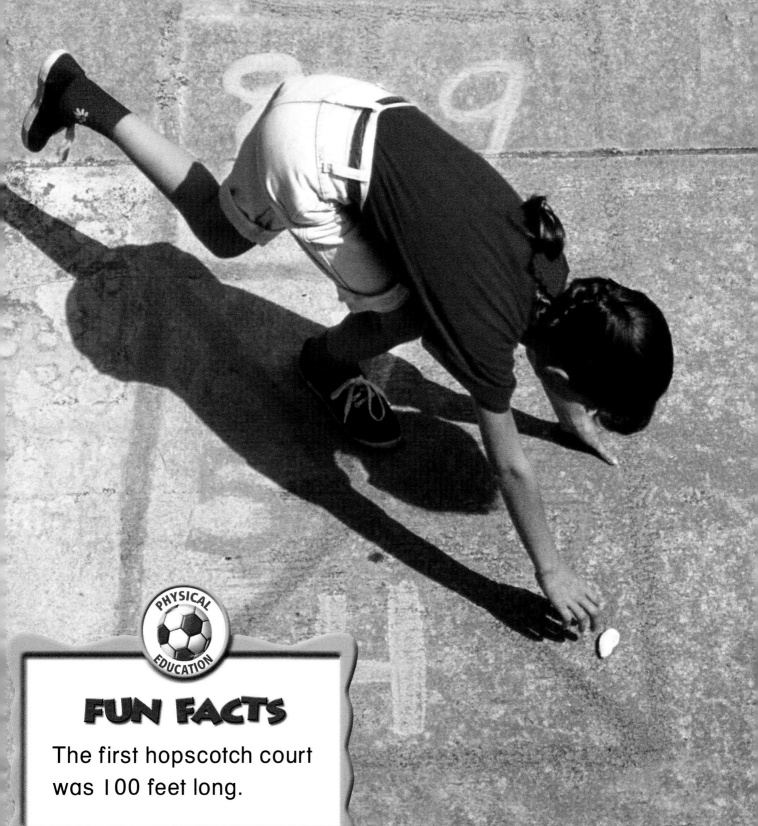

PHYSICAL EDUCATION

FUN FACTS

The first hopscotch court was 100 feet long.

✔️ Check What You Know

More, Less, Same
Count. Write the number.

1. Circle the number that is less.

_____   _____

2. Circle the number that is more.

_____   _____

3. Circle the 2 numbers that are the same.

_____   _____   _____

Order Numbers on a Number Line
Write the missing numbers.

4.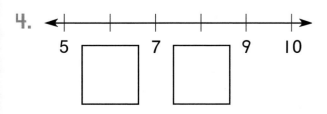

5.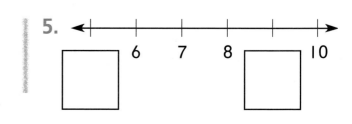

Use this page to review important skills needed for this chapter.

Name _____

Algebra: **Greater Than**

 Explore

43 and 47 have the same number of tens, but 47 has more ones.

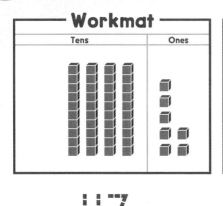

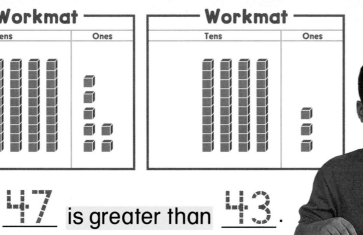

47 is greater than 43.

47 > 43

Connect

Use to show each number.
Circle the greater number. Write the numbers.

1.
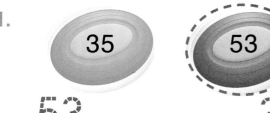

35   (53)

53 is greater than 35.

53 > 35

2.

56   46

_____ is greater than _____.

_____ > _____

3.

13   30

_____ is greater than _____.

_____ > _____

4.

66   69

_____ is greater than _____.

_____ > _____

Explain It • Daily Reasoning

To find the greater number, should you look
first at the ones or at the tens? Why?

Circle the greater number.
Write the numbers.
You can use ▭▭▭▭ ▯ .

1.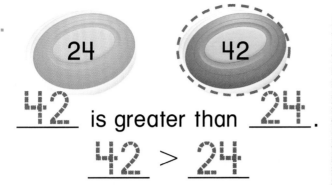

24   (42)

_42_ is greater than _24_ .

_42_ > _24_

2.   76   78

_____ is greater than _____ .

_____ > _____

3.   51   15

_____ is greater than _____ .

_____ > _____

4.   69   98

_____ is greater than_____ .

_____ > _____

5.   37   35

_____ is greater than _____ .

_____ > _____

6.   54   45

_____ is greater than _____ .

_____ > _____

Problem Solving
Application

7. Circle the numbers that are greater than 50.

14   83   94   44   62   70

 Write About It ● Use one of the numbers
you circled in Exercise 7 to complete ☐ > 50.

HOME ACTIVITY • Say two numbers that are less than 100. Ask your child which is greater. Then have him or her write the two numbers, using the *greater than* symbol (>).

Name _____

Algebra: **Less Than**

Explore

HANDS ON

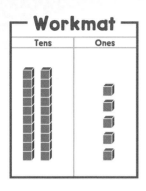

Workmat	
Tens	Ones

Workmat	
Tens	Ones

25 has fewer tens than 35.

__25__ is less than __35__.

__25__ < __35__

Connect

Use ▦ ▯ to show each number.
Circle the number that is less. Write the numbers.

1.

__65__ is less than __66__.

__65__ < __66__

2.
82   91

_____ is less than _____.

_____ < _____

3.
19   16

_____ is less than _____.

_____ < _____

4.
73   48

_____ is less than _____.

_____ < _____

Explain It ● Daily Reasoning

How could you find out which number is less
without using ▦ ▯ ?

Circle the number that is less.
Write the numbers. You can use .

1.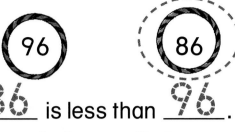

86 is less than 96.

86 < 96

2. 88   68

_____ is less than _____.

_____ < _____

3. 49   50

_____ is less than _____.

_____ < _____

4. 19   17

_____ is less than _____.

_____ < _____

5. 27   28

_____ is less than _____.

_____ < _____

6. 34   43

_____ is less than _____.

_____ < _____

Problem Solving
Application

7. Circle the numbers that are less than 50.

49   65   80   11   33   51

 Write About It • Use words to compare 50 and one of the numbers you circled in Exercise 7.

HOME ACTIVITY • Say two numbers that are less than 100. Ask your child which number is less. Then have him or her write the two numbers, using the *less than* symbol (<).

Algebra: **Use Symbols to Compare**

Explore

Compare the two numbers.

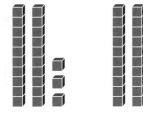

23 < 25

23 is less
than 25.

 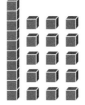

25 === 25

25 is equal
to 25.

26 > 25

26 is greater
than 25.

Connect

Compare the numbers.
Use to show each number.
Draw the ▬▬▬▬ .
Write <, >, or = in the circle.

1.

52 < 56

2.

56 ◯ 51

3.

17 ◯ 71

4.

37 ◯ 37

Explain It • Daily Reasoning

How can you show 71 in two ways? Explain.

Compare the numbers.
Use ▭▭▭ ▪ to show each number.
Draw the ▭▭▭ ▪.

Write <, >, or = in the circle.

> **REMEMBER**
>
> < means is less than.
>
> > means is greater than.
>
> = means is equal to.

1.

$21 \bigcirc 12$

2.

$46 \bigcirc 49$

3.

$38 \bigcirc 38$

4.

$55 \bigcirc 59$

Problem Solving

Algebra

Write <, >, or = in the circle.

5. 6 tens 4 ones $\bigcirc$ 60 + 4

6. 30 + 5 $\bigcirc$ 2 tens 5 ones

7. 9 tens 8 ones $\bigcirc$ 90 + 9

8. 40 + 3 $\bigcirc$ 4 tens 3 ones

 Write About It • What is the same about 91 and 99? What is different?

🔷 **HOME ACTIVITY** • Say two numbers that are less than 100. Ask your child to compare the numbers by writing them, using the symbols he or she learned in this lesson.

Order on a Number Line

Learn

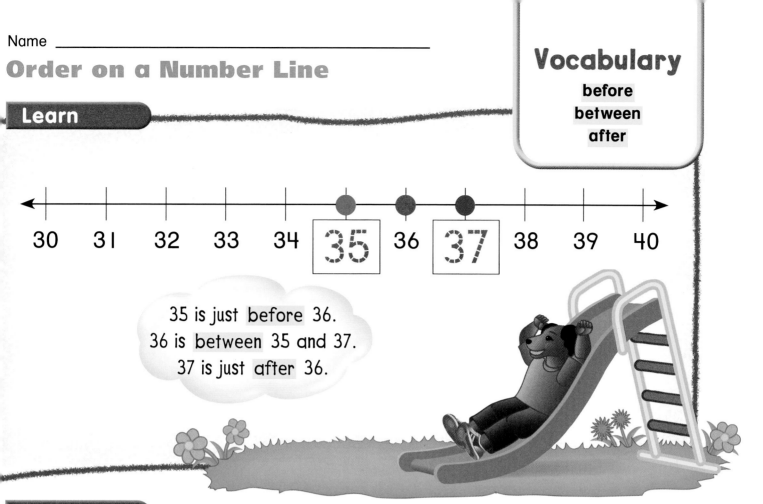

| 30 | 31 | 32 | 33 | 34 | 35 | 36 | 37 | 38 | 39 | 40 |

35 is just before 36.
36 is between 35 and 37.
37 is just after 36.

Check

Write the number that is just before, between,
or just after.

1. 47   48   49

2. ☐   60   61

3. 88   ☐   90

4. 66   ☐   68

5. 72   73   ☐

6. 98   99   ☐

Explain It • Daily Reasoning

What number comes just after 100?
Explain how you know.

Practice and Problem Solving

Write the number that is just
before, between, or just after.

1. 98 **99** 100

2. 11 [ ] 13

3. 39 [ ] 41

4. 54 [ ] 56

5. [ ] 31

6. 44 [ ]

7. [ ] 20

8. 79 [ ]

9. [ ] 58

10. 28 [ ]

Problem Solving
Visual Thinking

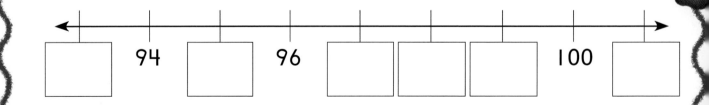

11. Write the missing numbers on the number line.

[ ] 94 [ ] 96 [ ] [ ] [ ] 100 [ ]

 Write About It • Explain how you found
the missing numbers in Exercise 11.

⬟ **HOME ACTIVITY** • Say a two-digit number. Ask your child to tell you the number that is just before
it and the number that is just after it. Then ask your child to use the word *between* to tell about
your number.

Count Forward and Backward

Vocabulary
count forward
count backward

Learn

52, <u>53</u>, <u>54</u> | 52, <u>51</u>, <u>50</u>

Count forward from 52. | Count backward from 52.

Check

Write the numbers.

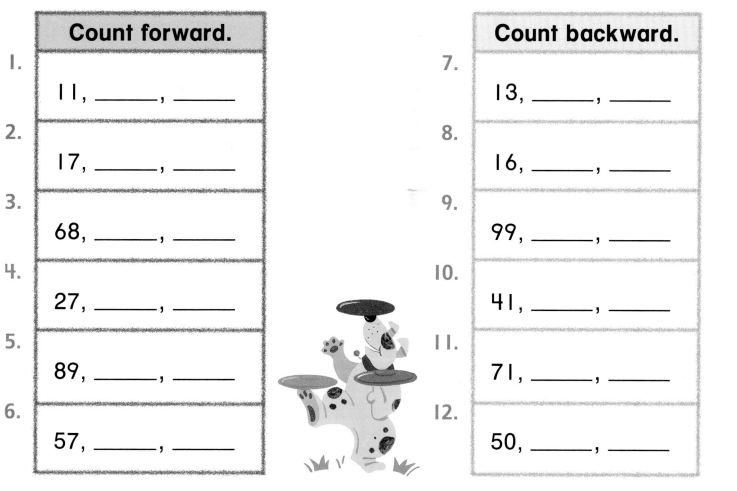

Count forward.

1. 11, _____, _____

2. 17, _____, _____

3. 68, _____, _____

4. 27, _____, _____

5. 89, _____, _____

6. 57, _____, _____

Count backward.

7. 13, _____, _____

8. 16, _____, _____

9. 99, _____, _____

10. 41, _____, _____

11. 71, _____, _____

12. 50, _____, _____

Explain It • Daily Reasoning

What number do you say when
you count backward from 1? Explain.

10, 11, 12, 13, 14, 15

Write the numbers.

Count forward.

1. 21, _____, _____, _____, _____, _____, _____, _____, _____

2. 45, _____, _____, _____, _____, _____, _____, _____, _____

3. 77, _____, _____, _____, _____, _____, _____, _____, _____

Count backward.

4. 20, _____, _____, _____, _____, _____, _____, _____, _____

5. 42, _____, _____, _____, _____, _____, _____, _____, _____

6. 67, _____, _____, _____, _____, _____, _____, _____, _____

Problem Solving
Application

7. These are lockers. Start on 27. Count forward. Write the number on each locker.

8. Tom's locker is 31. Circle Tom's locker.

 Write About It • Write a story telling how you get from locker 27 to Tom's locker.

HOME ACTIVITY • Say a two-digit number. Have your child count forward. Say a different two-digit number. Have your child count backward.

Name _____

Problem Solving Skill
Use a Model

Use the model 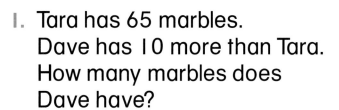 .
Find 10 more or 10 less.
Write the number.

To find 10 more, draw 1 more ten.

1. Tara has 65 marbles.
Dave has 10 more than Tara.
How many marbles does
Dave have?

___75___ marbles

2. Chen has 13 toy cars.
Anna has 10 less.
How many toy cars does
Anna have?

To find 10 less, cross out 1 ten.

_____ toy cars

3. Dan counted 25 children
on the playground.
Chris counted 10 more
than Dan. How many
children did Chris count?

_____ children

Problem Solving Practice

Use the model 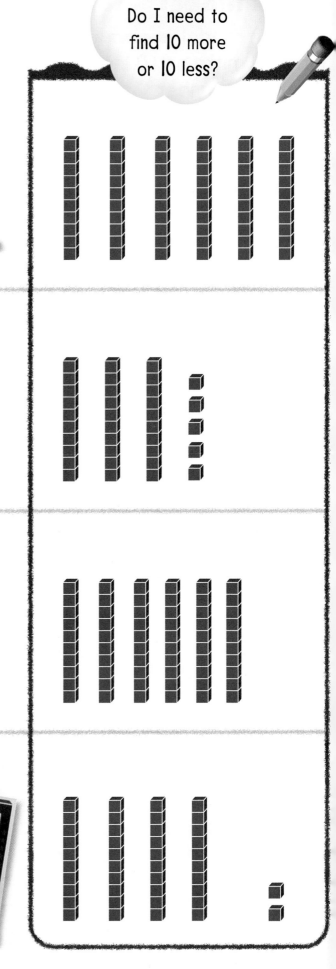.
Find 10 more or 10 less.
Write the number.

THINK:
Do I need to find 10 more or 10 less?

1. Pat has 60 toy trucks.
   Fred has 10 less.
   How many toy trucks
   does Fred have?

   _____ toy trucks

2. Music class has 35
   children. Art class has 10
   less. How many children
   are in art class?

   _____ children

3. Craig has 60 jacks.
   Brooke has 10 more
   than Craig. How many
   jacks does Brooke have?

   _____ jacks

4. Dave has 42 baseball
   cards. Kim has 10 more
   than Dave. How many
   baseball cards does
   Kim have?

   _____ baseball cards

 HOME ACTIVITY • Have your child tell how he or she used each model to solve the problem.

Name _____

Extra Practice

Circle the greater number.
Write the numbers.

1.   _____ > _____

Circle the number that is less.
Write the numbers.

2.   _____ < _____

---

3. Count forward.   68, _____, _____

4. Count backward.   41, _____, _____

Write the number that is just before, between,
or just after.

5.
29   [ ]   31

6.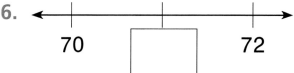
70   [ ]   72

7.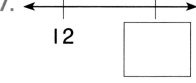
12   [ ]

8.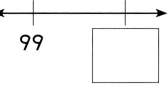
99   [ ]

9.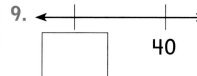
[ ]   40

Problem Solving

Use the model ▨▨▨▨ ▪ . Find 10
more or 10 less. Write the number.

10. Brad has 23 toy cars. Ken
    has 10 less. How many toy
    cars does Ken have?

    _____ toy cars

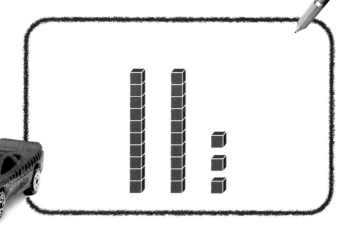

Review/Test

Concepts and Skills

Circle the greater number.
Write the numbers.

1. (61) 70   _____ > _____

Circle the number that is less.
Write the numbers.

2. 85 (99)   _____ < _____

3. Count forward.   90, _____, _____

4. Count backward.   63, _____, _____

Write the number that is just before, between,
or just after.

5.

   90 [ ] 92

6.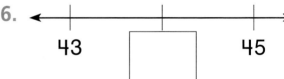

   43 [ ] 45

7.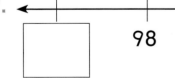

   [ ] 98

8.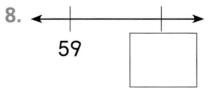

   59 [ ]

9.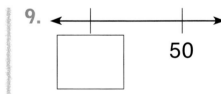

   [ ] 50

Problem Solving

Use the model ▭▭▭ ▪. Find 10
more or 10 less. Write the number.

10. Jose has 65 jacks. Elsa has 10
more. How many jacks does
Elsa have?

    _____ jacks

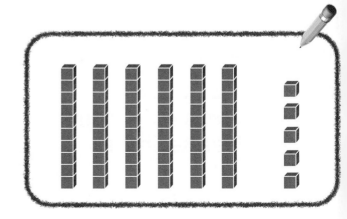

Getting Ready for the ★EOG Test
Chapters 1-11

Choose the answer for questions 1-4.

1. Which number is between 33 and 35?

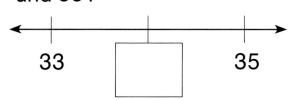

32	34	36	37
○	○	○	○

2. Which number is less than 24?

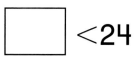

$\square < 24$

19	27	30	41
○	○	○	○

3. Which numbers are missing?

__20__ , __19__ , _____ , _____ , _____

18, 17, 16	19, 20, 21	21, 22, 23	21, 20, 19
○	○	○	○

4. Which is another way to write $9 - 3 = 6$?

$$\begin{array}{r} 9 \\ -4 \\ \hline 5 \end{array} \qquad \begin{array}{r} 9 \\ -3 \\ \hline 6 \end{array} \qquad \begin{array}{r} 9 \\ -2 \\ \hline 7 \end{array} \qquad \begin{array}{r} 9 \\ -1 \\ \hline 8 \end{array}$$

   ○   ○   ○   ○

Show What You Know

5. Find 10 less. Use the model to explain your answer.

April has 37 marbles.
Molly has 10 less.
How many marbles does Molly have?

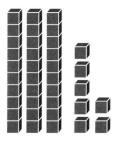

_____ marbles

MATH GAME

Greater Steps

Play with a partner.

You will need

2 ♟

2 🎲

1. Put your ♟ at START.

2. Toss the 🎲 and the 🎲 .

3. Use one number as tens and one number as ones. Can you make a number that solves the problem on your next step?

4. If you can, move your ♟ up to that step.

5. If you can not, your turn is over.

6. The first player to get to END wins.

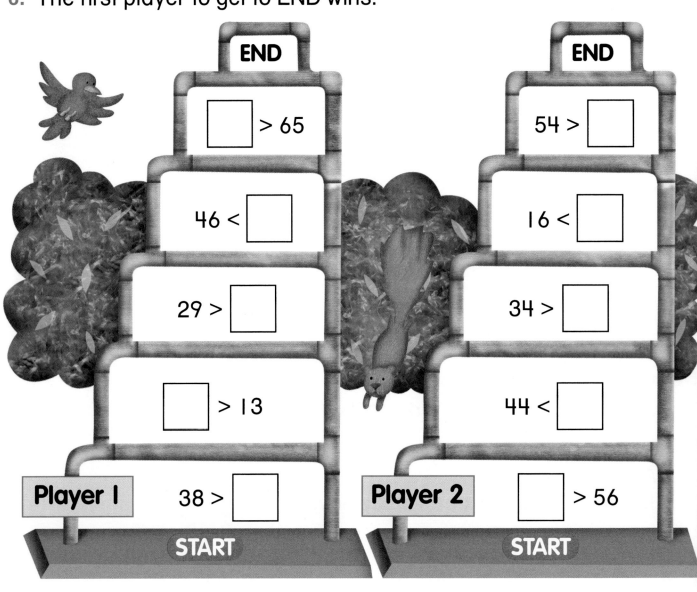

END

☐ > 65

46 < ☐

29 > ☐

☐ > 13

Player 1   38 > ☐

START

END

54 > ☐

16 < ☐

34 > ☐

44 < ☐

Player 2   ☐ > 56

START

CHAPTER 12

Number Patterns

FUN FACTS

The number of crayons in some boxes are all even numbers: 8, 16, 24, 32, 48, 64, and 96.

✔ Check What You Know

Count Orally Using a Hundred Chart

Touch and count. Color the last number counted.

1. Start at 1 and count to 30.
2. Start at 40 and count to 53.
3. Start at 92 and count to 98.

1	2	3	4	5	6	7	8	9	10
11	12	13	14	15	16	17	18	19	20
21	22	23	24	25	26	27	28	29	30
31	32	33	34	35	36	37	38	39	40
41	42	43	44	45	46	47	48	49	50
51	52	53	54	55	56	57	58	59	60
61	62	63	64	65	66	67	68	69	70
71	72	73	74	75	76	77	78	79	80
81	82	83	84	85	86	87	88	89	90
91	92	93	94	95	96	97	98	99	100

Ordinal Numbers

4. Circle the second cat.
5. Mark an X on the fifth cat.
6. Draw a line under the first cat.

Skip Count by 2s, 5s, and 10s

Learn

Skip count. Count the jars of paint by twos.
Write how many.

2 _____   4 _____   6 _____   _____   _____

12 _____   _____   _____   _____   _____ jars of paint

Check

Skip count. Count the fingers by fives. Write how many.

1.

5 _____   10 _____   _____   _____   _____   _____

35 _____   _____   _____   _____   _____ _____ fingers

Skip count. Count the toes by tens. Write how many.

2.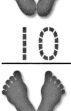

10 _____   20 _____   _____   _____   _____

_____   _____   _____   _____   _____ toes

Explain It • Daily Reasoning

What number comes after 100 when
you skip count by tens? Explain.

Skip count. Write how many.

1.

   <u>2</u>   ____   ____   ____   ____   ____   ____

2.

   <u>5</u>   ____   ____   ____   ____   ____   ____

3.

   <u>10</u>   ____   ____   ____   ____   ____   ____

Skip count. Write the missing numbers.

4.
   2, 4, 6, _____, _____, _____, 14, _____, 18

5.
   10, _____, 30, _____, _____, 60, 70, _____, 90

Problem Solving

Visual Thinking

6. Skip count.
   Each hand has 5 fingers.
   How many fingers are there in all?

   _____ fingers

 Write About It • Draw a picture to show skip counting by twos. Write the numbers.

🏠 **HOME ACTIVITY** • Draw 20 stars. Have your child circle groups of 2 and then count by twos to find the total. Repeat the activity for groups of 5.

Algebra: **Use a Hundred Chart to Skip Count**

Learn

Write the missing numbers. Count by tens.
Use ✏️ to color the numbers you say.

Start on 10. Count forward by tens.

1	2	3	4	5	6	7	8	9	10
11	12	13	14	15	16	17	18	19	
21	22	23	24	25	26	27	28	29	
31	32	33	34	35	36	37	38	39	
41	42	43	44	45	46	47	48	49	
51	52	53	54	55	56	57	58	59	
61	62	63	64	65	66	67	68	69	
71	72	73	74	75	76	77	78	79	
81	82	83	84	85	86	87	88	89	
91	92	93	94	95	96	97	98	99	

Check

1. Count again. Count by fives.
   Use 🖍️ to color the numbers you say.

Explain It • Daily Reasoning

What patterns do you see?
How could you make a new pattern?

Write the missing numbers. Count by twos.
Use to color the numbers you say.

1.

1	2	3	4	5		7		9	
11		13		15		17		19	
21		23		25		27		29	
31		33		35		37		39	
41		43		45		47		49	
51		53		55		57		59	
61		63		65		67		69	
71		73		75		77		79	
81		83		85		87		89	
91		93		95		97		99	

Problem Solving
Mental Math

Solve.

Sunday, Monday, Tuesday, Wednesday

2. Today is Sunday. Rosa saves 10 pennies
   every day. How many pennies will she have
   after she adds pennies for Wednesday? _____ pennies

Write About It • Look at Exercise 2.
How many pennies will Rosa have after
she adds pennies for Saturday?

🏠 **HOME ACTIVITY** • Have your child explain how to use the hundred chart to count by fives.

Name _____

Algebra: **Patterns on a Hundred Chart**

Start on 2. Count forward by tens.

Learn

1	2	3	4	5	6	7	8	9	10
11	12	13	14	15	16	17	18	19	20
21	22	23	24	25	26	27	28	29	30
31	32	33	34	35	36	37	38	39	40
41	42	43	44	45	46	47	48	49	50
51	52	53	54	55	56	57	58	59	60
61	62	63	64	65	66	67	68	69	70
71	72	73	74	75	76	77	78	79	80
81	82	83	84	85	86	87	88	89	90
91	92	93	94	95	96	97	98	99	100

Check

Start on the given number. Count forward
by tens. Write the numbers you say.

1. Start on 1.

 11, 21, _____, _____, _____, _____, _____, _____, _____

Explain It • Daily Reasoning

What pattern do you see? Explain.

Start on the given number. Count forward by tens. Write the numbers you say. Use a hundred chart if you need to.

1. Start on 7.

   __17__, __27__, ____, ____, ____, ____, ____, ____, ____

2. Start on 9.

   __19__, ____, ____, ____, ____, ____, ____, ____, ____

3. Start on 5.

   ____, ____, ____, ____, ____, ____, ____, ____, ____

4. Start on 3.

   ____, ____, ____, ____, ____, ____, ____, ____, ____

5. Start on 6.

   ____, ____, ____, ____, ____, ____, ____, ____, ____

Problem Solving

Logical Reasoning

6. Write the missing numbers.

   94, 84, 74, 64, ____, 44, ____, ____, 14, ____

7. Write the missing numbers.

   98, 88, ____, 68, ____, ____, ____, 28, ____, ____

 Write About It • What pattern can help you count forward by tens from any number?

🏠 **HOME ACTIVITY** • Say any number less than 10. Ask your child to start on that number and count forward by tens.

Name _____

Even and Odd

Learn

What pattern can you find in even and odd numbers?

An **even** number of objects can be grouped into pairs.

4

5

An **odd** number of objects has one left over.

Check

Use 🎲 to show each number.
Circle **even** or **odd**.

1.	1	even	(odd)	2.	2	even	odd
3.	3	even	odd	4.	4	even	odd
5.	5	even	odd	6.	6	even	odd
7.	7	even	odd	8.	8	even	odd
9.	9	even	odd	10.	10	even	odd

Explain It • Daily Reasoning

Color the numbers.   odd ▭▱   even ▬▬

1	2	3	4	5	6	7	8	9	10

What pattern do even and odd numbers make?

Color ▭▭▭ or ▭▭▭ to continue the pattern.

1.

1	2	3	4	5	6	7	8	9	10
11	12	13	14	15	16	17	18	19	20
21	22	23	24	25	26	27	28	29	30
31	32	33	34	35	36	37	38	39	40
41	42	43	44	45	46	47	48	49	50

Write **even** or **odd**.
You can use 🎲 to help.

_____

2. Are the red numbers even or odd? _____

_____

3. Are the blue numbers even or odd? _____

Problem Solving
Application

4. Start with 2. Skip count by twos.   _____
Do you say even or odd numbers? _____

5. Start with 10. Skip count by tens.   _____
Do you say even or odd numbers? _____

Write About It ● Skip count by fives to 50.
Write the numbers. Circle the odd numbers.
What pattern do you see?

 HOME ACTIVITY • Give your child a group of 20 small objects, such as beans. Have him or her count the objects and tell how many. Then have your child pair the objects and tell whether the number is even or odd.

Name _____

Problem Solving Strategy
Find a Pattern

Find a pattern to solve.

I star has 5 points.

┌─────────────────────────────────────┐
│ How many points do 5 stars have?   │
└─────────────────────────────────────┘

UNDERSTAND

What do you want to find out?

Circle the question.

PLAN

Make a chart to find the pattern.

SOLVE

Use the chart. Count by fives.

number of stars	1	2	3	4	5
number of points	5	10	15		

5 stars have __25__ points.

CHECK

Does your answer make sense? Explain.

Find a pattern to solve. Write how many.

1. I dog has two ears.
   How many ears do 5 dogs have?

number of dogs	1	2	3	4	5
number of ears	2	4			

5 dogs have _____ ears.

Find a pattern to solve.
Write how many.

1. 1 flower has 10 petals.
   How many petals do 5 flowers have?

number of flowers	1	2	3	4	5
number of petals	10	20			

5 flowers have _____ petals.

2. 1 bunny has 2 ears.
   How many ears do 7 bunnies have?

number of bunnies	1	2	3	4	5	6	7
number of ears	2						

7 bunnies have _____ ears.

3. 1 starfish has 5 arms.
   How many arms do 6 starfish have?

number of starfish	1	2	3	4	5	6
number of arms	5					

6 starfish have _____ arms.

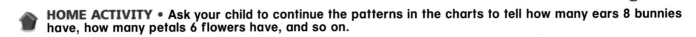

HOME ACTIVITY • Ask your child to continue the patterns in the charts to tell how many ears 8 bunnies have, how many petals 6 flowers have, and so on.

Ordinal Numbers

Learn

first   second   third   fourth   fifth   sixth   seventh   eighth   ninth   tenth

Check

Circle to show order.

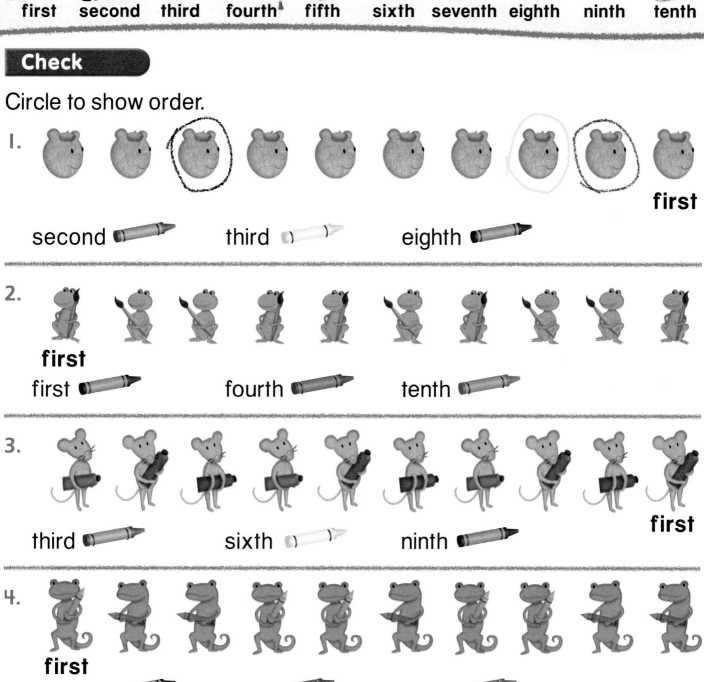

1.

first

second 🖍️   third 🖍️   eighth 🖍️

2.

first

first 🖍️   fourth 🖍️   tenth 🖍️

3.

first

third 🖍️   sixth 🖍️   ninth 🖍️

4.

first

second 🖍️   fifth 🖍️   ninth 🖍️

Explain It • Daily Reasoning

If you are eighth in line, how many people are in front of you? Explain.

1. Color to show order.

| first | second | third | fifth | seventh | tenth |

first

first

first

Problem Solving
Application

2. Color the bee that is second from the hive .
   Color the bee that is fourth from the hive .

Write About It • Draw 10 flowers in a row.
Label one **first**. Circle the flower that is eighth.
Tell how you know.

HOME ACTIVITY • Ask your child to show you which butterfly in the picture is fourth in line.

Extra Practice

1. Write the missing numbers. Count by twos.
   Use 🖍 to color the numbers you say.

21			24		26		28		30
	32			35				39	

2. Count again. Count by fives.
   Use 🖍 to color the numbers you say.

3. Count again. Count by tens.
   Use 🖍 to circle the numbers you say.

4. Color the numbers.
   odd 🖍   even 🖍

11	12	13	14	15	16	17	18	19	20

5. Circle to show order.

fourth 🖍   sixth 🖍   eighth 🖍   ninth 🖍   **first**

Problem Solving

Find a pattern to solve. Write how many.

6. 1 box has 10 crayons.
   How many crayons do 6 boxes have?

number of boxes	1	2	3	4	5	6
number of crayons	10					

6 boxes have _____ crayons.

Name _____

✔ Review/Test

Concepts and Skills

1. Write the missing numbers. Count by twos.
   Use 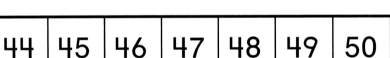 to color the numbers you say.

1	2	3	4				8	9	10
	12			15	16	17			

2. Count again. Count by fives.
   Use ✏ to color the numbers you say.

3. Count again. Count by tens.
   Use ✏ to circle the numbers you say.

4. Color the numbers.
   odd ✏   even ✏

41	42	43	44	45	46	47	48	49	50

5. Circle to show order.

first

second ✏   fifth ✏   ninth ✏   tenth ✏

Problem Solving

Find a pattern to solve.
Write how many.

6. 1 face has 2 eyes.
   How many eyes do
   5 faces have?

number of faces	1	2	3	4	5
number of eyes	2				

5 faces have _____ eyes.

Getting Ready for the ★EOG Test
Chapters 1–12

1. Count by fives. Which number is missing?

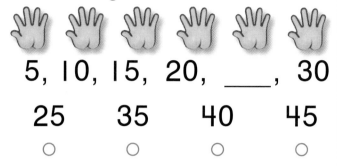

5, 10, 15, 20, ___, 30

  25   35   40   45
   ○   ○   ○   ○

2. Count by twos. Which number is missing?

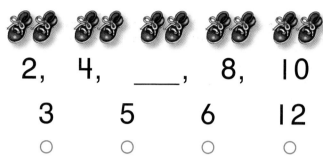

2, 4, ___, 8, 10

  3   5   6   12
 ○   ○   ○   ○

3. Which number is even?

   3   5   6   7
   ○   ○   ○   ○

4. Which is fourth?

first

○   ○   ○   ○

5. Which is just before 28?

28   27   30   36
○   ○   ○   ○

Show What You Know

6. How many ears are on 3 cats? Draw a picture to explain your answer.

Number of Cats	1	2	3
Number of Ears	2	4	

EOG TEST PREP

MATH GAME

Even Skips

Play with a partner.

You will need

2

1. Put your ♟ on START.

2. Toss the 🎲.

3. Move your ♟ that many spaces.

4. If you land on an odd number, your turn is over.

5. If you land on an even number, skip-count on by twos 3 times. Move to that number.

6. The first player to get to END wins.

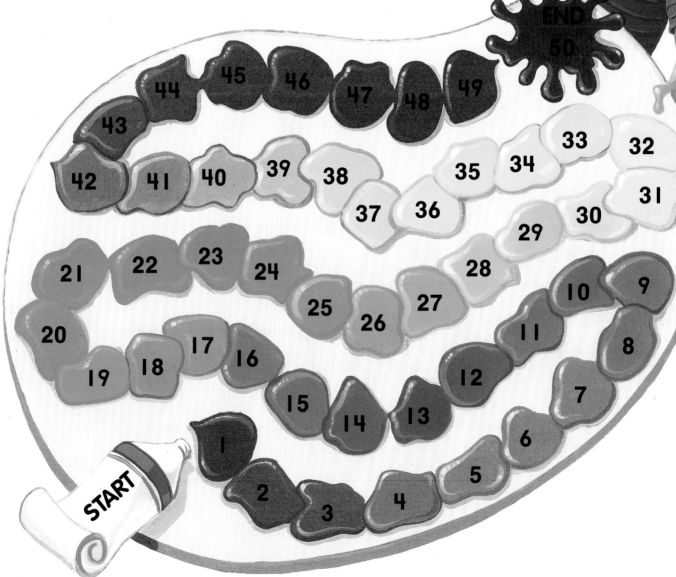

CHAPTER 13

Addition and Subtraction Facts to 12

FUN FACTS

You can walk through an outdoor rocket garden and see many rockets set on the ground in rows.

Name _____

✓ Check What You Know

Use a Number Line to Count On

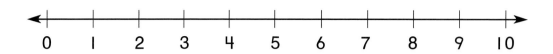

Use the number line. Count on to find the sum.

1. 2	2. 4	3. 6	4. 5	5. 8	6. 7
+2	+1	+3	+2	+1	+3

Use Doubles

Add. Then circle the doubles facts.

7. 4	8. 4	9. 2	10. 5	11. 2	12. 3
+3	+4	+3	+5	+4	+3

Use a Number Line to Count Back

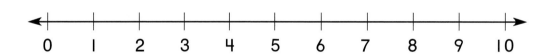

Use the number line. Count back to subtract.

13. 9	14. 6	15. 10	16. 8	17. 4	18. 10
−3	−3	− 2	−3	−2	− 1

Use this page to review important skills needed for this chapter.

Count On to Add

Learn

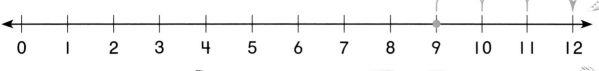

$$\begin{array}{r} \textcircled{9} \\ +3 \\ \hline 12 \end{array}$$

Start on 9. Then move
3 spaces to the right.
10, 11, 12

Start with the greater number.
Count on to add.

Check

Circle the greater number.
Use the number line. Count on to add.

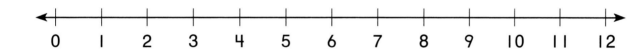

1. $\begin{array}{r}\textcircled{5}\\+3\\\hline\end{array}$
2. $\begin{array}{r}2\\+7\\\hline\end{array}$
3. $\begin{array}{r}3\\+8\\\hline\end{array}$
4. $\begin{array}{r}9\\+1\\\hline\end{array}$
5. $\begin{array}{r}3\\+9\\\hline\end{array}$
6. $\begin{array}{r}7\\+3\\\hline\end{array}$

7. $\begin{array}{r}8\\+1\\\hline\end{array}$
8. $\begin{array}{r}2\\+9\\\hline\end{array}$
9. $\begin{array}{r}9\\+2\\\hline\end{array}$
10. $\begin{array}{r}8\\+2\\\hline\end{array}$
11. $\begin{array}{r}1\\+7\\\hline\end{array}$
12. $\begin{array}{r}4\\+3\\\hline\end{array}$

13. $\begin{array}{r}3\\+7\\\hline\end{array}$
14. $\begin{array}{r}5\\+2\\\hline\end{array}$
15. $\begin{array}{r}3\\+6\\\hline\end{array}$
16. $\begin{array}{r}8\\+3\\\hline\end{array}$
17. $\begin{array}{r}6\\+2\\\hline\end{array}$
18. $\begin{array}{r}2\\+8\\\hline\end{array}$

Explain It • Daily Reasoning

Why is it easier to start with the greater
number when you count on?

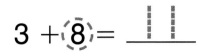

$$3 + 8 = \underline{}$$

Start on 8. Move
3 spaces to the right.
9, 10, 11

Circle the greater number.
Use the number line. Count on to add.

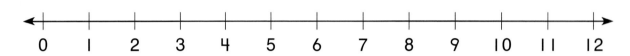

1. $6 + 2 = \underline{}$

2. $3 + 7 = \underline{}$

3. $9 + 3 = \underline{}$

4. $1 + 8 = \underline{}$

5. $6 + 3 = \underline{}$

6. $8 + 2 = \underline{}$

7. $2 + 9 = \underline{}$

8. $3 + 5 = \underline{}$

9. $7 + 2 = \underline{}$

10. $3 + 4 = \underline{}$

11. $9 + 1 = \underline{}$

12. $5 + 2 = \underline{}$

Problem Solving
Application

Count on to solve. Draw a picture to check.

13. Ann Lee saved 6¢.
Carol saved 3¢.
How much did
they save in all?   _____¢

 Write About It • Make up an
addition story about this picture.
Then write the number sentence.

HOME ACTIVITY • With your child, make flash cards for the addition facts for sums through 12.
Practice the facts together.

Name _____

Doubles and Doubles Plus 1

Vocabulary
doubles
doubles plus one

Learn

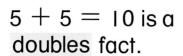

$$5$$
$$+5$$
$$\overline{10}$$

$$5$$
$$+6$$
$$\overline{11}$$

6 + 5 = 11 is a doubles plus one fact, too.

5 + 5 = 10 is a doubles fact.

5 + 6 = 11 is a doubles plus one fact.

Check

Write the three sums.
Then circle the doubles fact.

1.
$$\begin{array}{r} 3 \\ +3 \\ \hline 6 \end{array}$$
$$\begin{array}{r} 3 \\ +4 \\ \hline \end{array}$$
$$\begin{array}{r} 4 \\ +3 \\ \hline \end{array}$$

2.
$$\begin{array}{r} 4 \\ +4 \\ \hline \end{array}$$
$$\begin{array}{r} 4 \\ +5 \\ \hline \end{array}$$
$$\begin{array}{r} 5 \\ +4 \\ \hline \end{array}$$

3.
$$\begin{array}{r} 2 \\ +2 \\ \hline \end{array}$$
$$\begin{array}{r} 2 \\ +3 \\ \hline \end{array}$$
$$\begin{array}{r} 3 \\ +2 \\ \hline \end{array}$$

4.
$$\begin{array}{r} 1 \\ +1 \\ \hline \end{array}$$
$$\begin{array}{r} 1 \\ +2 \\ \hline \end{array}$$
$$\begin{array}{r} 2 \\ +1 \\ \hline \end{array}$$

5.
$$\begin{array}{r} 0 \\ +0 \\ \hline \end{array}$$
$$\begin{array}{r} 0 \\ +1 \\ \hline \end{array}$$
$$\begin{array}{r} 1 \\ +0 \\ \hline \end{array}$$

6.
$$\begin{array}{r} 5 \\ +5 \\ \hline \end{array}$$
$$\begin{array}{r} 5 \\ +6 \\ \hline \end{array}$$
$$\begin{array}{r} 6 \\ +5 \\ \hline \end{array}$$

Explain It ● Daily Reasoning

How does knowing the sum for 4 + 4 help
you find the sums for 4 + 5 and 5 + 4?

Write the sums.

1. $2 + 2 =$ __4__,   so $2 + 3 =$ __5__

2. $1 + 1 =$ ____,   so $2 + 1 =$ ____

3. $5 + 5 =$ ____,   so $5 + 6 =$ ____

4. $4 + 4 =$ ____,   so $5 + 4 =$ ____

5. $0 + 0 =$ ____,   so $0 + 1 =$ ____

6. $3 + 3 =$ ____,   so $3 + 4 =$ ____

Problem Solving

Logical Reasoning

Solve. Draw a picture to check.

7. Pat has 3 .
   Bob has double that many.
   Sue has double what Bob has.

   How many does each person have?

   _____    _____   _____

   Pat   Bob   Sue

 Write About It • Look at Exercise 7.
Explain how you got your answers.

HOME ACTIVITY • Have your child tell you the doubles facts and the doubles plus one facts for 2, 3, 4, and 5. For example, 2 + 2 = 4, so 2 + 3 = 5.

Algebra: **Add 3 Numbers**

Explore

4

$2 + 2 + 6 =$ __10__

8

$2 + 2 + 6 =$ __10__

The sums
are the same!

Connect

Use . Add the blue numbers first.
Write the sums.

1. $3 + 2 + 5 =$ ____ $3 + 2 + 5 =$ ____

2. $5 + 2 + 2 =$ ____ $5 + 2 + 2 =$ ____

3. $9 + 0 + 3 =$ ____ $9 + 0 + 3 =$ ____

4. $3 + 3 + 2 =$ ____ $3 + 3 + 2 =$ ____

5. $1 + 5 + 3 =$ ____ $1 + 5 + 3 =$ ____

6. $3 + 6 + 2 =$ ____ $3 + 6 + 2 =$ ____

Explain It ● Daily Reasoning

The numbers to be added are 6, 2, and 1.
Which numbers will you add first? Why?

6

1

2

Circle the two numbers you add first.
Write the sum.

1.

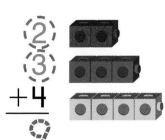

$$\begin{array}{r} ②\\ ③\\ +4\\ \hline 9 \end{array}$$

$$\begin{array}{r} 5\\ +4\\ \hline 9 \end{array}$$

2.

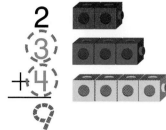

$$\begin{array}{r} 2\\ ③\\ +④\\ \hline 9 \end{array}$$

$$\begin{array}{r} 2\\ +7\\ \hline 9 \end{array}$$

3.
$$\begin{array}{r} 2\\ 5\\ +1 \end{array}$$

4.
$$\begin{array}{r} 3\\ 4\\ +3 \end{array}$$

5.
$$\begin{array}{r} 1\\ 1\\ +6 \end{array}$$

6.
$$\begin{array}{r} 7\\ 2\\ +1 \end{array}$$

7.
$$\begin{array}{r} 2\\ 1\\ +6 \end{array}$$

8.
$$\begin{array}{r} 6\\ 1\\ +4 \end{array}$$

9.
$$\begin{array}{r} 3\\ 5\\ +2 \end{array}$$

10.
$$\begin{array}{r} 2\\ 5\\ +5 \end{array}$$

11.
$$\begin{array}{r} 3\\ 2\\ +3 \end{array}$$

12.
$$\begin{array}{r} 4\\ 5\\ +0 \end{array}$$

Problem Solving

Mental Math

Add in your head. Draw to check.

13. Tim has 2 dogs. Steve has 3 cats. Greg has 6 fish. How many pets do the boys have in all?

_____ pets

 Write About It • Look at Exercise 13. Which numbers did you decide to add first? Tell why.

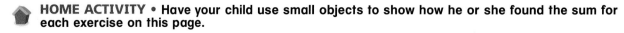

Problem Solving Strategy
Write a Number Sentence

5 children ride bicycles.

4 children join them.

How many children are riding bicycles now?

UNDERSTAND

What do you want to find out?

Circle the question.

PLAN

What facts do you need?

Underline them.

SOLVE

Write a number sentence to solve.

__5__ $\oplus$ __4__ $\bigodot$ __9__ children

CHECK

Does your answer make sense?

Draw a picture to check.

Write a number sentence.
Draw a picture to check.

THINK:
Where do I put the numbers in my sentence?

1. Jim saw 4 boats.
   Then he saw 3 more.
   How many boats did
   he see in all?

____ $\bigcirc$ ____ $\bigcirc$ ____ boats

Problem Solving Practice

Write a number sentence.
Draw a picture to check.

THINK:
Where do I put the numbers in my sentence?

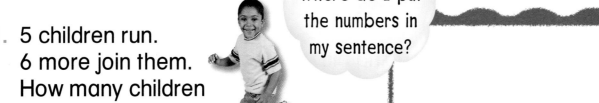

1. 5 children run.
   6 more join them.
   How many children
   are running now?

   ___ ◯ ___ ◯ ___ children

2. Lilly sees 7 cars.
   Then she sees 3 more.
   How many cars does
   she see in all?

   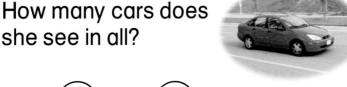

   ___ ◯ ___ ◯ ___ cars

3. 9 children go for a walk.
   3 more children join them.
   How many children are
   walking now?

   ___ ◯ ___ ◯ ___ children

4. Ross has 2 toy rockets.
   Ida gives him 7 more.
   How many toy rockets
   does Ross have now?

   ___ ◯ ___ ◯ ___ toy rockets

HOME ACTIVITY • Give your child 1 to 9 small objects all alike, such as paper clips. Then add several more, to a total of no more than 12. Have your child write an addition sentence about them. Repeat, using different numbers.

Count Back to Subtract

Learn

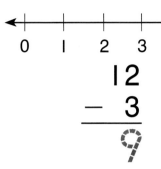

$$\begin{array}{r} 12 \\ -\ 3 \\ \hline 9 \end{array}$$

Start at 12. Then move
3 spaces to the left.
11, 10, 9

Start at 12. Count back to subtract.

Check

Use the number line to count back.
Write the difference.

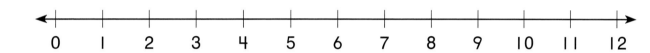

1. $\begin{array}{r}10\\-\ 2\\\hline\end{array}$	2. $\begin{array}{r}8\\-1\\\hline\end{array}$	3. $\begin{array}{r}6\\-2\\\hline\end{array}$	4. $\begin{array}{r}9\\-2\\\hline\end{array}$	5. $\begin{array}{r}7\\-2\\\hline\end{array}$	6. $\begin{array}{r}8\\-2\\\hline\end{array}$
7. $\begin{array}{r}11\\-\ 3\\\hline\end{array}$	8. $\begin{array}{r}10\\-\ 3\\\hline\end{array}$	9. $\begin{array}{r}9\\-3\\\hline\end{array}$	10. $\begin{array}{r}6\\-1\\\hline\end{array}$	11. $\begin{array}{r}8\\-3\\\hline\end{array}$	12. $\begin{array}{r}7\\-1\\\hline\end{array}$
13. $\begin{array}{r}10\\-\ 1\\\hline\end{array}$	14. $\begin{array}{r}11\\-\ 2\\\hline\end{array}$	15. $\begin{array}{r}9\\-1\\\hline\end{array}$	16. $\begin{array}{r}7\\-3\\\hline\end{array}$	17. $\begin{array}{r}6\\-3\\\hline\end{array}$	18. $\begin{array}{r}5\\-3\\\hline\end{array}$

Explain It • Daily Reasoning

How can you find the difference for
$10 - 3$ without using a number line?

$10 - 3$

Count back to subtract.

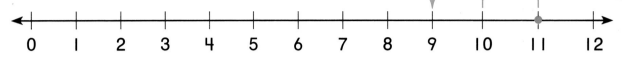

0 1 2 3 4 5 6 7 8 9 10 11 12

$11 - 2 = \underline{9}$

Start at 11.
Then move 2 spaces
to the left.
10, 9

Count back to subtract. Write the difference.
You can use the number line to help.

0 1 2 3 4 5 6 7 8 9 10 11 12

1. $12 - 3 = \underline{}$

2. $9 - 3 = \underline{}$

3. $10 - 2 = \underline{}$

4. $9 - 2 = \underline{}$

5. $10 - 3 = \underline{}$

6. $11 - 3 = \underline{}$

7. $10 - 1 = \underline{}$

8. $11 - 2 = \underline{}$

9. $6 - 3 = \underline{}$

10. $7 - 3 = \underline{}$

11. $9 - 1 = \underline{}$

12. $8 - 3 = \underline{}$

Problem Solving

Application

Write a number sentence to solve.
Use the number line to help.

13. There are 12 cars in the
parking lot. 2 cars leave.
How many cars are
still in the parking lot?

5 6 7 8 9 10 11 12

$\underline{} \bigcirc \underline{} \bigcirc \underline{}$ cars

 Write About It • Look at Exercise 13. Explain
how you used the number line to subtract.

HOME ACTIVITY • Help your child use the number line on this page to practice any subtraction facts he or she missed in this lesson.

Name _____

Subtract to Compare

Learn

How many more red cars than blue cars are there?

There are 2 more red cars than blue cars.

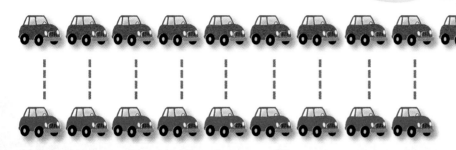

$$\begin{array}{r} 11 \\ -9 \\ \hline 2 \end{array}$$

Check

Draw lines to match. Write the difference.

1. How many fewer small boats than big boats are there?

$$\begin{array}{r} 12 \\ -8 \\ \hline \end{array}$$

2. How many more green bikes than yellow bikes are there?

$$\begin{array}{r} 10 \\ -7 \\ \hline \end{array}$$

Explain It • Daily Reasoning

Which group in the picture has more? How can you prove your answer?

Draw lines to match.
Write the difference.

1.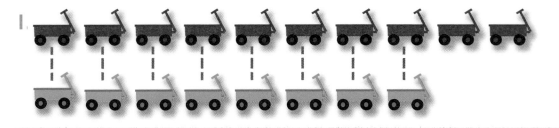

$$\begin{array}{r} 10 \\ -\ 8 \\ \hline 2 \end{array}$$

2.

$$\begin{array}{r} 11 \\ -\ 7 \\ \hline \end{array}$$

3.

$$\begin{array}{r} 12 \\ -\ 9 \\ \hline \end{array}$$

4.

$$\begin{array}{r} 12 \\ -\ 7 \\ \hline \end{array}$$

Problem Solving

Application

Solve. Draw a picture to check.

5. Margie has 10 cars.
   Jake has 6 cars.
   How many more cars
   does Margie have?

   _____ more cars

 Write About It • Look at Exercise 5.
Explain how you got your answer.

HOME ACTIVITY • Set out two groups of objects, one with more objects than the other. Have your child show how to use matching to subtract to find out how many more are in the larger group.

Name _____

Extra Practice

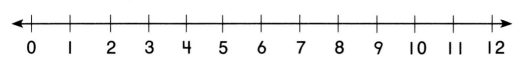

0 1 2 3 4 5 6 7 8 9 10 11 12

| Circle the greater number. Count on to add. | Count back to subtract. Write the difference. |

1. 8
   +3

2. 8
   +2

3. 2
   +5

4. 9
   −2

5. 8
   −3

6. 10
   − 3

Write all the sums. Then circle the doubles facts.

7. 2 + 2 = ___

8. 4 + 3 = ___

9. 5 + 5 = ___

Circle the two numbers you added first.
Write the sum.

10. 3 + 2 + 1 = _____

11. 7 + 1 + 2 = _____

Draw lines to match.
Write the difference.

12.

   10
   − 6

Problem Solving

Write a number sentence.
Draw a picture to check.

13. 6 children are on the bus.
    2 more children get on.
    How many children are
    on the bus?

____◯____◯____ children

Name _____

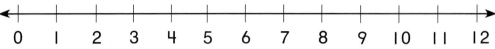 Review/Test

Concepts and Skills

```
<---+---+---+---+---+---+---+---+---+---+---+---+--->
    0   1   2   3   4   5   6   7   8   9  10  11  12
```

Circle the greater number.
Count on to add.

Count back to subtract.
Write the difference.

1.   9
   +3

2.   9
   +2

3.   3
   +6

4.   11
   − 2

5.   10
   − 3

6.   12
   − 3

Write all the sums. Then circle the doubles facts.

7. 4 + 4 = ___

8. 5 + 4 = ___

9. 3 + 3 = ___

Circle the two numbers you add first.
Write the sum.

10. 5 + 5 + 2 = ____

11. 4 + 4 + 2 = ____

Draw lines to match.
Write the difference.

10
− 4

12.

Problem Solving

Write a number sentence.
Draw a picture to check.

13. 7 children run. 3 more
    children join them. How many
    children are running now?

____ ◯ ____ ◯ ____ children

Name _____

1.
$$\begin{array}{r} 10 \\ -\ 3 \\ \hline \end{array}$$

5 ○   7 ○   13 ○   15 ○

---

2. Which does the number line show?

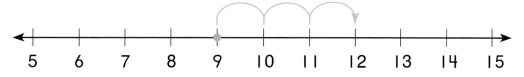

5   6   7   8   9   10   11   12   13   14   15

$9 - 2 = 7$ ○ $9 - 3 = 6$ ○ $2 + 9 = 11$ ○ $3 + 9 = 12$ ○

---

3. Which is a doubles plus 1 fact?

$3 + 3 = 6$ ○ $3 + 4 = 7$ ○ $5 + 5 = 10$ ○ $7 + 4 = 11$ ○

---

4. Which is the sum?

$3 + 4 + 2 = $ _____

8 ○   9 ○   10 ○   11 ○

---

5. Which tells how many more apples than pears there are?

$7 - 5 = 2$ ○ $8 - 5 = 3$ ○

$5 + 2 = 7$ ○ $5 + 3 = 8$ ○

Show What You Know

6. Write the number sentence. Draw a picture to explain your answer.

Kate picks 4 pumpkins. Edna picks 5 pumpkins. How many pumpkins do they pick in all?

____ ◯ ____ ◯ ____ pumpkins

MATH GAME

Boats Full of Facts

Play with a partner.

You will need

2 🎯   🎲

1. Put your 🎯 at START.

2. Spin the 🎯 .

3. Move your 🎯 that many boats.

4. Find the sum or difference.

5. Take that many 🎲 .

6. When the first player gets to END, count 🎲 .

7. The player with more 🎲 wins.

START

$3 + 7$ $9 - 4$ $11 - 6$ $\begin{array}{r} 7 \\ + 4 \\ \hline \end{array}$

$11 - 2$ $2 + 7$ $10 - 3$ $\begin{array}{r} 8 \\ + 5 \\ \hline \end{array}$ $\begin{array}{r} 12 \\ - 7 \\ \hline \end{array}$

END

$\begin{array}{r} 9 \\ + 3 \\ \hline \end{array}$ $4 + 4$ $5 + 6$ $12 - 9$ $\begin{array}{r} 9 \\ - 3 \\ \hline \end{array}$ $3 + 8$

CHAPTER 14

Practice Addition and Subtraction

SOCIAL STUDIES

FUN FACTS

A square picnic table with 4 long benches can seat between 10 to 12 people.

Theme: A Picnic

Name _____

✅ Check What You Know

Sums to 10

Add. Write the sums.

1.
$$\begin{array}{r} 2 \\ +8 \\ \hline \end{array} \qquad \begin{array}{r} 8 \\ +2 \\ \hline \end{array}$$

2.
$$\begin{array}{r} 6 \\ +3 \\ \hline \end{array} \qquad \begin{array}{r} 3 \\ +6 \\ \hline \end{array}$$

3.
$$\begin{array}{r} 7 \\ +1 \\ \hline \end{array} \qquad \begin{array}{r} 1 \\ +7 \\ \hline \end{array}$$

4.
$$\begin{array}{r} 4 \\ +5 \\ \hline \end{array} \qquad \begin{array}{r} 5 \\ +4 \\ \hline \end{array}$$

5.
$$\begin{array}{r} 3 \\ +7 \\ \hline \end{array} \qquad \begin{array}{r} 7 \\ +3 \\ \hline \end{array}$$

6.
$$\begin{array}{r} 8 \\ +0 \\ \hline \end{array} \qquad \begin{array}{r} 0 \\ +8 \\ \hline \end{array}$$

Subtraction to 10

Subtract. Circle the pair of facts
if they use the same numbers.

7.
$$\begin{array}{r} 9 \\ -2 \\ \hline \end{array} \qquad \begin{array}{r} 9 \\ -7 \\ \hline \end{array}$$

8.
$$\begin{array}{r} 8 \\ -0 \\ \hline \end{array} \qquad \begin{array}{r} 8 \\ -8 \\ \hline \end{array}$$

9.
$$\begin{array}{r} 10 \\ -4 \\ \hline \end{array} \qquad \begin{array}{r} 10 \\ -5 \\ \hline \end{array}$$

10.
$$\begin{array}{r} 7 \\ -6 \\ \hline \end{array} \qquad \begin{array}{r} 7 \\ -2 \\ \hline \end{array}$$

11.
$$\begin{array}{r} 8 \\ -2 \\ \hline \end{array} \qquad \begin{array}{r} 8 \\ -6 \\ \hline \end{array}$$

12.
$$\begin{array}{r} 10 \\ -3 \\ \hline \end{array} \qquad \begin{array}{r} 10 \\ -7 \\ \hline \end{array}$$

Subtract across. Subtract down.

13.

9	4	
6	2	

14.

10	3	
8	2	

Use this page to review important skills needed for this chapter.

Name _____

Algebra: **Related Addition and Subtraction Facts**

Vocabulary
related facts

Explore

Related facts use the same numbers.

$$8 + 4 = 12$$

$$12 - 4 = 8$$

Connect

Use ▨ ▨ to show related facts.
Complete the chart.

	Use Add ▨ ▨	Write the sum.	Take away	Write the subtraction sentence.
1.	6 3	$6 + 3 = \underline{9}$	3	$\underline{9} \ominus \underline{3} \ominus \underline{6}$
2.	7 5	$7 + 5 = \underline{}$	7	$\underline{}\bigcirc\underline{}\bigcirc\underline{}$
3.	4 6	$4 + 6 = \underline{}$	4	$\underline{}\bigcirc\underline{}\bigcirc\underline{}$
4.	3 8	$3 + 8 = \underline{}$	8	$\underline{}\bigcirc\underline{}\bigcirc\underline{}$
5.	6 6	$6 + 6 = \underline{}$	6	$\underline{}\bigcirc\underline{}\bigcirc\underline{}$

Explain It • Daily Reasoning

How can knowing an addition fact help you remember a subtraction fact?

Practice and Problem Solving

Write each sum or difference.
Circle the related facts in each row.

1. (7 + 2 = _9_)   5 + 2 = _7_   (9 – 2 = _7_)

2. 8 + 4 = ___   12 – 4 = ___   10 – 4 = ___

3. 11 – 4 = ___   9 + 1 = ___   10 – 1 = ___

4. 10 – 7 = ___   3 + 7 = ___   7 + 4 = ___

5. 6 + 5 = ___   12 – 5 = ___   11 – 5 = ___

6. 9 + 3 = ___   8 – 4 = ___   12 – 3 = ___

Problem Solving

Algebra

7. Circle three numbers that you can use to write a pair of related facts. Write the number sentences.    5 7 8 12

___ ◯ ___ ◯ ___   ___ ◯ ___ ◯ ___

Write About It • Look at Exercise 7. Write the other related addition and subtraction sentences.

 HOME ACTIVITY • Give your child an addition problem, such as 4 + 5, and ask him or her to tell you the sum (9). Then ask your child to tell you a related subtraction fact (9 – 5 = 4 or 9 – 4 = 5).

Fact Families to 12

8, 3, and 11 are the numbers in this fact family.

Vocabulary
fact family

HANDS ON Explore

8, 3, and 11 are the numbers in this fact family.

$8 + 3 = 11$

$3 + 8 = 11$

$11 - 3 = 8$

$11 - 8 = 3$

Connect

Use . Add or subtract.
Write the numbers in the fact family.

1.
$7 + 4 = \underline{11}$

$4 + 7 = \underline{11}$

$11 - 4 = \underline{7}$

$11 - 7 = \underline{4}$

| 7 | 4 | 11 |

2.
$8 + 4 = \underline{}$

$4 + 8 = \underline{}$

$12 - 4 = \underline{}$

$12 - 8 = \underline{}$

| | | |

3.
$5 + 4 = \underline{}$

$4 + 5 = \underline{}$

$9 - 4 = \underline{}$

$9 - 5 = \underline{}$

| | | |

4.
$6 + 5 = \underline{}$

$5 + 6 = \underline{}$

$11 - 5 = \underline{}$

$11 - 6 = \underline{}$

| | | |

Explain It • Daily Reasoning

How many facts are in the fact family for 12, 6, and 6?
Use  to prove your answer.

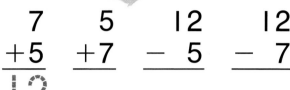

Practice and Problem Solving

Add or subtract.
Write the numbers in the fact family.

1.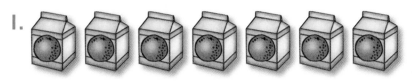

$$\begin{array}{r} 7 \\ +5 \\ \hline 12 \end{array} \qquad \begin{array}{r} 5 \\ +7 \\ \hline \end{array} \qquad \begin{array}{r} 12 \\ -5 \\ \hline \end{array} \qquad \begin{array}{r} 12 \\ -7 \\ \hline \end{array}$$

☐ ☐ ☐

2.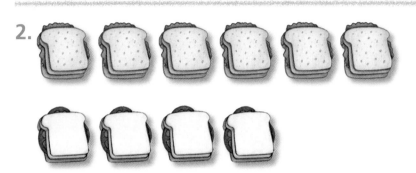

$$\begin{array}{r} 6 \\ +4 \\ \hline \end{array} \qquad \begin{array}{r} 4 \\ +6 \\ \hline \end{array} \qquad \begin{array}{r} 10 \\ -4 \\ \hline \end{array} \qquad \begin{array}{r} 10 \\ -6 \\ \hline \end{array}$$

☐ ☐ ☐

3.

$$\begin{array}{r} 9 \\ +3 \\ \hline \end{array} \qquad \begin{array}{r} 3 \\ +9 \\ \hline \end{array} \qquad \begin{array}{r} 12 \\ -9 \\ \hline \end{array} \qquad \begin{array}{r} 12 \\ -3 \\ \hline \end{array}$$

☐ ☐ ☐

Problem Solving

Logical Reasoning

Solve the riddle. Write the number.

4. When I am added to 4, we make 10.
   What number am I?

   _____

 Write About It • Write a number sentence
that shows your answer for Exercise 4. Then
write the rest of the fact family.

🏠 **HOME ACTIVITY** • Tell your child an addition fact with a sum of 12 or less. Have your child tell the
other number sentences in the fact family.

Name _____

Sums and Differences to 12

Learn

These are some ways to find sums and differences.

count on
$7 + 2 = 9$

count back
$10 - 2 = 8$

doubles
$5 + 5 = 10$

related facts
$5 + 3 = 8$ and $8 - 3 = 5$

Check

Write the sum or difference.

1. $7 + 2 = \underline{9}$

2. $11 - 3 = \underline{}$

3. $6 - 0 = \underline{}$

4. $7 + 3 = \underline{}$

5. $10 - 2 = \underline{}$

6. $12 - 6 = \underline{}$

7. $5 + 3 = \underline{}$

8. $9 + 0 = \underline{}$

9. $9 - 2 = \underline{}$

10. $11 - 2 = \underline{}$

11. $8 - 4 = \underline{}$

12. $10 + 2 = \underline{}$

13. $6 + 3 = \underline{}$

14. $9 - 5 = \underline{}$

15. $8 - 8 = \underline{}$

16. $4 + 3 = \underline{}$

17. $11 - 5 = \underline{}$

18. $6 + 6 = \underline{}$

19. $4 + 5 = \underline{}$

Explain It • Daily Reasoning

How could knowing $12 - 3 = 9$ help you find the difference for $12 - 4$?

$12 - 4$

Write the sum or difference.

1. $\begin{array}{r} 8 \\ +4 \\ \hline 12 \end{array}$	2. $\begin{array}{r} 10 \\ -3 \\ \hline \end{array}$	3. $\begin{array}{r} 6 \\ +6 \\ \hline \end{array}$	4. $\begin{array}{r} 12 \\ -7 \\ \hline \end{array}$	5. $\begin{array}{r} 3 \\ +8 \\ \hline \end{array}$	6. $\begin{array}{r} 8 \\ -5 \\ \hline \end{array}$
7. $\begin{array}{r} 9 \\ -4 \\ \hline \end{array}$	8. $\begin{array}{r} 11 \\ -2 \\ \hline \end{array}$	9. $\begin{array}{r} 3 \\ +5 \\ \hline \end{array}$	10. $\begin{array}{r} 12 \\ -4 \\ \hline \end{array}$	11. $\begin{array}{r} 5 \\ +5 \\ \hline \end{array}$	12. $\begin{array}{r} 7 \\ -3 \\ \hline \end{array}$
13. $\begin{array}{r} 6 \\ +2 \\ \hline \end{array}$	14. $\begin{array}{r} 10 \\ -6 \\ \hline \end{array}$	15. $\begin{array}{r} 4 \\ +3 \\ \hline \end{array}$	16. $\begin{array}{r} 11 \\ -8 \\ \hline \end{array}$	17. $\begin{array}{r} 3 \\ +7 \\ \hline \end{array}$	18. $\begin{array}{r} 9 \\ +1 \\ \hline \end{array}$
19. $\begin{array}{r} 5 \\ +7 \\ \hline \end{array}$	20. $\begin{array}{r} 11 \\ -6 \\ \hline \end{array}$	21. $\begin{array}{r} 6 \\ +3 \\ \hline \end{array}$	22. $\begin{array}{r} 10 \\ -5 \\ \hline \end{array}$	23. $\begin{array}{r} 7 \\ +4 \\ \hline \end{array}$	24. $\begin{array}{r} 6 \\ +5 \\ \hline \end{array}$

Problem Solving
Visual Thinking

25. Write the fact family that tells about the picture.

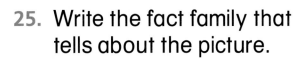

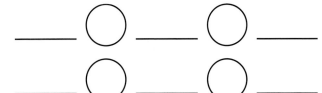

 Write About It ● How would your fact family be different if there were 1 more cherry in the second row?

Algebra: **Missing Numbers**

Learn

What is the missing number?

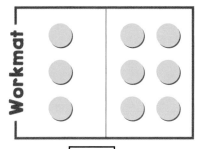

$3 + \boxed{} = 9$

$3 + \boxed{6} = 9$

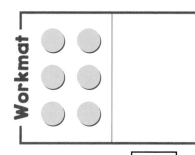

$9 - 3 = \boxed{}$

$9 - 3 = \boxed{6}$

Check

Write the missing number.
Use ⬤ if you need to.

Use a related fact to help you.

1. $6 + \boxed{} = 10$ $\qquad$ $10 - 6 = \boxed{}$

2. $\boxed{} + 3 = 6$ $\qquad$ $6 - 3 = \boxed{}$

3. $8 + \boxed{} = 12$ $\qquad$ $12 - 8 = \boxed{}$

4. $\boxed{} + 5 = 11$ $\qquad$ $11 - 5 = \boxed{}$

5. $5 + \boxed{} = 12$ $\qquad$ $12 - 5 = \boxed{}$

Explain It • Daily Reasoning

Use ⬤ to show why you can solve
$\boxed{} + 5 = 9$ by using subtraction.

Write the missing number.
Use ⬤ if you need to.

1.

$2 + \boxed{5} = 7$ $7 - 2 = \boxed{5}$

2.

$\boxed{} + 3 = 9$ $9 - 3 = \boxed{}$

3.

$7 + \boxed{} = 10$ $10 - 7 = \boxed{}$

4.

$\boxed{} + 7 = 8$ $8 - 7 = \boxed{}$

5.

$8 + \boxed{} = 9$ $9 - 8 = \boxed{}$

6.

$\boxed{} + 5 = 8$ $8 - 5 = \boxed{}$

7.

$3 + \boxed{} = 11$ $11 - 3 = \boxed{}$

Problem Solving

Algebra

8. What is the missing number?

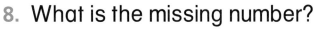

$$\blacksquare = \underline{\hspace{2cm}}$$

$$\begin{array}{cccc} 9 & \blacksquare & 11 & 11 \\ +\,\blacksquare & +\,9 & -\,9 & -\,\blacksquare \\ \hline 11 & 11 & \blacksquare & 9 \end{array}$$

 Write About It • Look at Exercise 8.
Write the numbers that are in the fact
family. Explain how you know.

 HOME ACTIVITY • Put 12 small items in a bag. Have your child remove some, count them, and tell
how many are left in the bag. Repeat.

Name _____

Problem Solving
Choose a Strategy

You can use different ways to
solve a problem.

Scott ate 4 hot dogs.
Tal also ate 4 hot dogs.
How many hot dogs did they eat in all?

Make a model.	Draw a picture.	Write a number sentence.
		$4 + 4 = 8$
_8_ hot dogs	_8_ hot dogs	_8_ hot dogs

Choose a way to solve each problem.
Make a model 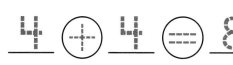, draw a picture 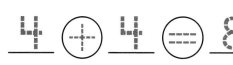,
or write a number sentence 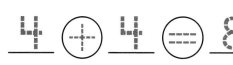.
Show your work.

THINK:
Which way do
I want to solve
this problem?

1. 8 ants are on the picnic table.
   3 go away.
   How many ants are there now?

   _5_ ants

2. The basket has 11 apples.
   Jose takes 2 apples.
   How many apples are there now?

   _____ apples

Problem Solving Practice

Choose a way to solve each problem.
Make a model ◼, draw a picture 🖍,
or write a number sentence ✏️.
Show your work.

THINK:
What is another way to solve the problem?

1. Meg's mom makes 12 muffins.
   Her family eats 9 muffins.
   How many muffins are left?

   _____ muffins

2. Sara sets out 9 plates.
   Children take 3 plates.
   How many plates are left?

   _____ plates

3. There are 4 pretzels.
   Hans brings 3 more pretzels.
   How many pretzels are there now?

   _____ pretzels

4. Rick eats 4 cherries.
   Peter eats 6 cherries.
   How many do they eat in all?

   _____ cherries

🔶 **HOME ACTIVITY** • Ask your child to explain how he or she solved each problem on this page. Then ask him or her to show a different way to solve each problem.

Name _____

Extra Practice

Write each sum or difference.
Circle the related facts.

1. $10 - 2 =$ _____ $9 + 3 =$ _____ $12 - 3 =$ _____

Add or subtract. Write the numbers in the fact family.

2. $7 + 4 =$ _____

       $4 + 7 =$ _____

       $11 - 4 =$ _____

       $11 - 7 =$ _____

□ □ □

3. $6 + 3 =$ _____

       $3 + 6 =$ _____

       $9 - 3 =$ _____

       $9 - 6 =$ _____

□ □ □

Write the sum or difference.

4. $\begin{array}{r} 8 \\ +1 \\ \hline \end{array}$
5. $\begin{array}{r} 11 \\ -5 \\ \hline \end{array}$
6. $\begin{array}{r} 12 \\ -4 \\ \hline \end{array}$
7. $\begin{array}{r} 6 \\ +4 \\ \hline \end{array}$
8. $\begin{array}{r} 3 \\ +4 \\ \hline \end{array}$
9. $\begin{array}{r} 10 \\ -2 \\ \hline \end{array}$

Write the missing number.

10.   □ $+ 5 = 11$ $11 - 5 =$ □

Problem Solving

Choose a way to solve the problem.

11. Lily has 8 cherries.
Her friend gives her 3 cherries.
How many does Lily have now?

_____ cherries

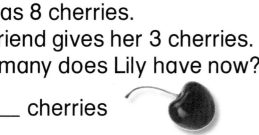

✔ Review/Test

Concepts and Skills

Write each sum or difference.
Circle the related facts.

1. $4 + 7 =$ ___ $11 - 7 =$ ___ $11 - 2 =$ ___

Add or subtract. Write the numbers in the fact family.

2. $4 + 8 =$ ___

   $8 + 4 =$ ___

   $12 - 8 =$ ___

   $12 - 4 =$ ___

3. $6 + 5 =$ ___

   $5 + 6 =$ ___

   $11 - 5 =$ ___

   $11 - 6 =$ ___

Write the sum or difference.

4. $\begin{array}{r} 9 \\ +1 \\ \hline \end{array}$ 5. $\begin{array}{r} 12 \\ -\ 6 \\ \hline \end{array}$ 6. $\begin{array}{r} 10 \\ -\ 4 \\ \hline \end{array}$ 7. $\begin{array}{r} 7 \\ +5 \\ \hline \end{array}$ 8. $\begin{array}{r} 4 \\ +5 \\ \hline \end{array}$ 9. $\begin{array}{r} 11 \\ -\ 3 \\ \hline \end{array}$

Write the missing number.

10. $8 + \boxed{} = 12$ $12 - 8 = \boxed{}$

Problem Solving

Choose a way to solve the problem.

11. Alex has 12 pretzels.
    He gives 4 pretzels to friends.
    How many pretzels are left?

    _____ pretzels

Name _____

Choose the answer for questions 1 – 5.

1.
$$\begin{array}{r} 12 \\ -\ 5 \\ \hline \end{array}$$

18 ○   17 ○

8 ○   7 ○

2.
$$\begin{array}{r} 5 \\ +6 \\ \hline \end{array}$$

1 ○   2 ○

10 ○   11 ○

3. Which is the missing number?

$6 + \boxed{} = 10$

2 ○   4 ○   6 ○   8 ○

4. Gabe had 11 berries. He ate 4. Which number sentence tells how many berries Gabe has left?

$11 - 7 = 4$ ○ $11 - 4 = 7$ ○ $7 + 4 = 11$ ○ $4 + 7 = 11$ ○

5. Which is a way to make 9?

$4 + 2$ ○ $5 + 4$ ○ $4 + 1$ ○ $4 + 3$ ○

Show What You Know

6. Write four number sentences that are in the same fact family. Draw a picture of each number sentence to explain.

IT'S IN THE BAG
Animals Picnic Basket

PROJECT Create a slide-through picnic basket of addition and subtraction facts.

You Will Need

- Large brown bag
- Pattern tracer
- Cardboard sentence strip
- Scissors

Directions

1 Put the bag flat in front of you. Place the pattern at the top of the bag. Trace around the pattern.

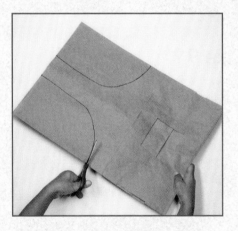

2 Cut on the lines you drew.

3 Put the end of the facts strip in the left side. Push it through to the other side.

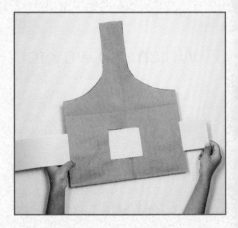

4 Decorate your picnic basket. Draw and write addition and subtraction facts on the strip so they show in the basket's window.

The Animals' Picnic

BY DAVID MCPHAIL

This book will help me review doubles.

This book belongs to _____.

All the animals were having
a picnic.

One mouse invited one mouse.

They went by bike.

B

Two sheep invited two sheep.

They went by car.

Three rabbits invited three rabbits.

They went by wheelbarrow.

Four ants invited four ants.

They walked.

E

The ants got there first.

Roanoke Island, NC

At the Aquarium

There are three North Carolina aquariums. You can find them at Roanoke Island, Pine Knoll Shores, and Fort Fisher.

Buses bring many people to visit the aquariums.

Use the graph to answer the questions.

Aquarium	Buses of Visitors in One Week						
Roanoke Island	🚌	🚌					
Pine Knoll Shore	🚌	🚌	🚌	🚌	🚌	🚌	🚌
Fort Fisher	🚌	🚌	🚌				

1 How many buses went to Roanoke Island? _____ buses

2 How many more buses went to Pine Knoll Shores than Fort Fisher? _____ buses

3 How many buses in all went to the aquariums? _____ buses

4 Did more buses go to Pine Knoll Shores or go to Roanoke Island and Fort Fisher together? _____

CHALLENGE

Represent Numbers in Different Ways

This number is shown in three different ways.

Show each number three different ways.

Number	Use ■. Draw to show.	Draw a picture.	Write a name for the number.
1. **7**			__ ◯ __
2. **10**			__ ◯ __
3. **8**			__ ◯ __
4. **12**			__ ◯ __

✓ Study Guide and Review

Vocabulary

Write how many **tens** and **ones**.
Write the number in a different way.

1.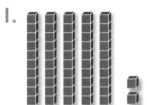

_____ tens _____ ones = _____

_____ + _____

2.

_____ tens _____ ones = _____

_____ + _____

Skills and Concepts

Circle the number that is greater.
Write the numbers.

3.

_____ is greater than _____.

_____ > _____

4.

_____ is greater than _____.

_____ > _____

Circle the number that is less.
Write the numbers.

5.

_____ is less than _____.

_____ < _____

6.

_____ is less than _____.

_____ < _____

Sort. Draw to complete the picture graph.

7.

Lunches We Like						
hot dog						
pizza						
soup						

Count by fives. Write the missing numbers.

8. 5, 10, _____, _____, 25, _____, _____, 40

Add or subtract. Think of a related fact to help.

9.   8   10.   10   11.   9   12.   5   13.   6   14.   11
    $+\,4$ $-\,5$ $+\,3$ $-\,5$ $+\,6$ $-\,2$

Problem Solving

Write the number sentence.
Draw a picture to check.

15. There are 12 eggs.
    Dad cooks 6 of them.
    How many eggs are left?

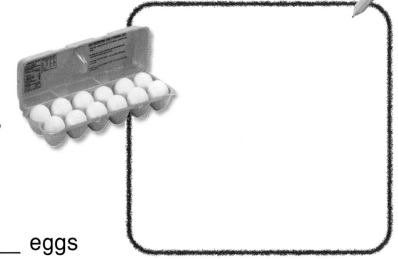

_____ ◯ _____ ◯ _____ eggs

Performance Assessment

Buying Fish

Megan and her sister Erin bought some fish at the pet store.

- Erin bought 1 more fish than Megan.

- Megan bought fewer than 7 fish.

Write a doubles-plus-one sentence that fits this math story.

Show your work.

TECHNOLOGY

Calculator • Skip Counting

You can use a to skip count.

Skip count by twos.

Press   .

Read the number 2 .

Press = .

Read the number 4 .

Press = .

Read the number 6 .

So, count 2 , 4 , 6 to count by twos.

Practice and Problem Solving

Use a .

1. Skip count by threes.

   Press   = = = = = =

   ☐ ☐ ☐ ☐ ☐ ☐

2. Count by adding the next larger number each time.

   Press ON/C 1 + 2 = + 3 = + 4 =

   ☐   ☐   ☐

Dear Family,

In Unit 3 we learned about graphs, numbers to 100, and facts to 12. Here is a game for us to play together. This game will give me a chance to share what I have learned.

Love,

_____

Directions

1. Cover each apple with a penny.
2. Pick up 1 penny.
3. Use the number on that apple. Tell an addition or subtraction fact that uses doubles or doubles plus one.
4. Put the penny on the graph to show the kind of fact you made.
5. Take turns until a row is full. Look at the graph. Count the number of doubles facts and doubles plus one facts.
6. Tell which kind of fact you made more of. Play again.

Materials
21 pennies or beans

Double the Apples

How We Doubled the Apples

doubles							
doubles plus 1							

Dear Family,

During the next few weeks, we will learn about solid figures, plane shapes, and patterns. We will also learn more about addition and subtraction to 20. Here is important math vocabulary and a list of books to share.

Love,

_____

Vocabulary

rectangle
square
circle
triangle
sphere
cone
cylinder
pyramid
cube
rectangular prism

Vocabulary Power

Solid Figures:

rectangular prism   sphere

cone   cylinder

pyramid   cube

Plane Shapes:

rectangle square   circle   triangle

BOOKS TO SHARE

To read about geometry and patterns with your child, look for these books in your library.

When a Line Bends... A Shape Begins, by Rhonda Gowler Greene, Houghton Mifflin, 2001.

Circus Shapes, by Stuart J. Murphy, HarperCollins, 1998.

The Very Busy Spider, by Eric Carle, Penguin Putnam, 1999.

A Fair Bear Share, by Stuart J. Murphy, HarperCollins, 1998.

 Visit *The Learning Site* for additional ideas and activities. **www.harcourtschool.com**

CHAPTER 15

Solid Figures and Plane Shapes

FUN FACTS

Most sand castles are built from a pile of sand that has been packed down. Then molds can be placed on top.

Name _____

✅ Check What You Know

Sort Solid Figures

Color the shape blue.

Color the shape red.

Color the shape yellow.

Color the  shape green.

1.

2.

3.

4.

5.

6.

Sort Plane Shapes

Circle the same shape.

7.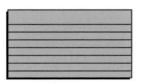

8.

Use this page to review important skills needed for this chapter.

Name _____

Solid Figures

HANDS ON

Explore

Vocabulary

cylinder	sphere
pyramid	cone
rectangular prism	cube

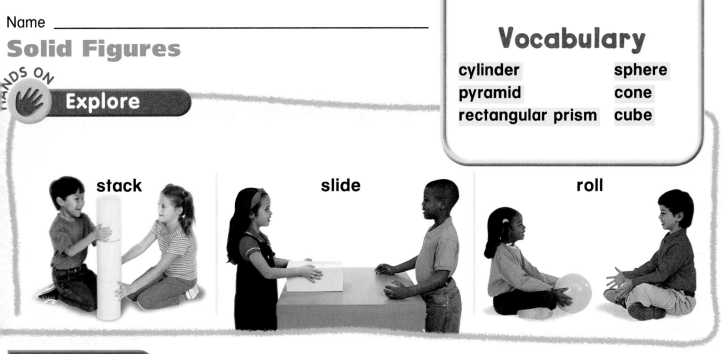

stack   slide   roll

Connect

Use solids. Sort. Write **yes** or **no**.

	Does it stack?	roll?	slide?
1. sphere	no		
2. cone			
3. cube			
4. cylinder			
5. pyramid			
6. rectangular prism			

Explain It ● Daily Reasoning

Which solids roll? Tell why.

cube   pyramid   rectangular prism

These can slide.

sphere   cone   cylinder

These are round and curved. They roll.

Use solids.

1. Color each solid that will stack.

2. Color each solid that will roll.

3. Color each solid that will slide.

Problem Solving

Logical Reasoning

4. Cross out the solid that does not belong. Circle the sentence that tells why.

It will not stack.

It will not roll.

 Write About It ● Draw something in your classroom that will roll. Tell why.

 HOME ACTIVITY • Find objects that are shaped like the solids on this page. Work with your child to find out which ones will stack, roll, and slide.

Name _____

Faces and Corners

Vocabulary

corner

face

HANDS ON Explore

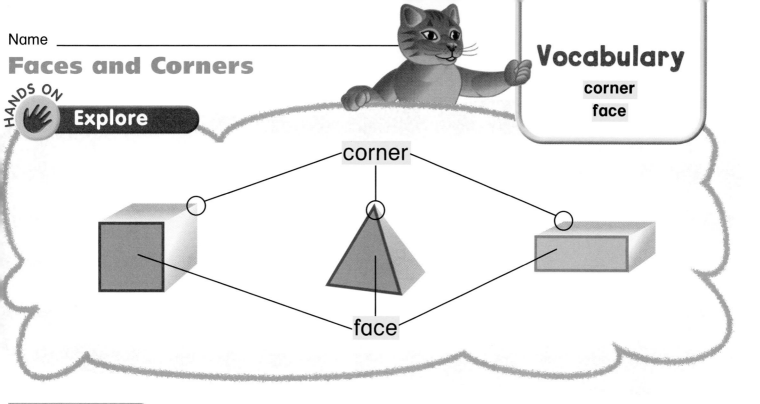

corner

face

Connect

Sort solids by the number of corners or faces.
Color the pictures that match the sentence.

1. I have 6 faces.

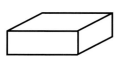

2. I have 5 faces.

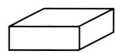

3. I have 8 corners.

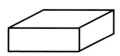

4. I have 5 corners.

Explain It ● Daily Reasoning

How are a sphere and a
rectangular prism different?

Use solids.
Circle the pictures that match the sentence.

1. These solids have 6 faces.

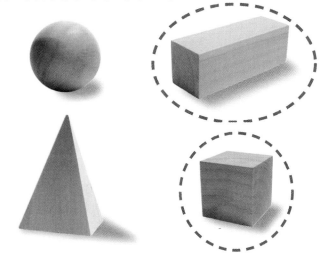

2. This solid has 5 corners.

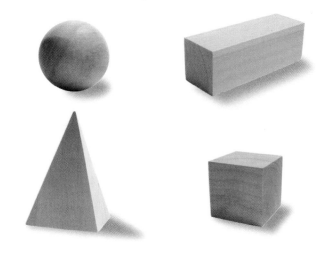

3. These solids have 8 corners.

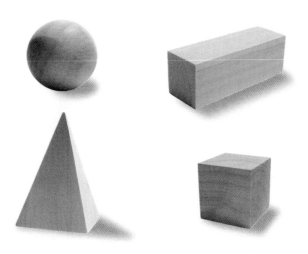

4. This solid has 5 faces.

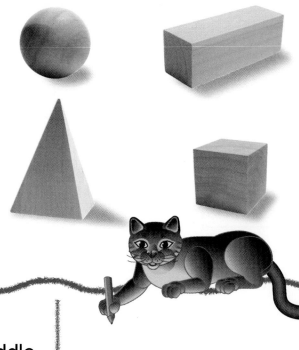

Problem Solving

Logical Reasoning

5. Draw the solid that solves the riddle.

   I am curved.

   I am shaped like a beach ball.

 Write About It • Find 5 cubes
in the classroom. Describe them.

🔶 **HOME ACTIVITY** • Find objects that are shaped like the solids on this page. Have your child count
the faces of each object.

Plane Shapes on Solid Figures

HANDS ON Explore

circle

square

triangle

rectangle

Vocabulary

circle
square
triangle
rectangle

Connect

Use solids. Trace around each one.
Write the name of the shape you drew.

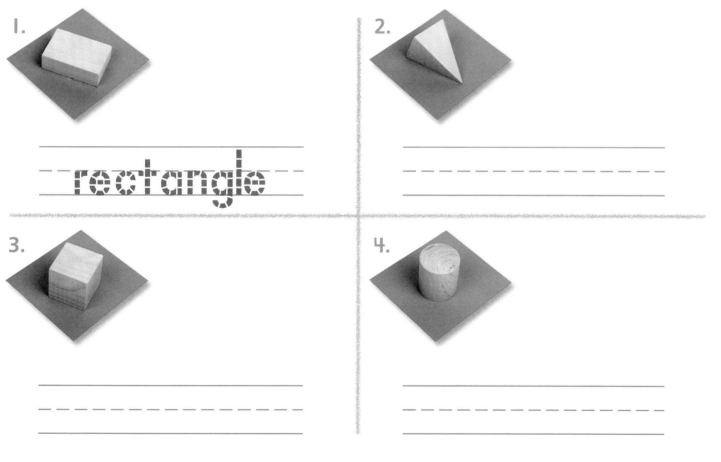

1. rectangle

2. _____

3. _____

4. _____

Explain It • Daily Reasoning

What two shapes can you
trace from this pyramid?

Draw a house.
Use at least one ☐, one ◯, one △, and one ☐.

1. Color ☐ ✏️ .

2. Color ◯ ✏️ .

3. Color △ ✏️ .

4. Color ☐ ✏️ .

Problem Solving

Visual Thinking

5. Draw a small rectangle.

6. Draw a large triangle.

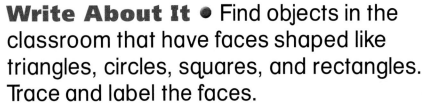

Write About It ● Find objects in the classroom that have faces shaped like triangles, circles, squares, and rectangles. Trace and label the faces.

HOME ACTIVITY • Gather some objects that are solid figures, such as a box and a can. Have your child place each on a sheet of paper, trace the faces and name the shape he or she drew.

Name _____

Sort and Identify Plane Shapes

Vocabulary
side
corner

Explore

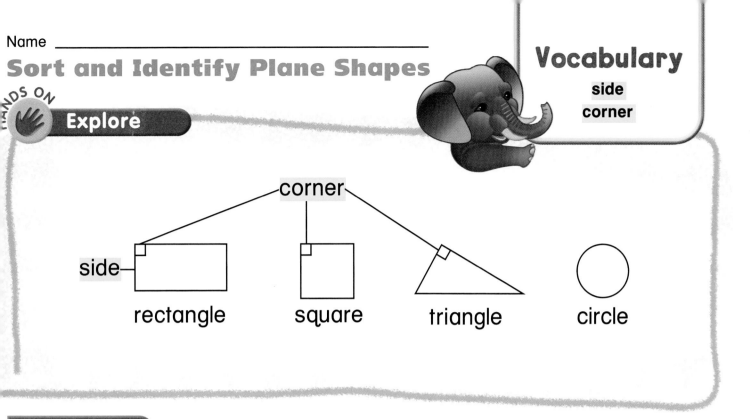

corner

side—

rectangle   square   triangle   circle

Connect

Use shapes. Sort by the number of sides and
corners. Draw the shapes. Write the names.

1. Find a shape with
   4 sides and 4 corners.

_____

____ rectangle ____

2. Find a different shape with
   4 sides and 4 corners.

_____

_____

3. Find a shape with 0 corners.

_____

_____

4. Find a shape with
   3 sides and 3 corners.

_____

_____

Explain It ● Daily Reasoning

How are a rectangle and a square alike?

Use to trace each side.
Use to circle each corner.
Write how many sides and corners there are.

1.

__4__ sides

__4__ corners

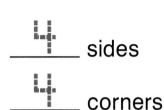

2.

_____ sides

_____ corners

3.

_____ sides

_____ corners

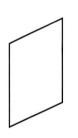

4.

_____ sides

_____ corners

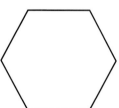

5.

_____ sides

_____ corners

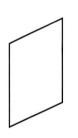

6.

_____ sides

_____ corners

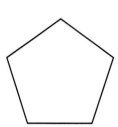

Problem Solving

Visual Thinking

7. Draw one line inside each shape to make 2 triangles.

    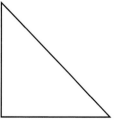

Write About It • Draw a shape that has
4 corners. Draw two lines inside the shape to
make 4 triangles.

HOME ACTIVITY • Ask your child to draw a shape that has 3 sides and 3 corners (triangle).
Ask your child to draw a shape that has 4 sides and 4 corners (rectangle or square).

Name _____

Problem Solving Strategy
Make a Model

How many make a ?

UNDERSTAND

What do you need to find out?

Read the question again.

PLAN

How can you solve the problem?

Use pattern blocks to make a model.

SOLVE

Write how many you use.

__2__ make a .

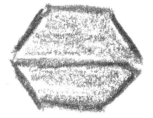

CHECK

How do you know that your answer is correct?

Cover the with to check.

Use pattern blocks to
make a model.
Draw to show your model.
Write how many pattern
blocks you use.

1. How many make a ?

_____

Use pattern blocks to make a model.
Draw to show your model.
Write how many pattern blocks you use.

Keep in Mind!
Understand
Plan
Solve
Check

1. How many ◆ make a ⬡ ?

_____ ◆

2. How many ▲ make a ◆ ?

_____ ▲

3. How many ▲ make a ▱ ?

_____ ▲

4. How many ▲ and ◆ make a ⬡ ?

_____ ▲ and _____ ◆

HOME ACTIVITY • Have your child explain how he or she figured out Exercises 1–4.

260 two hundred sixty

Name _____

Extra Practice

Use solids to sort.

1. Color each solid that will roll.
   Circle the solids that have 6 faces.
   Draw a line under the solid that
   has 5 corners.

2. Use to color the rectangle.
   Use to color the triangle.

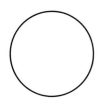 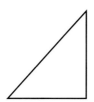 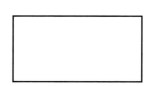

Write how many sides and corners there are.

3.

_____ sides

_____ corners

4.

_____ corners

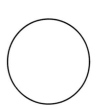

Problem Solving

Use pattern blocks to make a model.
Draw to show your model.
Write how many pattern blocks
you use.

5. How many ▲ make a ◆ ?

_____ ▲

✅ Review/Test

Concepts and Skills

Use solids to sort.

1. Color each solid that will stack.
   Circle the solid that has 5 faces.
   Draw a line under the solids that
   have 8 corners.

2. Use to color the circle.
   Use to color the square.

 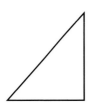 

Write how many sides and corners there are.

3.

_____ sides

_____ corners

4.

_____ sides

_____ corners

Problem Solving

Use pattern blocks to make a model.
Draw to show your model. Write how
many pattern blocks you use.

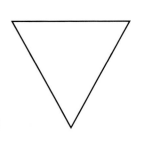

5. How many and ▲ make
   ⬛ ?

_____ and _____ ▲

Getting Ready for the EOG Test
Chapters 1–15

Choose the answer for questions 1– 5.

1. Which did the fewest children choose?

Fruits We Like				
🍎 apples	🍎	🍎	🍎	
🍌 bananas	🍌	🍌		
🍒 cherries	🍒	🍒	🍒	🍒

apples ○   cherries ○

bananas ○   grapes ○

---

2. Which solid has 6 faces and stacks?

      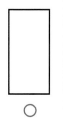

○   ○   ○   ○

3. How many faces are on a ?

○ 1   ○ 6

○ 4   ○ 8

---

4. Which shape is a circle?

  ○   ○   ○   ○

5. Which shape has 3 sides and 3 corners?

 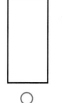 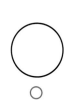

○   ○   ○   ○

Show What You Know

6. Use and .

How many make a ?

Draw a picture to explain.

_____

MATH GAME

Make That Shape

Play with a partner.

1. Each player puts 3  in a row.

2. Spin the ⬤.

3. Take 1 block of that shape.

4. If you can, fit it on a ⬡. If you can not fit it, put it back.

5. The first player to cover all 3 ⬡ wins.

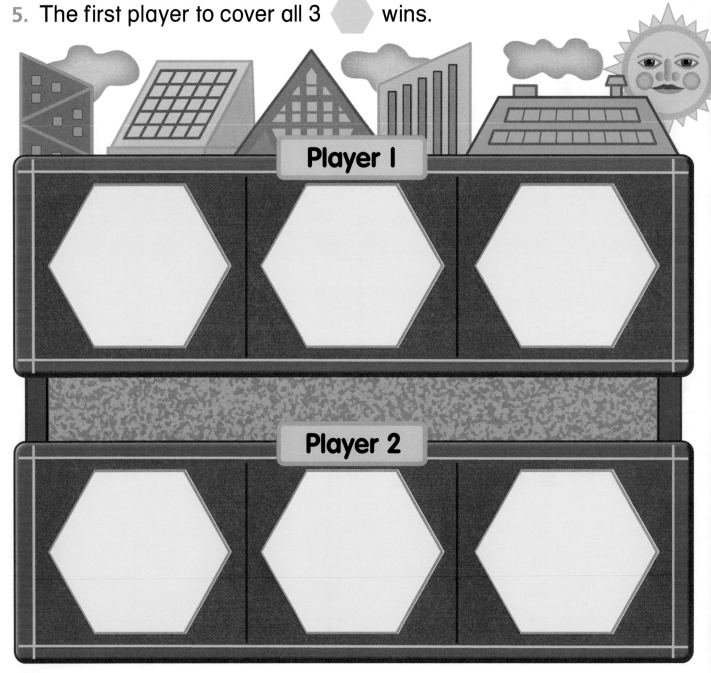

FUN FACTS

Butterflies have two sides that look alike.

Name _____

✔ Check What You Know

Plane Shapes in Different Positions

Color the triangles blue. Color the squares red.
Color the rectangles orange.

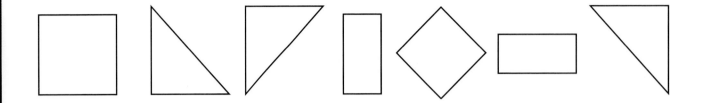

Above, Below, Over, Under

Circle the bird that is above the plane.
Mark an X on the bird that is below the
plane. Draw the sun over the
plane. Draw a cloud under
the plane.

Read Simple Patterns

Copy the pattern. Use 2 colors.

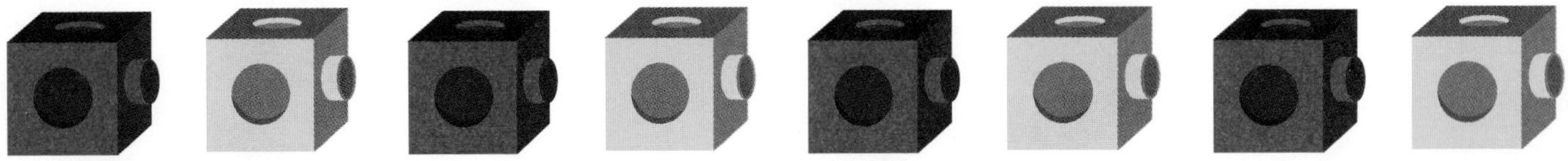

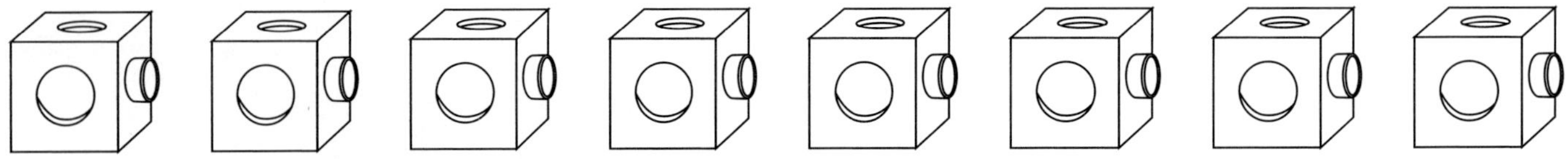

Use this page to review important skills needed for this chapter.

Open and Closed

Learn

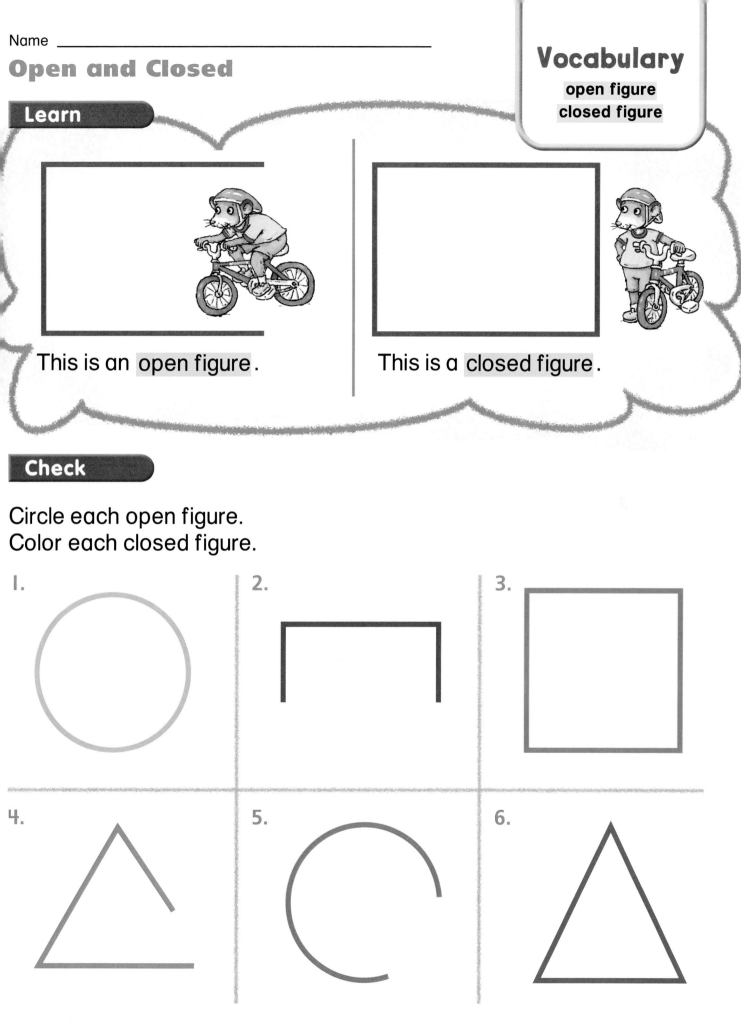

This is an open figure .

This is a closed figure .

Check

Circle each open figure.
Color each closed figure.

1.

2.

3.

4.

5.

6.

Explain It • Daily Reasoning

How are open and closed figures different?

Circle each open figure.
Color each closed figure.

1.

2.

3.

4.

5.

6.

7.

8.

9.

Problem Solving
Application

10. Draw a face. Use only closed figures.

 Write About It • Look at Exercise 10.
Which closed figures did you use?
Write about the face you drew.

⬠ **HOME ACTIVITY** • Have your child find three objects at home whose outlines are closed figures, for example, the outline of a window.

Name _____

Problem Solving Skill
Use a Picture

Vocabulary

above   below
close by   over
near   far
next to   beside
to the left of
to the right of

Follow the directions.

1. The [School] is above the 🚪.

   Draw a ☀ above the 🏫.

2. The ⚽ is below the 🛝.

   Draw a 🌷 below the ⛸.

3. The 🚩 is close by the 🏫.

   Draw a 🚗 close by the 🕯.

4. The 🦋 is over the 🌳.

   Draw a 🕊 over the 🌳.

Problem Solving Practice

Follow the directions.

1. The is near the .

   Draw a near the  .

2. The is far from the .

   Draw a far from the .

3. The 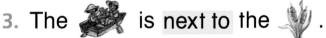 is next to the .

   Draw a next to the .

4. The 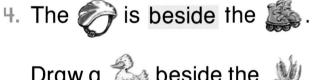 is beside the  .

   Draw a beside the .

5. The is to the left of

   the .

   Draw a to the left of

   the .

6. The is to the right of

   the .

   Draw a to the right of

   the .

Give and Follow Directions

Vocabulary

up	left
down	right

Learn

From **Start**, go right 3.
Go up 2.
Where are you?

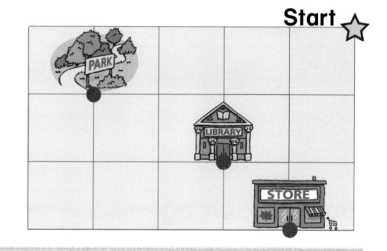

Up

Left

Right

Down

Start

I'm at the school!

Check

Follow the directions in order.
Draw the path. Write the place.

1. Go down 1. Go left 4.
   Where are you?

   _____

   _ _ _ _ _ _ _ _ _ _ _

   _____

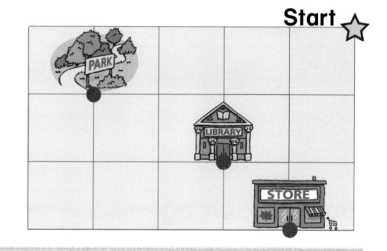

Start

2. Go right 2. Go up 1. Go right 2.
   Go up 1. Where are you?

   _____

   _ _ _ _ _ _ _ _ _ _ _

   _____

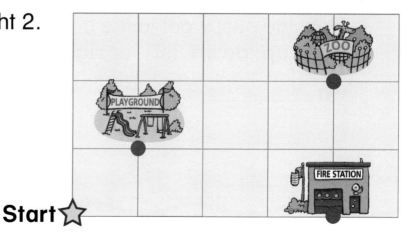

Start

Explain It • Daily Reasoning

How could you go from the
playground to the zoo? Is there
more than one way? Explain.

Get me to the ZOO.

Follow the directions in order.
Draw the path. Write the place.

1. Go right 3. Go up 2.
   Go left 1. Go down 1.
   Where are you?

   _____

   - - - - - - - - - - - -

   _____

Start ☆

---

2. Go left 4. Go down 1.
   Go right 3. Go down 1.
   Where are you?

   _____

   - - - - - - - - - - - -

   _____

Start ☆

Problem Solving

Visual Thinking

3. Help the puppy get to the bones.
   Write **up**, **down**, **left**, or **right.**

   Go _____ 3.

   Go _____ 2.

   Go _____ 2.

   Start ☆

 Write About It • Choose a place in your
school. Make a map. Tell how to get there.
Then draw the path.

🏠 **HOME ACTIVITY** • Ask your child to tell another way the puppy could get to the bones in Exercise 3.

272 two hundred seventy-two

Symmetry

HANDS ON

Explore

1. Fold your paper.

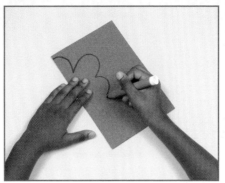

2. Start at the fold. Draw a shape.

3. Cut along the line.

4. Open your shape.

5. Draw a line down the middle.

The line down the middle is called a line of symmetry. It shows two parts that match.

Connect

Draw a line of symmetry to show two matching parts.

1.

2.

Explain It • Daily Reasoning

Fold a shape on the line of symmetry. How can you tell if the two parts match?

Draw a line of symmetry to
show two matching parts.

1.

2.

3.

4.

5.

6.

7.

8.

9.

Problem Solving
Visual Thinking

10. Draw a different line of symmetry on each square.

Write About It • Look at Exercise 10.
Hold a mirror on each line of symmetry.
Write about what you see.

HOME ACTIVITY • Find objects that are symmetrical. Have your child trace the line of symmetry
of each with a finger.

Name _____

Slides and Turns

HANDS ON

Explore

You can move your suitcase.

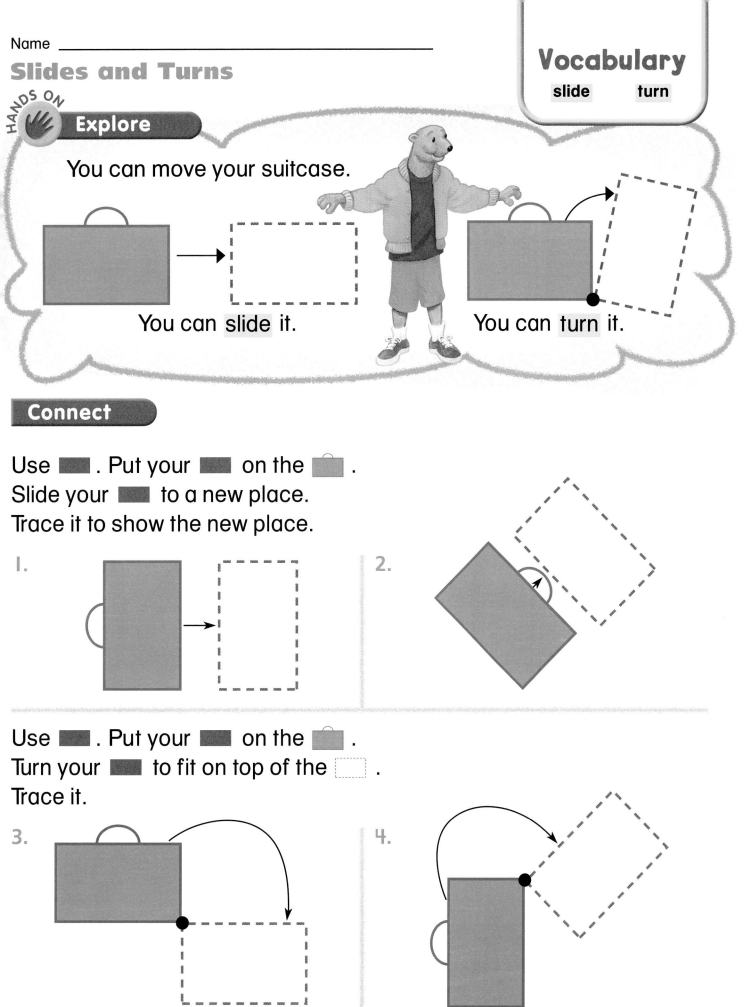

You can slide it.

You can turn it.

Connect

Use ▬. Put your ▬ on the ▭.
Slide your ▬ to a new place.
Trace it to show the new place.

1.

2.

Use ▬. Put your ▬ on the ▭.
Turn your ▬ to fit on top of the ▭.
Trace it.

3.

4.

Explain It ● Daily Reasoning

How is a slide different from a turn?

Circle **slide** or **turn** to name the move.

1.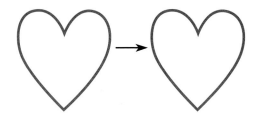

    slide   turn

2.

    slide   turn

3.

    slide   turn

4.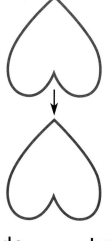

    slide   turn

Problem Solving
Application

5. Marie drew this train. Draw what it looks like to slide the train to the right.

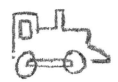

 Write About It • Look at Exercise 5. Write about how you moved the train. Use the word **slide**.

 HOME ACTIVITY • Gather items with simple shapes, such as boxes and pot lids. Ask your child to slide a certain item. Then ask your child to turn a different item. Repeat.

Name _____

Extra Practice

Draw the path. Draw the shape.

1. Go down 2. Go right 1.

Start ☆

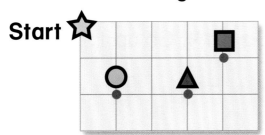

Where are you? _____

2. Go left 2. Go up 1.

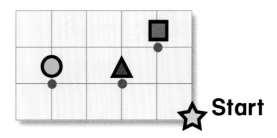

☆ **Start**

Where are you? _____

Draw a line of symmetry to show two matching parts.

3.

4.

Circle **slide** or **turn** to name the move.

5.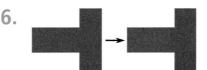

slide   turn

6.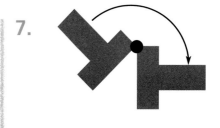

slide   turn

7.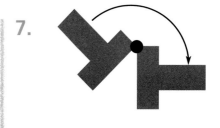

slide   turn

Problem Solving

Follow the directions.

8. Draw a ☀ above the .

9. Draw a ⬤ beside the 🛋 .

10. Draw a 🌳 near the .

Name _____

✅ Review/Test

Concepts and Skills
Draw the path. Draw the shape.

1. Go down 2. Go right 3.

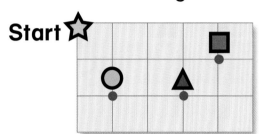

Where are you? _____

2. Go left 4. Go up 1.

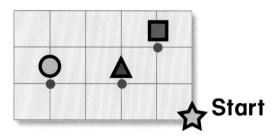

Where are you? _____

Draw a line of symmetry to show two matching parts.

3.

4.

Circle **slide** or **turn** to name the move.

5.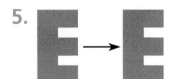

slide   turn

6.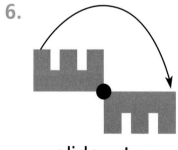

slide   turn

7.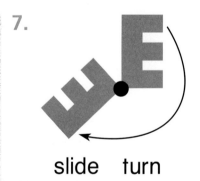

slide   turn

Problem Solving
Follow the directions.

8. Draw ⭐ over the 🚢 .

9. Draw a 🐟 below the 🚢 .

10. Draw a 🛟 to the left of the 🚢 .

1.

Start ⭐

Go left 1. Go down 3.
Where are you?

○　　　○　　　○　　　○

2. Which shows a slide?

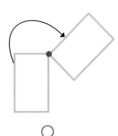　　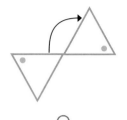

○　　　　　　　○

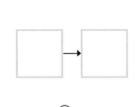　　

○　　　　　　　○

---

3. Which shape does not have a line of symmetry?

　　　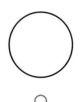　　　　　　

○　　　　　　○　　　　　　○　　　　　　○

Show What You Know

4.

Explain what you drew.

_____

_____

_____

_____

Draw a 🔵 next to the 🛝 .

Draw a 🐦 over the 🛝 .

Draw a 🌼 close by the 🛒 .

Draw a 🧍 to the left of the 🧍 .

Name _____

MATH GAME

On the Map

Play with a partner.

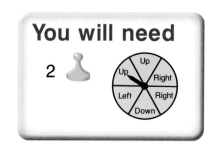

You will need

2

1. Put your ♟ on HOME.
2. Spin the ⟳.
3. Move 2 spaces in that direction.
4. If you can not move 2 spaces in that direction, your turn is over.
5. The first player to get to SCHOOL wins.

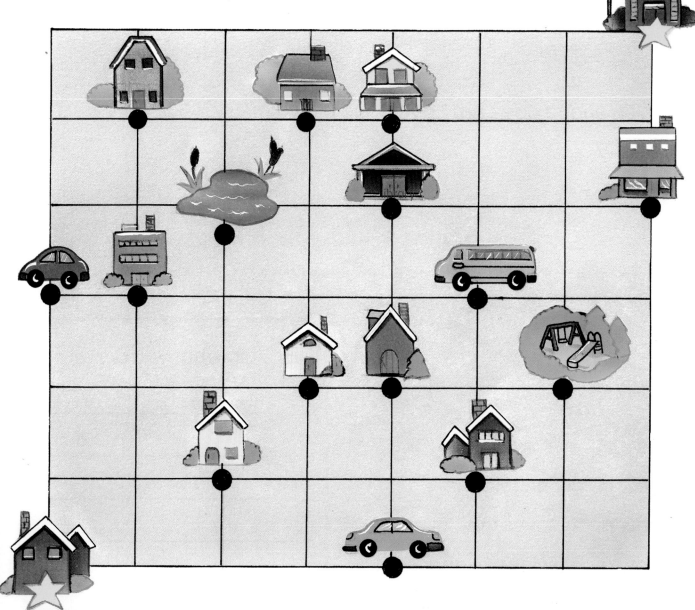

SCHOOL

HOME

SCIENCE

FUN FACTS

A mother zebra guards her young for about 13 months so she can learn the stripe pattern.

✓ Check What You Know

Copy and Extend Patterns

Color the counters to copy the pattern.
Then color what most likely comes next.

1.

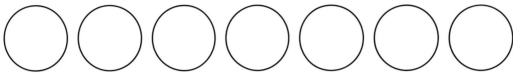

2.

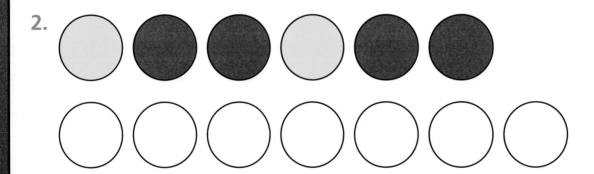

3.

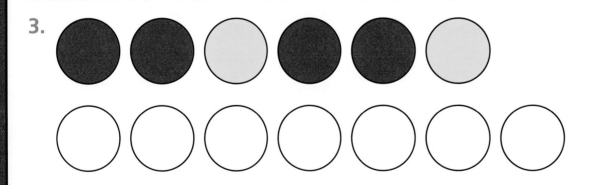

4.

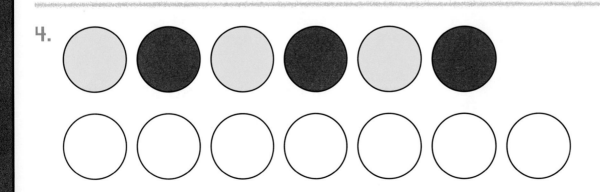

Use this page to review important skills needed for this chapter.

Name _____

Algebra: **Describe and Extend Patterns**

Learn

I can find a pattern on my shirt.
yellow, blue, yellow, blue, yellow, blue

I can find a pattern on my shirt.
pink, blue, orange, pink, blue, orange

Check

Find the pattern. Then color to continue it.

1.

2.

3.

4.

5.

6.

7.

8.

9.

Explain It ● Daily Reasoning

How did you know what color would be next in the pattern?

Find the pattern. Then color to continue it.

1.

2.

3.

4.

5.

Problem Solving
Visual Thinking

Draw and color to continue the pattern.

6.

Write About It • Look at Exercise 6.
Use the same shapes. Make a new pattern
with a different color.

HOME ACTIVITY • With your child, look for patterns in clothing, wallpaper, and gift wrap.
Have your child explain the patterns to you.

Algebra: **Pattern Units**

Vocabulary

pattern unit

Explore

The **pattern unit** repeats over and over in the pattern.

This pattern unit is two shapes long.

Connect

Use shapes to copy the pattern.
Then circle the pattern unit.

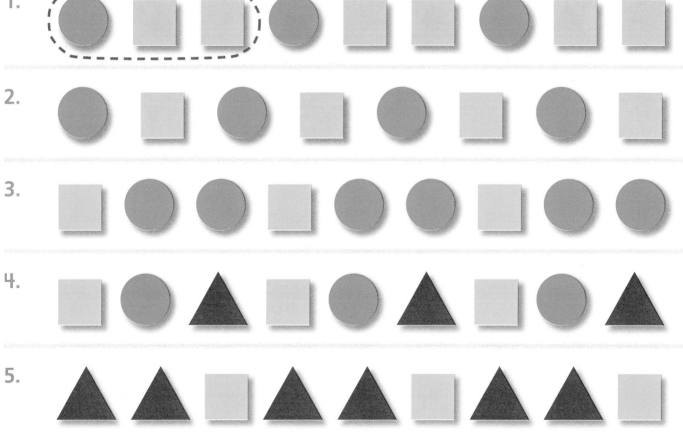

1.

2.

3.

4.

5.

Explain It • Daily Reasoning

How do you know how long the pattern unit is?

Circle the pattern unit.

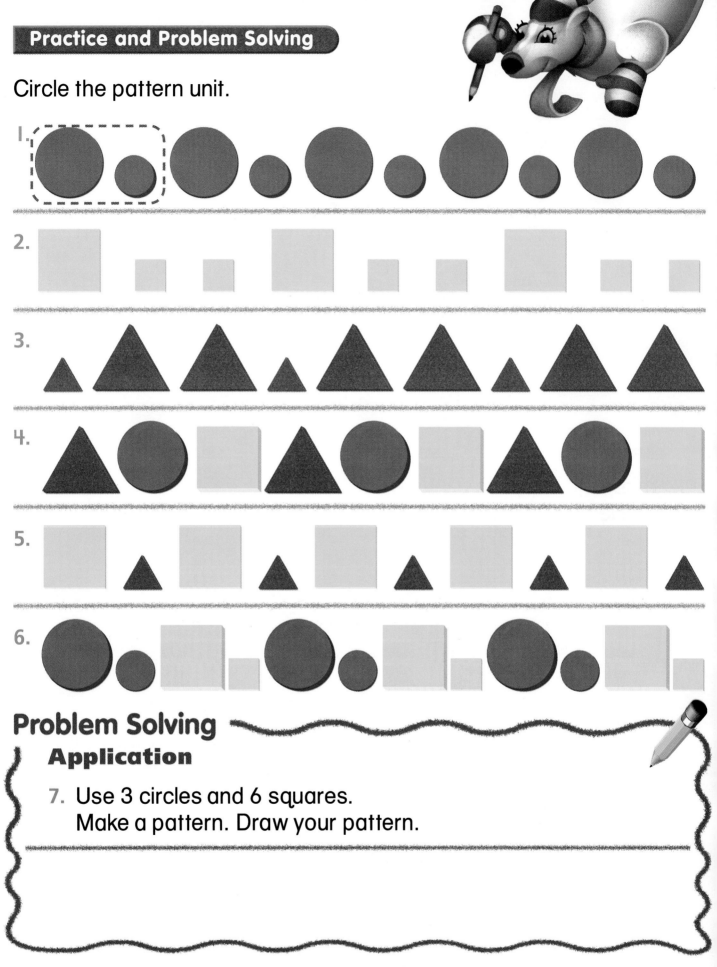

Problem Solving

Application

7. Use 3 circles and 6 squares.
   Make a pattern. Draw your pattern.

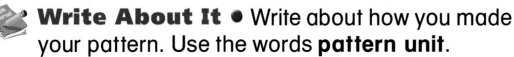

Write About It • Write about how you made
your pattern. Use the words **pattern unit**.

HOME ACTIVITY • Ask your child to draw a pattern and circle the pattern unit to show how the pattern unit repeats.

286 two hundred eighty-six

Name _____

Algebra: **Make New Patterns**

Explore

Use the same shapes
to make a different pattern.
Draw your new pattern.

Connect

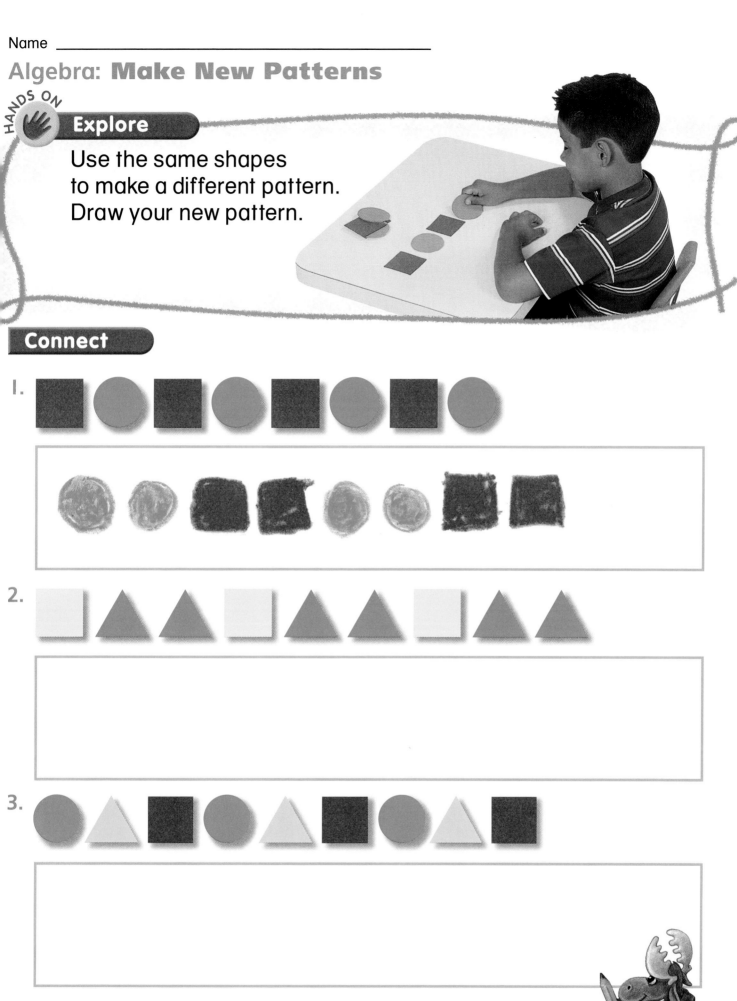

1.

2.

3.

Explain It • Daily Reasoning

How are your patterns the same as the
ones shown? How are they different?

Use the same shapes to make a different pattern.
Draw your new pattern.

1.

2.

3.

Problem Solving

Logical Reasoning

4. Find the pattern.
   Draw what comes next.

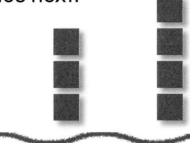

 Write About It ● Use ➡ → .
Make your own pattern.

⬠ HOME ACTIVITY • Have your child arrange objects in a pattern and then explain the pattern to you.

Problem Solving Skill
Correct a Pattern

Find the mistake in the pattern.

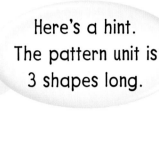

Here's a hint. The pattern unit is 3 shapes long.

Then the last triangle should be a red square.

Each pattern unit is 3 shapes long.
Find the pattern.
Circle the mistake. Draw the correct shape.

1.

2.

3.

4.

5.

PROBLEM SOLVING

Find the pattern.
Circle the mistake.
Draw the correct shape.

Each pattern unit
is 3 shapes long.

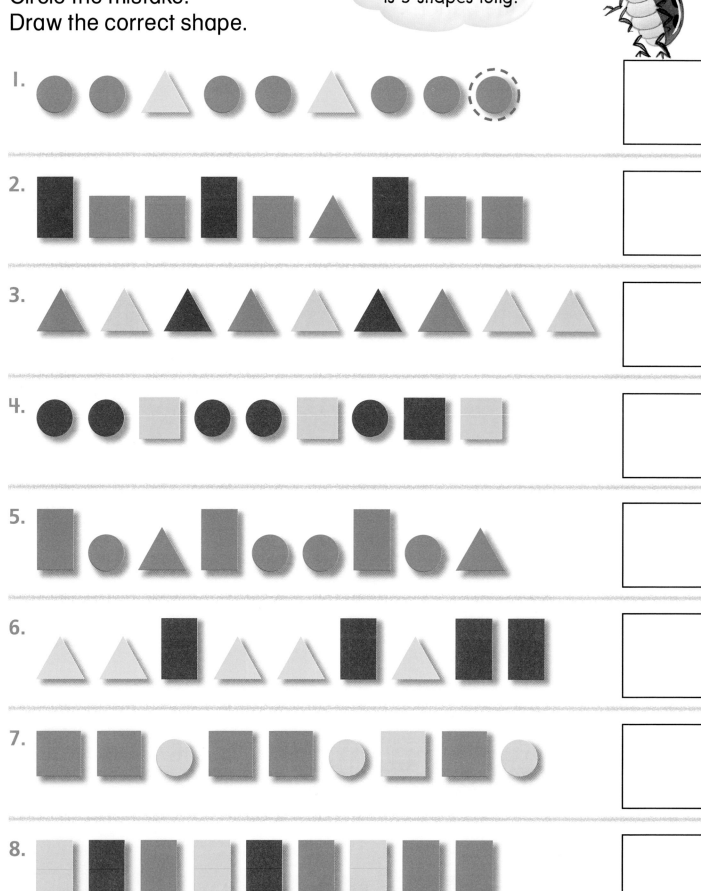

1.

2.

3.

4.

5.

6.

7.

8.

HOME ACTIVITY • Arrange objects in a pattern. Change one of the objects so that there is a mistake in the pattern. Have your child find and correct the mistake.

290 two hundred ninety

Name _____

Problem Solving Skill
Transfer Patterns

You can show the same pattern in a different way.

Use shapes to show the same pattern.
Draw the shapes.

1.

$$\bigcirc \; \square \; \bigcirc \; \square \; \bigcirc \; \square \; \bigcirc \; \square \; \bigcirc \; \square$$

2.

3.

Problem Solving Practice

Use shapes to show the same pattern.
Draw the shapes.

1.

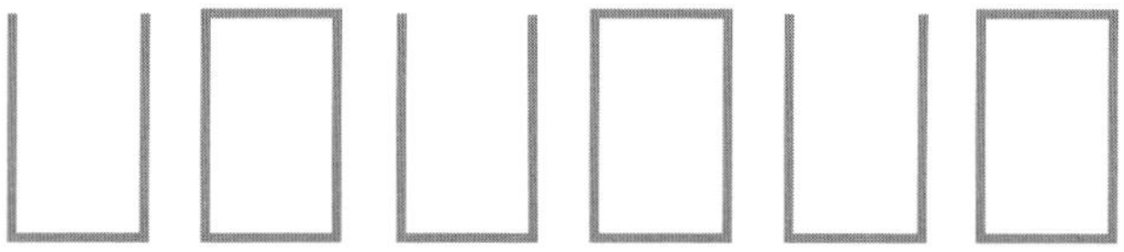

2.

3.

4.

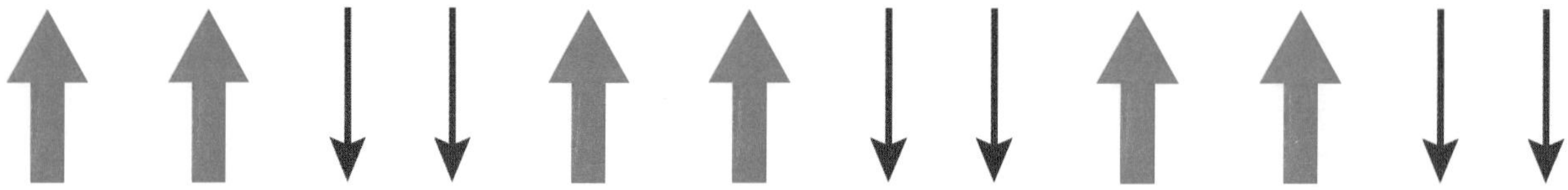

HOME ACTIVITY • Arrange objects in a pattern. Have your child use different objects to show the same pattern.

Extra Practice

Name _____

Find the pattern. Then color to continue it.

1.

2.

3.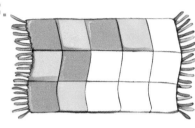

4. Circle the pattern unit.

5. Use the same shapes to make a different pattern.
Draw your new pattern.

Problem Solving

Find the pattern.
Circle the mistake. Draw the correct shape.

> Each pattern unit is 3 shapes long.

6.

7.

✓ Review/Test

Concepts and Skills

Find the pattern. Then color to continue it.

1.

2.

3.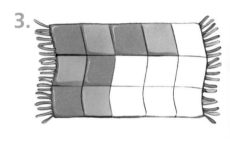

4. Circle the pattern unit.

5. Use the same shapes to make a different pattern.
   Draw your new pattern.

Problem Solving

6. Use shapes to show the same pattern.
   Draw the shapes.

Getting Ready for the ⭐EOG Test
Chapters 1–17

Choose the answer for questions 1– 3.

1. Which shows the right way to continue the pattern?

2. Find the pattern unit.
   Which is the mistake in the pattern?

3. How many faces are on a ▱ ?

   2   5   6   7
   ○   ○   ○   ○

Show What You Know

4. Use different shapes to show the same pattern. Draw and explain your new pattern.

MATH GAME

Pattern Play

Play with a partner.

You will need

AttriLinks

1. Spin the ⊙. Take any AttriLink that matches that shape or color.

2. Take turns until each player has three links.

3. Use these to make a pattern unit of shapes or colors. Draw your pattern unit. You will make your pattern on the table.

4. Spin again. If that shape or color is in your unit, use it in your pattern where you can.

5. The first player to repeat his or her pattern unit two times wins.

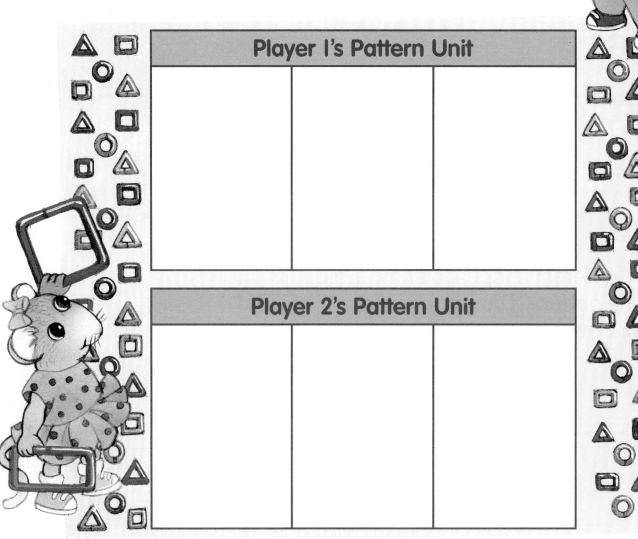

Player 1's Pattern Unit

Player 2's Pattern Unit

Addition Facts and Strategies

FUN FACTS

Each paw has 5 toes and 5 claws.

✓ Check What You Know

Count On to Add

Circle the greater number.
Use the number line. Count on to add.

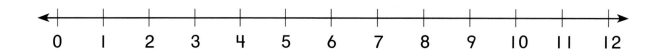

0 1 2 3 4 5 6 7 8 9 10 11 12

1. 8
    +2

2. 3
    +6

3. 1
    +6

4. 7
    +3

5. 2
    +9

6. 2
    +7

Doubles and Doubles Plus 1

Write the three sums.
Then circle the doubles fact.

7. 2   2   3
    +2   +3   +2

8. 4   4   5
    +4   +5   +4

Add 3 Numbers

Circle the two numbers you add first.
Write the sum.

9.   2
     4
     +4

10. 3
     1
     +6

11. 4
     3
     +4

12. 3
     0
     +5

13. 6
     2
     +1

14. 5
     5
     +2

Use this page to review important skills needed for this chapter.

Doubles and Doubles Plus 1

Vocabulary
doubles
doubles plus one

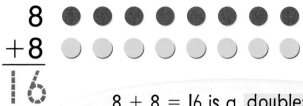

Explore

```
 8   ● ● ● ● ● ● ● ●
+8   ○ ○ ○ ○ ○ ○ ○ ○
16
```

8 + 8 = 16 is a doubles fact.
8 + 9 = 17 is a doubles plus one fact.

```
 8   ● ● ● ● ● ● ● ●
+9   ○ ○ ○ ○ ○ ○ ○ ○ ○
17
```

Connect

Use ○. Write the sums.

1.
```
  5      5
 +5     +6
```

2.
```
  2      3
 +2     +2
```

3.
```
  7      7
 +7     +8
```

4.
```
  0      0
 +0     +1
```

5.
```
  6      7
 +6     +6
```

6.
```
  3      3
 +3     +4
```

7.
```
  4      4
 +4     +5
```

8.
```
  8      9
 +8     +8
```

9.
```
  9      9
 +9    +10
```

Explain It ● Daily Reasoning

What are two ways you could
find the sum for 10 + 10?

Write the sums.

1. $4 + 4 = \underline{8}$, so $5 + 4 = \underline{9}$

2. $7 + 7 = \underline{\hspace{1cm}}$, so $7 + 8 = \underline{\hspace{1cm}}$

3. $5 + 5 = \underline{\hspace{1cm}}$, so $6 + 5 = \underline{\hspace{1cm}}$

4. $9 + 9 = \underline{\hspace{1cm}}$, so $9 + 10 = \underline{\hspace{1cm}}$

5. $1 + 1 = \underline{\hspace{1cm}}$, so $1 + 2 = \underline{\hspace{1cm}}$

6. $3 + 3 = \underline{\hspace{1cm}}$, so $4 + 3 = \underline{\hspace{1cm}}$

7. $8 + 8 = \underline{\hspace{1cm}}$, so $8 + 9 = \underline{\hspace{1cm}}$

Problem Solving

Algebra

Write the missing numbers.

8.
$$\begin{array}{r} 5 \\ + \square \\ \hline 10 \end{array} \qquad \begin{array}{r} 5 \\ + \square \\ \hline 11 \end{array}$$

9.
$$\begin{array}{r} 2 \\ + \square \\ \hline 4 \end{array} \qquad \begin{array}{r} 2 \\ + \square \\ \hline 5 \end{array}$$

10.
$$\begin{array}{r} 6 \\ + \square \\ \hline 12 \end{array} \qquad \begin{array}{r} 6 \\ + \square \\ \hline 13 \end{array}$$

 Write About It • Look at Exercises 8, 9, and 10.
Explain the pattern you see.

🏠 **HOME ACTIVITY** • Have your child tell you the doubles facts and the doubles plus one facts
for 6, 7, 8, and 9 (6 + 6 = 12, 6 + 7 = 13; 7 + 7 = 14, 7 + 8 = 15; and so on).

10 and More

Explore

Workmat

$$\begin{array}{r} 10 \\ + 5 \\ \hline 15 \end{array}$$

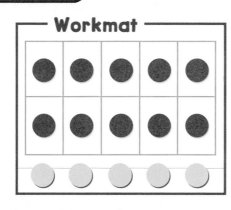

I can use a ten frame to show 10 + 5.

Connect

Use ⚪ and Workmat 7 to add.
Draw the ⚪. Write the sum.

1.
$$\begin{array}{r} 10 \\ + 7 \\ \hline 17 \end{array}$$

2.
$$\begin{array}{r} 10 \\ + 3 \\ \hline \end{array}$$
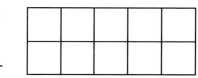

3.
$$\begin{array}{r} 10 \\ + 8 \\ \hline \end{array}$$

4.
$$\begin{array}{r} 10 \\ + 4 \\ \hline \end{array}$$
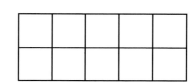

5.
$$\begin{array}{r} 10 \\ + 6 \\ \hline \end{array}$$
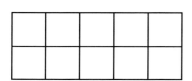

6.
$$\begin{array}{r} 10 \\ + 2 \\ \hline \end{array}$$
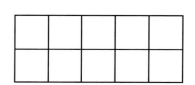

Explain It • Daily Reasoning

What happens when you add 10 to any number less than 10?

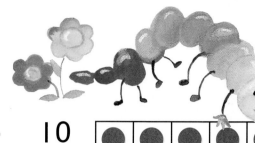

Write the sum.

1.
$$\begin{array}{r} 10 \\ +\ 9 \\ \hline 19 \end{array}$$

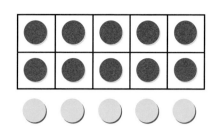

2.
$$\begin{array}{r} 10 \\ +\ 4 \\ \hline \end{array}$$

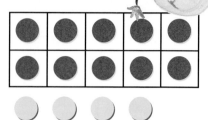

3.
$$\begin{array}{r} 10 \\ +\ 1 \\ \hline \end{array}$$

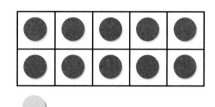

4.
$$\begin{array}{r} 10 \\ +\ 6 \\ \hline \end{array}$$

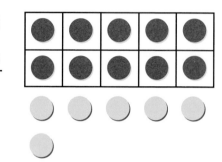

5.
$$\begin{array}{r} 10 \\ +\ 2 \\ \hline \end{array}$$

6.
$$\begin{array}{r} 10 \\ +\ 7 \\ \hline \end{array}$$

7.
$$\begin{array}{r} 10 \\ +\ 3 \\ \hline \end{array}$$

8.
$$\begin{array}{r} 10 \\ +\ 5 \\ \hline \end{array}$$

9.
$$\begin{array}{r} 10 \\ +\ 8 \\ \hline \end{array}$$

10.
$$\begin{array}{r} 10 \\ +\ 0 \\ \hline \end{array}$$

Problem Solving

Logical Reasoning

Choose a way to solve.

11. Jan plants 18 flowers in two rows. She plants 10 in the first row. How many are in the second row?

_____ flowers

 Write About It • Look at Exercise 11. Explain how a row of 10 helped you.

HOME ACTIVITY • Ask your child to tell the sums for 10 + 1 through 10 + 9 (10 + 1 = 11, 10 + 2 = 12, and so on).

Make 10 to Add

Vocabulary
make a ten

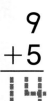 **Explore**

Find the sum for 9 + 5.

Show 9.
Then show 5.

$$\begin{array}{r} 9 \\ +5 \\ \hline 14 \end{array}$$

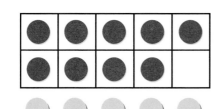

Make a ten.
Move 1 counter into the ten frame.

$$\begin{array}{r} 10 \\ +4 \\ \hline 14 \end{array}$$

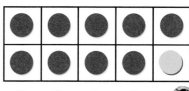

Connect

Use ◯ and Workmat 7.
Show the numbers and add. Then make a ten and add.

1.
$$\begin{array}{r} 9 \\ +7 \\ \hline \end{array}$$
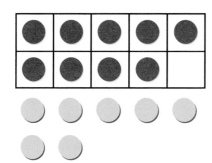

$$\begin{array}{r} 10 \\ +\ 6 \\ \hline \end{array}$$
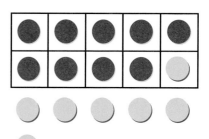

2.
$$\begin{array}{r} 9 \\ +4 \\ \hline \end{array}$$
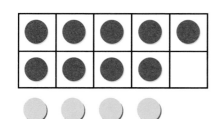

$$\begin{array}{r} 10 \\ +\ 3 \\ \hline \end{array}$$
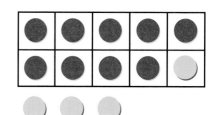

3.
$$\begin{array}{r} 9 \\ +6 \\ \hline \end{array}$$
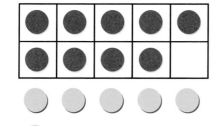

$$\begin{array}{r} 10 \\ +\ 5 \\ \hline \end{array}$$
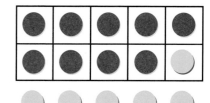

Explain It • Daily Reasoning

How do you know that 9 + 3 = 10 + 2?
Use ◯ to prove your answer.

9 + 3   10 + 2

Use ◯ and Workmat 7.
Show the numbers and add. Then make a ten and add.

1.
$$\begin{array}{r} 9 \\ +9 \\ \hline 18 \end{array}$$
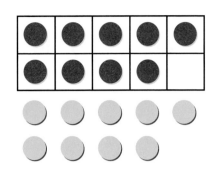

$$\begin{array}{r} 10 \\ +\ 8 \\ \hline 18 \end{array}$$
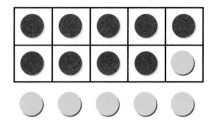

2.
$$\begin{array}{r} 9 \\ +2 \\ \hline \end{array}$$
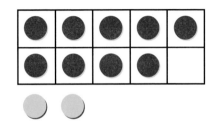

$$\begin{array}{r} 10 \\ +\ 1 \\ \hline \end{array}$$
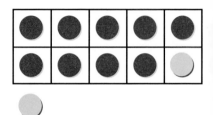

3.
$$\begin{array}{r} 9 \\ +8 \\ \hline \end{array}$$
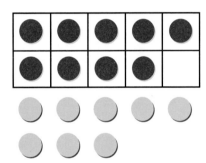

$$\begin{array}{r} 10 \\ +\ 7 \\ \hline \end{array}$$
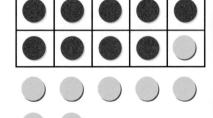

Problem Solving
Mental Math

Solve in your head.
Draw a picture to check.

4. There were 9 pine cones on the ground. Then 5 more pine cones fell. How many pine cones were on the ground then?

_____ pine cones

 Write About It • Look at Exercise 4.
Explain how to make a ten to add 9 + 5.

🏠 HOME ACTIVITY • Ask your child to tell the sums for 9 + 1 through 9 + 9 (9 + 1 = 10, 9 + 2 = 11, and so on).

Name _____

Use Make a 10

 Explore

Find the sum for 7 + 4.

First show 7. Then show 4.
Fill up the ten frame to add.

$$\begin{array}{r} 7 \\ +4 \\ \hline 11 \end{array}$$

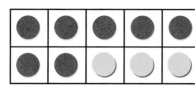

You made a ten
and have 1 extra.
10 + 1 = 11

Connect

Use ◯ and Workmat 7 to add.
Start with the greater number.
Draw the ◯. Write the sum.

1.
$$\begin{array}{r} 5 \\ +8 \\ \hline 13 \end{array}$$

2.
$$\begin{array}{r} 7 \\ +6 \\ \hline \end{array}$$

3.
$$\begin{array}{r} 8 \\ +4 \\ \hline \end{array}$$

4.
$$\begin{array}{r} 5 \\ +6 \\ \hline \end{array}$$

5.
$$\begin{array}{r} 8 \\ +7 \\ \hline \end{array}$$

6.
$$\begin{array}{r} 7 \\ +5 \\ \hline \end{array}$$

Explain It • Daily Reasoning

How do you make a ten to add two numbers?

Use  and Workmat 7 to add.
Start with the greater number.

1.
```
   6
 + 8
 ___
  14
```
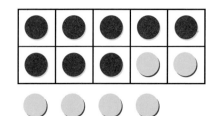

2.
```
   9
 + 6
 ___
```

3.
```
   3
 + 8
 ___
```

4.
```
   5
 + 7
 ___
```

5.
```
   8
 + 9
 ___
```

6.
```
   8
 + 5
 ___
```

7.
```
   9
 + 7
 ___
```

8.
```
   4
 + 7
 ___
```

9.
```
   8
 + 6
 ___
```

10.
```
   3
 + 9
 ___
```

11.
```
   4
 + 8
 ___
```

12.
```
   5
 + 9
 ___
```

13.
```
   9
 + 4
 ___
```

14.
```
   6
 + 7
 ___
```

15.
```
   7
 + 8
 ___
```

16.
```
   7
 + 9
 ___
```

17.
```
   2
 + 9
 ___
```

18.
```
   6
 + 5
 ___
```

19.
```
   6
 + 8
 ___
```

Problem Solving

Logical Reasoning

Choose a way to solve.

20. Josh needs to plant 15 seeds. He has 8 seeds. How many more seeds does he need?

_____ more seeds

 Write About It ● Look at Exercise 20.

Complete the number sentence. $8 + \boxed{} = 10 + 5$

HOME ACTIVITY • Ask your child to read a problem on this page and tell how to solve it by making a ten. For example, solve 8 + 4 by making it 10 + 2.

Algebra: **Add 3 Numbers**

Learn

You can add three numbers in any order.

 ⑦
③
$+4$
14

7
③
$+④$
14

You can make a ten.
$7 + 3 = 10$
$10 + 4 = 14$

You can use doubles.
$3 + 4 = 7$
$7 + 7 = 14$

Check

Circle the numbers you add first.
Write the sum.

1. $\begin{array}{r} 2 \\ 7 \\ +3 \\ \hline \end{array}$

2. $\begin{array}{r} 8 \\ 4 \\ +4 \\ \hline \end{array}$

3. $\begin{array}{r} 9 \\ 3 \\ +1 \\ \hline \end{array}$

4. $\begin{array}{r} 8 \\ 3 \\ +3 \\ \hline \end{array}$

5. $\begin{array}{r} 4 \\ 7 \\ +3 \\ \hline \end{array}$

6. $\begin{array}{r} 6 \\ 5 \\ +4 \\ \hline \end{array}$

7. $\begin{array}{r} 2 \\ 2 \\ +7 \\ \hline \end{array}$

8. $\begin{array}{r} 2 \\ 5 \\ +5 \\ \hline \end{array}$

9. $\begin{array}{r} 4 \\ 2 \\ +6 \\ \hline \end{array}$

10. $\begin{array}{r} 8 \\ 8 \\ +1 \\ \hline \end{array}$

11. $\begin{array}{r} 8 \\ 2 \\ +7 \\ \hline \end{array}$

12. $\begin{array}{r} 4 \\ 3 \\ +4 \\ \hline \end{array}$

Explain It • Daily Reasoning

Look at Exercise 1. Add two different numbers first.
Did the sum change? Why or why not?

Circle the numbers you add first.
Write the sum.

1. 1
   ⟨5⟩
   +⟨5⟩
   ___
   11

2. 8
   2
   +1
   ___

3. 6
   3
   +7
   ___

4. 1
   2
   +9
   ___

5. 8
   2
   +6
   ___

6. 1
   7
   +7
   ___

7. 4
   9
   +6
   ___

8. 9
   6
   +1
   ___

9. 3
   6
   +3
   ___

10. 4
    4
    +2
    ___

11. 8
    4
    +2
    ___

12. 3
    5
    +5
    ___

13. 6
    1
    +6
    ___

14. 8
    1
    +9
    ___

15. 5
    7
    +3
    ___

Problem Solving
Application

16. Kim picks 3 pink flowers.
    Tod picks 7 yellow flowers.
    Chris picks 5 purple flowers.
    How many flowers in all do
    the children pick?

    _____ flowers

 Write About It • Look at Exercise 16.
Explain how you could make a ten. How could
that help you solve the problem?

 HOME ACTIVITY • Have your child use pennies to show how to add three numbers.

Name _____

Problem Solving Skill
Use Data from a Table

This table tells how many animals children saw at camp.

Animals		Number
chipmunks		6
rabbits		2
squirrels		4
deer		3

Use the table to answer the questions. Write a number sentence to solve.

1. How many deer and squirrels did they see?

   __7__ deer and squirrels

   __3__ $\oplus$ __4__ $\ominus$ __7__

2. How many more chipmunks than deer did they see?

   _____ more chipmunks

   _____ $\bigcirc$ _____ $\bigcirc$ _____

3. How many more deer than rabbits did they see?

   _____ more deer

   _____ $\bigcirc$ _____ $\bigcirc$ _____

4. How many chipmunks and rabbits did they see?

   _____ chipmunks and rabbits

   _____ $\bigcirc$ _____ $\bigcirc$ _____

5. How many small animals did they see in all?

   > Find the numbers for small animals.

   _____ small animals

   ____ $\bigcirc$ ____ $\bigcirc$ ____ $\bigcirc$ ____

This table tells how many birds
children saw at camp.

Birds	Number
owl	1
robins	5
blue jays	4
blackbirds	7

Use the table to answer
the questions. Write a
number sentence to solve.

1. How many robins and blue jays
   did they see in all?

   _____ robins and blue jays

   ___ ◯ ___ ◯ ___

2. How many more robins
   than owls did they see?

   _____ more robins

   ___ ◯ ___ ◯ ___

3. How many blackbirds and owls
   did they see in all?

   _____ blackbirds and owls

   ___ ◯ ___ ◯ ___

4. How many more blackbirds
   than robins did they see?

   _____ more blackbirds

   ___ ◯ ___ ◯ ___

5. How many birds did they
   see that were not blue?

   Find the numbers for
   birds that are not blue.

   _____ birds

   ___ ◯ ___ ◯ ___ ◯ ___

HOME ACTIVITY • Ask your child to explain how he or she solved each problem.

Name _____

Extra Practice

Write the sum.

1.
$$3 \atop +3$$
$$\quad 3 \atop +4$$

2.
$$6 \atop +6$$
$$\quad 6 \atop +7$$

3.
$$5 \atop +5$$
$$\quad 5 \atop +6$$

4.
$$9 \atop +4$$

5.
$$9 \atop +6$$

6.
$$8 \atop +4$$

7.
$$8 \atop +8$$

8.
$$2 \atop +7$$

9.
$$7 \atop +7$$

10.
$$6 \atop +4$$

11.
$$4 \atop +5$$

12.
$$4 \atop +4$$

13.
$$7 \atop +8$$

14.
$$2 \atop 7 \atop +3$$

15.
$$4 \atop 2 \atop +6$$

16.
$$8 \atop 6 \atop +1$$

17.
$$3 \atop 7 \atop +3$$

Problem Solving

This table tells how many animals children saw.
Use the table to answer the question.

18. How many animals did the children see in all?

___ ◯ ___ ◯ ___ ◯ ___

 animals

Animals		Number
rabbits		3
deer		7
squirrels		4

Name _____

✅ Review/Test

Concepts and Skills

Write the sum.

1.
   $$4 \atop +4$$ $$4 \atop +5$$

2. $$8 \atop +8$$ $$8 \atop +9$$

3. $$7 \atop +7$$ $$8 \atop +7$$

4. 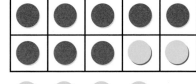 $$8 \atop +6$$

5. 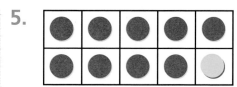 $$9 \atop +7$$

6. $$9 \atop +5$$

7. $$6 \atop +6$$

8. $$5 \atop +5$$

9. $$9 \atop +9$$

10. $$7 \atop +5$$

11. $$5 \atop +6$$

12. $$8 \atop +8$$

13. $$8 \atop +9$$

14. $$7 \\ 2 \\ +2$$

15. $$3 \\ 4 \\ +7$$

16. $$9 \\ 7 \\ +1$$

17. $$4 \\ 8 \\ +4$$

Problem Solving

This table tells how many animals children saw.
Use the table to answer the question.

18. How many animals did the children see in all?

_____ animals

Animals		Number
chipmunks		6
rabbits		6
squirrels		4

312 three hundred twelve

CHAPTER 18 · REVIEW/TEST

Name _____

Choose the answer for questions 1–5.

1. $7 + 7 = 14$, so $7 + 8 =$ __?__

14	15	16	17
○	○	○	○

2. Which shows the sum of $10 + 9$?

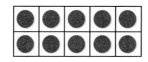 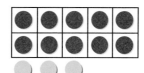 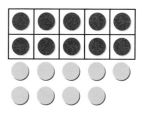

○   ○   ○   ○

3. The table shows how many vegetables the children picked.

   How many more cucumbers than beans did they pick?

2	4	5	8
○	○	○	○

Vegetables Picked	
beans	8
cucumbers	12
tomatoes	5

4.
$$\begin{array}{r} 9 \\ 1 \\ +3 \\ \hline \end{array}$$

10	12	13	15
○	○	○	○

5. Which is the missing number?

$$8 + \boxed{} = 13$$

3	5	7	8
○	○	○	○

Show What You Know

6. Use the ten frame. Draw counters to explain how to make a ten to find the sum.

$$\begin{array}{r} 9 \\ +5 \\ \hline \end{array}$$

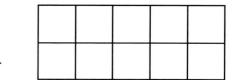

EOG TEST PREP

MATH GAME

Ten Plus

Play with a partner.

1. Put your ♟ at START.

2. Stack the 2 face down.

3. Start with 9. Take one number card.

4. Find the sum by making 10 first.

5. Say the number you add to 10 to get the sum.

6. Move your ♟ that many spaces.

7. The first player to get to END wins.

START

Move back 1.

Take 1 more turn.

END

Lose 1 turn.

Move forward 1.

CHAPTER 19

Subtraction Facts and Strategies

FUN FACTS

Hibiscus grows in many shades of its 7 basic colors: red, yellow, blue, pink, white, purple, and orange.

✓ Check What You Know

Count Back to Subtract

Count back to subtract. Write the difference.
You can use the number line to help.

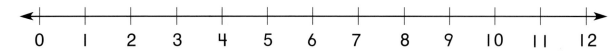

1. 8
−2

2. 9
−1

3. 11
− 3

4. 7
−1

5. 6
−2

6. 11
− 2

7. 12
− 3

8. 10
− 1

9. 9
−2

10. 8
−3

11. 7
−3

12. 6
−1

13. 10
− 2

14. 6
−3

15. 8
−1

16. 7
−2

17. 10
− 3

18. 9
−3

Related Addition and Subtraction Facts to 12

Write each sum or difference.
Circle the related facts in each row.

19. 12 − 4 = ___

20. 12 − 6 = ___

21. 8 + 4 = ___

22. 5 + 7 = ___

23. 11 − 7 = ___

24. 12 − 5 = ___

25. 9 − 6 = ___

26. 9 − 3 = ___

27. 5 + 3 = ___

Use a Number Line to Count Back

Vocabulary

count back

Learn

You can use the number line to help you count back.

Find the difference for 12 − 3.

Start at 12.
Count back 3 spaces.
11, 10, 9

$$12 - 3 = \underline{9}$$

Check

Count back to subtract. Write the difference.
Use the number line to help.

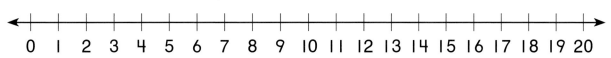

1.
$$9 - 2 = \underline{}$$

2.
$$10 - 1 = \underline{}$$

3.
$$8 - 3 = \underline{}$$

4.
$$11 - 3 = \underline{}$$

5.
$$7 - 1 = \underline{}$$

6.
$$6 - 3 = \underline{}$$

7.
$$8 - 2 = \underline{}$$

8.
$$11 - 2 = \underline{}$$

9.
$$10 - 3 = \underline{}$$

10.
$$9 - 1 = \underline{}$$

Explain It • Daily Reasoning

Pat drew this number line to find 10 − 2 and got 12. What mistake did she make?

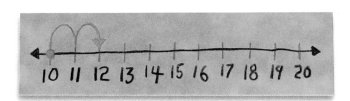

$$\begin{array}{r} 18 \\ -\ 9 \\ \hline 9 \end{array}$$

8 9 10 11 12 13 14 15 16 17 18 19 20

Use the number line to subtract.

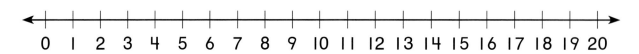

0 1 2 3 4 5 6 7 8 9 10 11 12 13 14 15 16 17 18 19 20

1. $\begin{array}{r} 20 \\ -10 \\ \hline \end{array}$ 2. $\begin{array}{r} 13 \\ -\ 6 \\ \hline \end{array}$ 3. $\begin{array}{r} 17 \\ -\ 9 \\ \hline \end{array}$ 4. $\begin{array}{r} 14 \\ -\ 5 \\ \hline \end{array}$ 5. $\begin{array}{r} 11 \\ -\ 3 \\ \hline \end{array}$ 6. $\begin{array}{r} 16 \\ -\ 9 \\ \hline \end{array}$

7. $\begin{array}{r} 15 \\ -\ 8 \\ \hline \end{array}$ 8. $\begin{array}{r} 18 \\ -\ 9 \\ \hline \end{array}$ 9. $\begin{array}{r} 11 \\ -\ 2 \\ \hline \end{array}$ 10. $\begin{array}{r} 12 \\ -\ 4 \\ \hline \end{array}$ 11. $\begin{array}{r} 14 \\ -\ 6 \\ \hline \end{array}$ 12. $\begin{array}{r} 13 \\ -\ 5 \\ \hline \end{array}$

13. $\begin{array}{r} 16 \\ -\ 7 \\ \hline \end{array}$ 14. $\begin{array}{r} 10 \\ -\ 2 \\ \hline \end{array}$ 15. $\begin{array}{r} 12 \\ -\ 3 \\ \hline \end{array}$ 16. $\begin{array}{r} 16 \\ -\ 8 \\ \hline \end{array}$ 17. $\begin{array}{r} 15 \\ -\ 9 \\ \hline \end{array}$ 18. $\begin{array}{r} 17 \\ -\ 8 \\ \hline \end{array}$

Problem Solving
Visual Thinking

19. Write the number sentence that tells about the number line.

_____ ◯ _____ ◯ _____

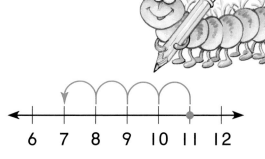

6 7 8 9 10 11 12

 Write About It ● Look at Exercise 19. Explain how you counted on the number line.

 HOME ACTIVITY • Ask your child to show how to subtract 18 − 9 on the number line.

Doubles Fact Families

Vocabulary

fact family

Learn

These facts use the same two numbers.
Together, they make a doubles fact family .

$$4 + 4 = \underline{8}$$

$$\underline{8} \bigcirc \underline{4} \bigcirc \underline{4}$$

Check

Write the sum for the doubles addition fact.
Write the subtraction fact that is in the same family.

1. $$6 + 6 = \underline{} \qquad \underline{} \bigcirc \underline{} \bigcirc \underline{}$$

2. $$3 + 3 = \underline{} \qquad \underline{} \bigcirc \underline{} \bigcirc \underline{}$$

3. $$8 + 8 = \underline{} \qquad \underline{} \bigcirc \underline{} \bigcirc \underline{}$$

4. $$5 + 5 = \underline{} \qquad \underline{} \bigcirc \underline{} \bigcirc \underline{}$$

5. $$9 + 9 = \underline{} \qquad \underline{} \bigcirc \underline{} \bigcirc \underline{}$$

6. $$7 + 7 = \underline{} \qquad \underline{} \bigcirc \underline{} \bigcirc \underline{}$$

Explain It • Daily Reasoning

Why are there only two facts in doubles
fact families?

$$\begin{array}{r} 9 \\ +9 \\ \hline 18 \end{array}$$

$$\begin{array}{r} 18 \\ -9 \\ \hline 9 \end{array}$$

Write the sum and difference for each pair.

1.
$$\begin{array}{r} 8 \\ +8 \\ \hline \end{array} \qquad \begin{array}{r} 16 \\ -8 \\ \hline \end{array}$$

2.
$$\begin{array}{r} 5 \\ +5 \\ \hline \end{array} \qquad \begin{array}{r} 10 \\ -5 \\ \hline \end{array}$$

3.
$$\begin{array}{r} 6 \\ +6 \\ \hline \end{array} \qquad \begin{array}{r} 12 \\ -6 \\ \hline \end{array}$$

4.
$$\begin{array}{r} 1 \\ +1 \\ \hline \end{array} \qquad \begin{array}{r} 2 \\ -1 \\ \hline \end{array}$$

5.
$$\begin{array}{r} 4 \\ +4 \\ \hline \end{array} \qquad \begin{array}{r} 8 \\ -4 \\ \hline \end{array}$$

6.
$$\begin{array}{r} 3 \\ +3 \\ \hline \end{array} \qquad \begin{array}{r} 6 \\ -3 \\ \hline \end{array}$$

7.
$$\begin{array}{r} 4 \\ -2 \\ \hline \end{array} \qquad \begin{array}{r} 2 \\ +2 \\ \hline \end{array}$$

8.
$$\begin{array}{r} 18 \\ -9 \\ \hline \end{array} \qquad \begin{array}{r} 9 \\ +9 \\ \hline \end{array}$$

9.
$$\begin{array}{r} 14 \\ -7 \\ \hline \end{array} \qquad \begin{array}{r} 7 \\ +7 \\ \hline \end{array}$$

Problem Solving

Logical Reasoning

Solve.

10. 16 children eat 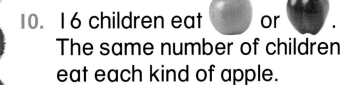 or . The same number of children eat each kind of apple.

How many eat ? _____

How many eat ? _____

 Write About It ● Explain your answer for Exercise 10.

HOME ACTIVITY • Say an addition doubles fact, such as 6 + 6 = 12. Have your child say the subtraction fact that is in the same fact family. (12 − 6 = 6)

Algebra: **Related Addition and Subtraction Facts**

Learn

You can use related facts to help
you find sums and differences.

$8 + 7 = 15$
$15 - 7 = 8$

$$\begin{array}{r} 8 \\ +7 \\ \hline 15 \end{array}$$

$$\begin{array}{r} 15 \\ -\ 7 \\ \hline 8 \end{array}$$

Check

Write the sum and difference for each pair.

1.
$$\begin{array}{r} 9 \\ +5 \\ \hline \end{array}$$
$$\begin{array}{r} 14 \\ -\ 9 \\ \hline \end{array}$$

2.
$$\begin{array}{r} 5 \\ +6 \\ \hline \end{array}$$
$$\begin{array}{r} 11 \\ -\ 6 \\ \hline \end{array}$$

3.
$$\begin{array}{r} 6 \\ +8 \\ \hline \end{array}$$
$$\begin{array}{r} 14 \\ -\ 8 \\ \hline \end{array}$$

4.
$$\begin{array}{r} 6 \\ +9 \\ \hline \end{array}$$
$$\begin{array}{r} 15 \\ -\ 6 \\ \hline \end{array}$$

5.
$$\begin{array}{r} 7 \\ +7 \\ \hline \end{array}$$
$$\begin{array}{r} 14 \\ -\ 7 \\ \hline \end{array}$$

6.
$$\begin{array}{r} 6 \\ +7 \\ \hline \end{array}$$
$$\begin{array}{r} 13 \\ -\ 7 \\ \hline \end{array}$$

7.
$$\begin{array}{r} 8 \\ +5 \\ \hline \end{array}$$
$$\begin{array}{r} 13 \\ -\ 5 \\ \hline \end{array}$$

8.
$$\begin{array}{r} 9 \\ +3 \\ \hline \end{array}$$
$$\begin{array}{r} 12 \\ -\ 9 \\ \hline \end{array}$$

9.
$$\begin{array}{r} 8 \\ +8 \\ \hline \end{array}$$
$$\begin{array}{r} 16 \\ -\ 8 \\ \hline \end{array}$$

Explain It • Daily Reasoning

What addition fact can help you find the
difference for $17 - 9$? Explain how it can help.

Write the sum and difference for each pair.

1.
```
   8      11
 +3     − 3
 ---    ---
  11      8
```

2.
```
   9      16
 +7     − 9
 ---    ---
```

3.
```
   9      17
 +8     − 8
 ---    ---
```

4.
```
   8      12
 +4     − 8
 ---    ---
```

5.
```
   9      13
 +4     − 4
 ---    ---
```

6.
```
   6      10
 +4     − 4
 ---    ---
```

7.
```
   7      12
 +5     − 5
 ---    ---
```

8.
```
   2      11
 +9     − 2
 ---    ---
```

9.
```
   9      18
 +9     − 9
 ---    ---
```

10.
```
   8      15
 +7     − 8
 ---    ---
```

11.
```
   6      12
 +6     − 6
 ---    ---
```

12.
```
   7      11
 +4     − 7
 ---    ---
```

Problem Solving
Application

Write a number sentence to solve.

13. 18 children are at a party.
     9 children go home.
     How many children
     are at the party now?

_____ children   _____ ◯ _____ ◯ _____

 Write About It • Look at Exercise 13.
 Write about how you solved the problem.

Name _____

Problem Solving Skill
Estimate Reasonable Answers

Tim has 10 carrots.
Bev has 9 carrots.
About how many carrots do they have in all?

about 5   about 10   (about 20)

> Each number is larger than 5. So **about 5** is too little.

> There are 9 more than 10. So **about 10** is too little.

> 10 + 9 is almost 10 + 10. So, **about 20** is the best estimate.

Circle the best estimate.

> Will 10 − 4 be more than 10 or less than 10?

1. Betty has 10 plums. She gives away 4 plums. About how many plums does Betty have now?

   about 5   about 10   about 15

2. 6 children work in the garden. 10 more come. About how many children are in the garden?

   about 5   about 10   about 15

3. Mark picks 4 peppers. He needs 13 in all. About how many more peppers does Mark need?

   about 1   about 10   about 20

4. Elena waters her garden for 16 minutes. Don waters his garden for 9 minutes. About how many more minutes does Elena water than Don?

   about 5   about 10   about 20

Problem Solving Practice

THINK:
Which estimate makes sense?

Circle the best estimate.

1. Tom plants 8 seeds.
   Then he plants 3 more.
   About how many seeds
   does he plant?

   about 5   about 10   about 15

2. Kris has 8 flowers.
   Mike brings 3 more.
   About how many flowers
   do they have in all?

   about 5   about 10   about 20

3. Becky picks 18 tomatoes.
   She gives 9 of them away.
   About how many tomatoes
   does Becky have left?

   about 2   about 10   about 20

4. Jason finds 4 ladybugs.
   Seena finds 10 more.
   About how many ladybugs
   do they find in all?

   about 5   about 10   about 15

5. Keesha picks 12 carrots.
   She eats 3 of them.
   About how many carrots
   does she have now?

   about 5   about 10   about 15

 HOME ACTIVITY • Ask your child how he or she chose the answer for each problem.

Name _____

Extra Practice

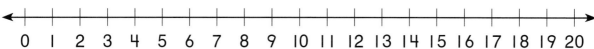

Write the difference.
Use the number line to help.

<----+---->
　　0　1　2　3　4　5　6　7　8　9　10　11　12　13　14　15　16　17　18　19　20

| 1. | 12
 − 3 | 2. | 14
 − 7 | 3. | 16
 − 7 | 4. | 15
 − 9 | 5. | 13
 − 6 |

Write the sum and difference for each pair.

6.　　6　　　12
　　+6　　　− 6

7.　　7　　　14
　　+7　　　− 7

8.　　5　　　11
　　+6　　　− 6

9.　　7　　　15
　　+8　　　− 8

Problem Solving

Circle the best estimate.

10. Drew planted 10 seeds.
Jess planted 9 seeds.
About how many did they
plant altogether?

about 5　　　　about 10　　　　about 20

✔ Review/Test

Concepts and Skills

Write the difference.
Use the number line to help.

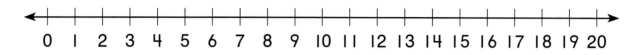

0 1 2 3 4 5 6 7 8 9 10 11 12 13 14 15 16 17 18 19 20

1.	2.	3.	4.	5.
15 − 9	18 − 9	14 − 6	16 − 8	17 − 8

Write the sum and difference for each pair.

6.
    8   16
  +8   − 8

7.
    9   18
  +9   − 9

8.
    8   14
  +6   − 6

9.
    8   17
  +9   − 9

Problem Solving

Circle the best estimate.

10. Juan has 8 flowers.
Joe has 3 flowers.
About how many flowers
do they have in all?

about 4   about 10   about 19

Name _____

Choose the answer for questions 1– 5.

1. Which does the number line show?

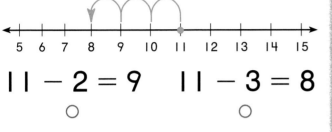

$11 - 2 = 9$ ○ $11 - 3 = 8$ ○

$9 + 2 = 11$ ○ $9 + 3 = 12$ ○

2. Which does the number line show?

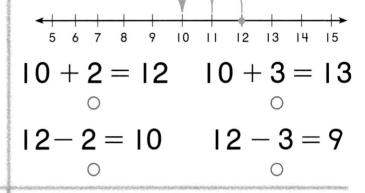

$10 + 2 = 12$ ○ $10 + 3 = 13$ ○

$12 - 2 = 10$ ○ $12 - 3 = 9$ ○

---

3. Which subtraction fact is in the same family as $9 + 9 = 18$?

$18 - 9 = 9$ ○ $17 - 9 = 8$ ○

$16 - 9 = 7$ ○ $9 - 9 = 0$ ○

4. Which is the best estimate?

Jack has 20 crayons.
He gives 6 away.
About how many crayons does Jack have left?

about 5 ○   about 15 ○   about 50 ○

---

5. Which is a different way to show $30 + 2$?

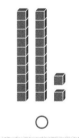 ○
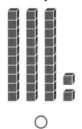 ○
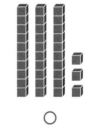 ○
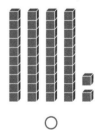 ○

Show What You Know

6. Find the sum and difference. Draw a picture to explain how the facts are related.

$8 + 8 =$ _____

_____ ◯ _____ ◯ _____

MATH GAME

Fact Family Bingo

Play with a partner.

1. Put 12 subtraction cards face down.

2. One player uses ⬤. The other player uses ⬤.

3. Take a card. Subtract. Use 🎲 to check.

4. If you are correct, cover 1 space with a counter.

5. Give an addition fact from that fact family.

6. If you are correct, cover 1 more space.

7. Play until all the spaces are covered.

8. The player with more counters wins.

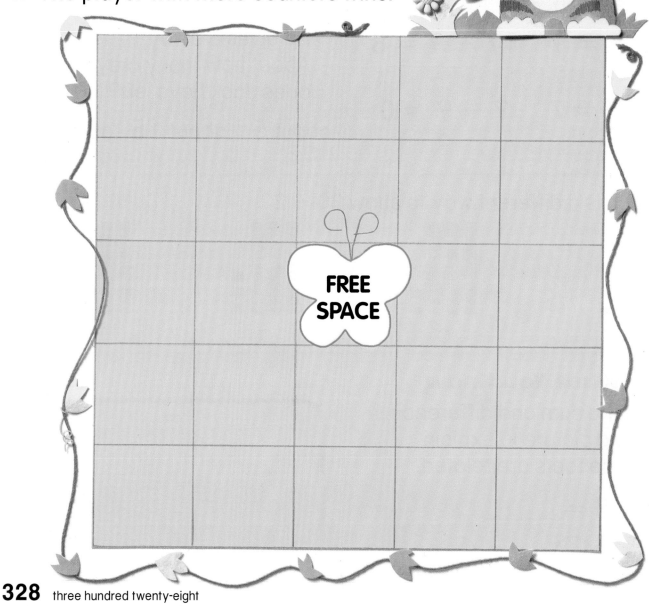

FREE SPACE

Addition and Subtraction Practice

FUN FACTS

Emperor penguin dads keep the eggs on top of their feet for up to 63 days without food, waiting for chicks to hatch.

Theme: Arctic Life

✔ Check What You Know

Fact Families to 12

Add or subtract.
Write the numbers in the fact family.

1. $3 + 8 = $ _____

    $8 + 3 = $ _____

    $11 - 3 = $ _____

    $11 - 8 = $ _____

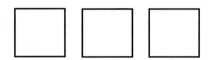

2. $3 + 9 = $ _____

    $9 + 3 = $ _____

    $12 - 3 = $ _____

    $12 - 9 = $ _____

Sums and Differences to 12

Write the sum or difference.

3. $6 + 4 = $ _____

4. $9 - 3 = $ _____

5. $10 - 6 = $ _____

6. $7 + 2 = $ _____

7. $8 + 4 = $ _____

8. $3 + 9 = $ _____

9. $\begin{array}{r} 9 \\ +2 \\ \hline \end{array}$
10. $\begin{array}{r} 12 \\ -8 \\ \hline \end{array}$
11. $\begin{array}{r} 11 \\ -4 \\ \hline \end{array}$
12. $\begin{array}{r} 12 \\ -6 \\ \hline \end{array}$
13. $\begin{array}{r} 5 \\ +4 \\ \hline \end{array}$
14. $\begin{array}{r} 10 \\ -10 \\ \hline \end{array}$

Name _____

Practice the Facts

There are many ways to find sums and differences!

I can count on, make a ten, or use doubles or doubles plus one to add.

I can count back or use a related fact to subtract.

$$\begin{array}{r} 6 \\ + 6 \\ \hline 12 \end{array}$$

$9 + 4 = 13$

10 11 12 13 14 15 16 17 18 19 20

$3 + 9 = 12$
$12 - 3 = 9$

Check

Add or subtract.

1. $\begin{array}{r} 9 \\ +5 \\ \hline 14 \end{array}$
2. $\begin{array}{r} 12 \\ - 3 \\ \hline \end{array}$
3. $\begin{array}{r} 7 \\ +9 \\ \hline \end{array}$
4. $\begin{array}{r} 13 \\ - 8 \\ \hline \end{array}$
5. $\begin{array}{r} 14 \\ - 5 \\ \hline \end{array}$
6. $\begin{array}{r} 9 \\ +9 \\ \hline \end{array}$

7. $\begin{array}{r} 5 \\ +8 \\ \hline \end{array}$
8. $\begin{array}{r} 11 \\ - 4 \\ \hline \end{array}$
9. $\begin{array}{r} 6 \\ +6 \\ \hline \end{array}$
10. $\begin{array}{r} 10 \\ - 4 \\ \hline \end{array}$
11. $\begin{array}{r} 13 \\ - 6 \\ \hline \end{array}$
12. $\begin{array}{r} 4 \\ +7 \\ \hline \end{array}$

13. $\begin{array}{r} 8 \\ +4 \\ \hline \end{array}$
14. $\begin{array}{r} 14 \\ - 7 \\ \hline \end{array}$
15. $\begin{array}{r} 5 \\ +7 \\ \hline \end{array}$
16. $\begin{array}{r} 18 \\ - 9 \\ \hline \end{array}$
17. $\begin{array}{r} 18 \\ - 8 \\ \hline \end{array}$
18. $\begin{array}{r} 10 \\ + 9 \\ \hline \end{array}$

Explain It • Daily Reasoning

What ways could you use to find the sum for 7 + 6? What ways could you use to find the difference for 12 − 3?

1. Solve the number puzzle.
   Write each sum or difference.
   The problems go across and down.

	16	−	8	=	8		15	−	7	=	
−	9			+	2					+	5
	7					+	8	=			
								−	9		
	10	+		=			17				
+	10					−	8				
		−	10	=					+	7	=

Problem Solving

Logical Reasoning

2. The sum for two of these numbers is 14.
   The difference for the same two numbers is 2.
   What are the two numbers?

5	8
6	9

   _____ and _____

 Write About It • Look at Exercise 2.
The sum for two other numbers is also 14.
What are the two numbers?
What is the difference for those numbers?

HOME ACTIVITY • With your child, make flash cards for the addition facts with sums of 10
through 20. Ask your child to choose a card, say the sum, and then tell you a related subtraction
fact. (For example: 8 + 7 = 15, 15 − 7 = 8)

Fact Families to 20

Vocabulary
fact family

Learn

Fact Family

$9 + 8 = 17$

So, $8 + 9 = 17$
$17 - 8 = 9$
$17 - 9 = 8$

You can use one fact in a fact family to help you write the other facts in the same family.

Check

Write the sum or difference.
Circle the two facts if they are in the same fact family.

1. $6 + 7 = \underline{13}$
   $13 - 6 = \underline{7}$

2. $18 + 2 = \underline{}$
   $20 - 10 = \underline{}$

3. $9 + 3 = \underline{}$
   $12 - 9 = \underline{}$

4. $10 + 9 = \underline{}$
   $10 - 3 = \underline{}$

5. $15 - 7 = \underline{}$
   $7 + 8 = \underline{}$

6. $5 + 9 = \underline{}$
   $14 - 5 = \underline{}$

7. $18 - 9 = \underline{}$
   $9 + 9 = \underline{}$

8. $19 - 9 = \underline{}$
   $9 + 2 = \underline{}$

Explain It • Daily Reasoning

Which facts are in the same family as $13 - 9 = 4$?
How do you know?

Practice and Problem Solving

Write the sum or difference.
Color all the facts in the same fact family to match.

1.
$$\begin{array}{r} 9 \\ +7 \\ \hline 16 \end{array}$$

2.
$$\begin{array}{r} 6 \\ +8 \\ \hline \end{array}$$

3.
$$\begin{array}{r} 17 \\ -9 \\ \hline \end{array}$$

4.
$$\begin{array}{r} 6 \\ +9 \\ \hline \end{array}$$

5.
$$\begin{array}{r} 15 \\ -6 \\ \hline \end{array}$$

6.
$$\begin{array}{r} 16 \\ -9 \\ \hline \end{array}$$

7.
$$\begin{array}{r} 8 \\ +6 \\ \hline \end{array}$$

8.
$$\begin{array}{r} 17 \\ -8 \\ \hline \end{array}$$

9.
$$\begin{array}{r} 8 \\ +9 \\ \hline \end{array}$$

10.
$$\begin{array}{r} 9 \\ +6 \\ \hline \end{array}$$

11.
$$\begin{array}{r} 16 \\ -7 \\ \hline \end{array}$$

12.
$$\begin{array}{r} 14 \\ -6 \\ \hline \end{array}$$

13.
$$\begin{array}{r} 14 \\ -8 \\ \hline \end{array}$$

14.
$$\begin{array}{r} 9 \\ +8 \\ \hline \end{array}$$

15.
$$\begin{array}{r} 15 \\ -9 \\ \hline \end{array}$$

16.
$$\begin{array}{r} 7 \\ +9 \\ \hline \end{array}$$

Problem Solving

Application

17. Write the number sentence that is missing from this fact family.

____ ◯ ____ ◯ ____

$$5 + 7 = 12$$
$$12 - 7 = 5$$
$$7 + 5 = 12$$

 Write About It • Look at Exercise 17.
Explain how you figured out the missing
number sentence.

⬠ **HOME ACTIVITY** • Say an addition or subtraction fact to your child. Ask him or her to tell another fact that is in the same fact family. (For example: 7 + 6 = 13, 13 − 6 = 7)

Name _____

Algebra: **Ways to Make Numbers to 20**

Explore

You can make the number 19 in different ways.

$$4 + 9 + 6$$

$$20 - 1$$

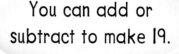

You can add or subtract to make 19.

$$15 + 4$$

Connect

Use .
Circle all the ways to make the number at the top.

1.

18
9 + 9
8 + 4 + 4
19 − 1
5 + 5 + 7
20 − 8
15 + 2
20 − 2

2.

20
13 + 6 + 1
5 + 4 + 10
20 − 0
14 + 6
5 + 7 + 8
12 + 7
2 + 8 + 7

Explain It • Daily Reasoning

Look at Exercise 2. What are
three other ways to make 20?

Use ▪▪▪.

Circle all the ways to make the number at the top.

1.

15
⟨6 + 4 + 5⟩
8 + 2 + 5
10 + 5
7 + 9
15 − 0

2.

17
6 + 10
17 − 0
5 + 5 + 7
18 − 0
7 + 10

3.

14
4 + 10
19 − 9
2 + 3 + 9
14 − 0
7 + 5 + 1

4.

16
6 + 4 + 6
10 + 6
17 + 1
8 + 8
7 + 3 + 5

Problem Solving
Application

5. Circle ways to show 12.

     6 + 7   twelve   ❄❄❄❄ ❄❄❄❄ ❄❄❄❄

 Write About It ● Use pictures, words, and numbers to show 13.

 HOME ACTIVITY • Ask your child to tell you three ways to make 20.

Name _____

Problem Solving Strategy
Make a Model

10 girls are sledding.
7 more come.
How many girls are sledding?

UNDERSTAND

What do you need to find out?

Circle the question.

PLAN

How will you solve this problem?

You can make a model.
Use and to show the groups of girls.

Workmat

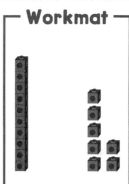

SOLVE

I have 10. I can count 7 more.

There are ___17___ girls.

CHECK

Does your answer make sense? Explain.

Use Workmat 1, , and .
Draw the and you use.
Write the answer.

THINK:
I have 17. How many more do I count to get to 20?

1. Tom's class has
20 children. 17 children
are here today. How many
children are absent?

_____ children

Problem Solving Practice

Use Workmat 1, 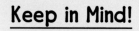, and .
Draw the and you use.
Write the answer.

1. 10 boys are skating.
There are 18 boys in all.
How many boys are not
skating?

_____ boys

2. Robin sees 9 children.
9 more are hiding.
How many children
are there in all?

_____ children

3. Kate makes 8 snowballs.
Then she makes 7 more.
How many snowballs
does she have now?

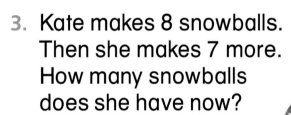

_____ snowballs

4. 15 mittens are missing.
Jan finds 5 mittens.
How many mittens are
still missing?

_____ mittens

🏠 **HOME ACTIVITY** • Ask your child how he or she decided to solve each problem.

Name _____

Extra Practice

Add or subtract.

1.	2.	3.	4.	5.	6.
7 +8	11 − 4	6 +6	16 − 7	13 − 8	5 +9

Write the sum or difference.
Circle the two facts if they are in the same fact family.

7. $10 + 0 =$ _____

$17 − 8 =$ _____

8. $7 + 9 =$ _____

$16 − 7 =$ _____

9. Use ▨ ▨ ▨.
Circle all the ways
to make the number
at the top.

20
$10 + 10$
$9 + 9$
$7 + 3 + 10$
$12 − 3$
$3 + 4 + 3$

Problem Solving

Use Workmat 1, ▨, and ▨.
Draw the ▨ and ▨ you use.
Write the answer.

10. Amy sees 8 children. 7 more
are hiding. How many children
are there in all?

_____ children

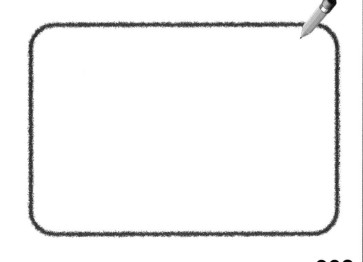

Name _____

 Review/Test

Concepts and Skills

Add or subtract.

1.	2.	3.	4.	5.	6.
6 $+7$	15 $-\ 5$	9 $+9$	14 $-\ 6$	17 $-\ 9$	10 $+\ 8$

Write the sum or difference.
Circle the pair of facts if they are in the same fact family.

7. $8 + 7 =$ _____

$15 - 8 =$ _____

8. $19 - 9 =$ _____

$9 + 9 =$ _____

9. Use ▦▦▦.
Circle all the ways
to make the number
at the top.

11
6 + 5
11 − 0
4 + 2 + 6
8 + 3
5 + 5 + 1

Problem Solving

Use Workmat 1, ▦, and ▦. Draw the
▦ and ▦ you use. Write the answer.

10. There are 15 children marching.
Some children leave. 9 children
are still marching. How many
children left?

_____ children

Name _____

Getting Ready for the ★EOG Test
Chapters 1–20

Choose the answer for questions 1–5.

1. Which object is shaped most like a sphere?

○   ○   ○   ○

---

2. What is the difference?

$18 - 9 =$ _____

6	7	8	9
○	○	○	○

---

3. What is the sum?

$10 + 6 =$ _____

13	15	16	20
○	○	○	○

---

4. Which fact is in the same family as $8 + 9 = 17$?

$17 - 8 = 9$ $17 - 7 = 10$ $9 - 8 = 1$ $1 + 8 = 9$

○   ○   ○   ○

---

5. Which is a way to make 18?

$9 + 8$ $9 + 4 + 5$ $10 + 7$ $10 - 6$

○   ○   ○   ○

Show What You Know

6. Solve. Draw 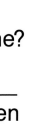 to explain.
   Write a number sentence.

   14 children play in the snow.
   6 children are still playing.
   How many children went home?

   children

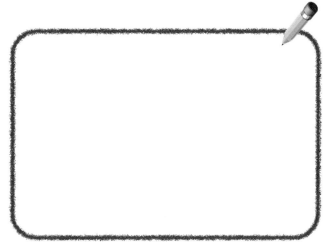

IT'S IN THE BAG
The Hungry Prince's Crown

PROJECT You will make a crown with your hardest math facts.

You Will Need

- Paper plate
- Pattern tracer
- Crayons
- Scissors

Directions

1 Put the paper plate upside down in front of you. Write your hardest math facts around the outside. Fold the paper plate in half.

2 Place the pattern on top of your plate. Trace the cut lines on your plate.

3 Cut on the lines you traced.

4 Open the plate. Fold back the points to make the top of the crown. Decorate your crown.

The Hungry Prince

written by Lucy Floyd
illustrated by Alexi Natchev

This book will help me review doubles plus one.

This book belongs to _____.

A

Once there was a very hungry prince.
"I have only 5 muffins," said the prince.
"I need MORE!"

The cook gave him 5 more.

"Now I have 5 + 5 = _____ muffins,"
said the hungry prince. "I still need more."

The cook gave him 1 more muffin. "Goody!" said the hungry prince.

"Now I have 5 + 6 = _____ muffins!"

He ate every one of them.

"I am still hungry," said the prince.
The cook gave him 6 rolls.
"I need MORE!" said the prince.

The cook gave him 6 more rolls.

"Now I have 6 + 6 = _____ rolls!" said
the hungry prince. "I still need more."

The cook gave him 1 more roll. "Goody!" said the hungry prince.

"Now I have 6 + 7 = _____ rolls!"

He ate every one of them.

"I am still hungry," said the prince.
The cook gave him 7 bagels.
"I need MORE!" said the prince.

The cook gave him 7 more bagels.

"Now I have 7 + 7 = _____ bagels!"
said the hungry prince. "I still need more."

The cook gave him 1 more bagel.
"Goody!" said the hungry prince.

"Now I have 7 + 8 = _____ bagels!
Should I eat them all?"

WHAT DID THE PRINCE DO?

The prince did eat them all!

Then he was a sick prince, but he was NOT a hungry prince any more!

Appalachian Trail, NC

On the Appalachian Trail

You can hike over 300 miles of the Appalachian Trail in North Carolina.

Two friends go hiking.

They use rocks and sticks to make patterns.

Appalachian Trail

Find the pattern.
Then color to continue it.

1 Find the pattern. Then color to continue it.

2 Use the pictures. Circle the pattern unit.

3 The pattern unit is three shapes long.
Use shapes to find the pattern.
Circle the mistake in the pattern.

CHALLENGE

Repeated Addition

Each bike has 2 wheels.
How many wheels are there in all?

You can add to find how many wheels there are.

__2__ + __2__ + __2__ + __2__ = __8__

Complete the number sentence.

1. Each boat has 2 sails.
   How many sails are there in all?

_____ + _____ + _____ + _____ + _____ = _____

2. Each car has 4 wheels.
   How many wheels are there in all?

_____ + _____ + _____ + _____ + _____ = _____

3. Each swing set has 3 swings.
   How many swings are there in all?

_____ + _____ + _____ + _____ = _____

Name _____

✓ Study Guide and Review

Vocabulary

Use  to color the **circles**.
Use  to color the **triangles**.
Use  to color the **rectangles** and **squares**.

1.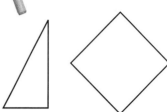

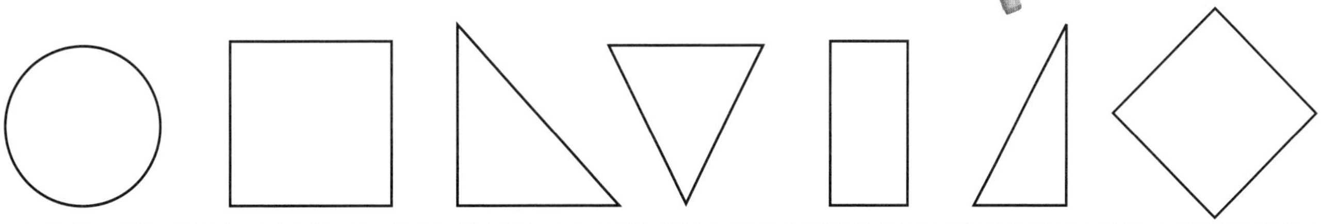

Skills and Concepts

Color each solid that will stack.

2.

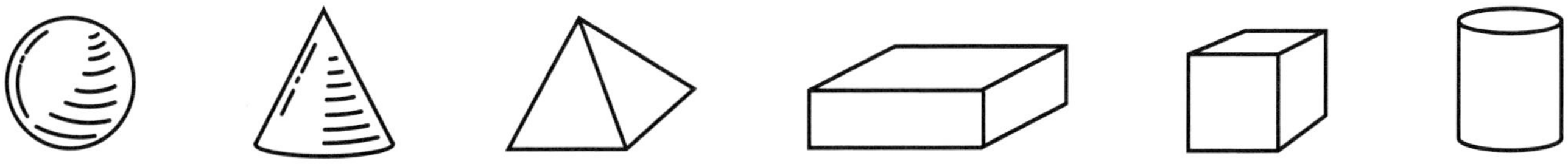

3. Write how many sides
   and corners.

   _____ sides

   _____ corners

4. Draw a line of symmetry to
   show two matching parts.

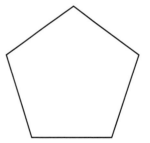

Write the sum.

5.   9
   + 5

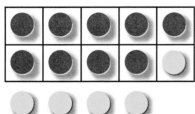

6.   8
   + 4

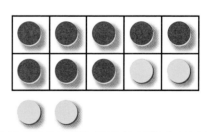

Add. Then subtract.

7.   9   10
   + 6   + 5

8.   7   10
   + 4   + 1

9.   8   10
   + 5   + 3

Subtract.

10.
$$15$$
$$-\ 7$$

11.
$$18$$
$$-\ 9$$

12.
$$20$$
$$-\ 10$$

13.
$$13$$
$$-\ 5$$

14.
$$17$$
$$-\ 8$$

15.
$$16$$
$$-\ 8$$

Write the sum for the doubles addition fact.
Write the subtraction fact that is in the same family.

16. $9 + 9 =$ _____   _____ ◯ _____ ◯ _____

17. $7 + 7 =$ _____   _____ ◯ _____ ◯ _____

18. $8 + 8 =$ _____   _____ ◯ _____ ◯ _____

Problem Solving

Find the pattern. Circle the mistake.
Draw the correct shape.

19.

20.

Name _____

Performance Assessment

How to Make a House

Sal had these blocks.

10	7	10	8
			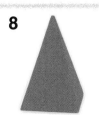

- He used 16 blocks to build a house.

- All the blocks he used had faces that were squares or triangles.

Draw 16 blocks Sal could have used. Write the number sentence to show the blocks he used.

Show your work.

Name _____

TECHNOLOGY

The Learning Site • Addition Surprise

1. Go to **www.harcourtschool.com**.

2. Click on 🐻.

3. Drag the first number tile to start.

Addition Surprise!

Drag this number tile to a square where the row and column add up to this sum.

+	0	1	2	3	4	5	6	7	8	9
0										
1										
2										
3										
4										
5										
6										
7										
8										
9										

Practice and Problem Solving

Use 🎲 🎲 🎲.
Circle all the ways to make the number at the top.

1.
16
8 + 9
4 + 14
8 + 8
14 + 2 + 2
11 + 5

2.
20
11 + 9
10 + 10
12 + 7
7 + 12 + 1
8 + 5 + 6

Write the sums. Circle the pair of facts
if they are in the same fact family.

3. 9 + 6 = _____

    10 + 5 = _____

4. 6 + 7 = _____

    7 + 6 = _____

Dear Family,

In Unit 4 we learned about geometry and about addition and subtraction to 20. Here is a game for us to play together. This game will give me a chance to share what I have learned.

Love,

_____

Directions
1. Put a game piece at START. Cover each button with a coin.
2. Your partner gives you directions such as, "Go down 2. Go left 1. Where are you?"
3. Move the game piece. Give your partner the coin where you land.
4. Take turns.
5. Play until all of the coins are taken.
6. The player with more coins wins.

Materials
- 10 pennies
- 10 nickels
- 10 dimes
- 2 game pieces or beans

Find the Pattern

START

LOOKING FORWARD
SCHOOL HOME CONNECTION

Dear Family,

During the next few weeks, we will learn about fractions, money, and time. Here is important math vocabulary and a list of books to share.

Love,

_____

Vocabulary Power

Two equal parts are halves.

one half
$\frac{1}{2}$ →
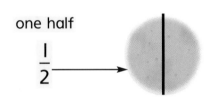

one third
$\frac{1}{3}$ →
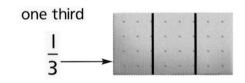

one fourth
$\frac{1}{4}$ →
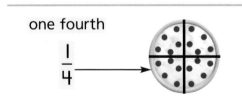

minute hand   hour hand

BOOKS TO SHARE

To read about fractions, money, and time with your child, look for these books in your library.

Eating Fractions,
by Bruce McMillan, Scholastic, 1991.

Fraction Action,
by Loreen Leedy, Holiday House, 1996.

26 Letters and 99 Cents,
by Tana Hoban, William Morrow, 1995.

Isn't It Time?
by Judy Hindley, Candlewick, 1996.

Visit *The Learning Site* for additional ideas and activities. **www.harcourtschool.com**

CHAPTER 21

Fractions

HEALTH

FUN FACTS

On an average size pizza, $\frac{1}{2}$ of the pizza's weight is crust and $\frac{1}{4}$ of the weight is cheese.

✔ Check What You Know

Equal Parts

Circle the shape that is divided into 2 equal parts.

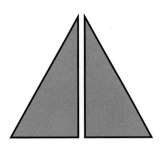 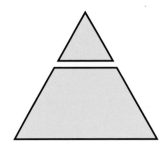 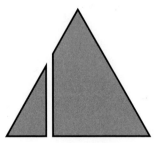

Circle the shape that is divided into 3 equal parts.

 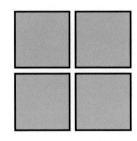 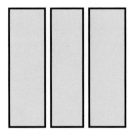

Circle the shape that is divided into 4 equal parts.

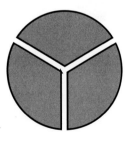 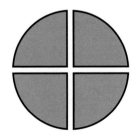 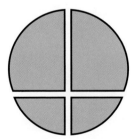

Halves

Vocabulary

$\frac{1}{2}$ one half

Learn

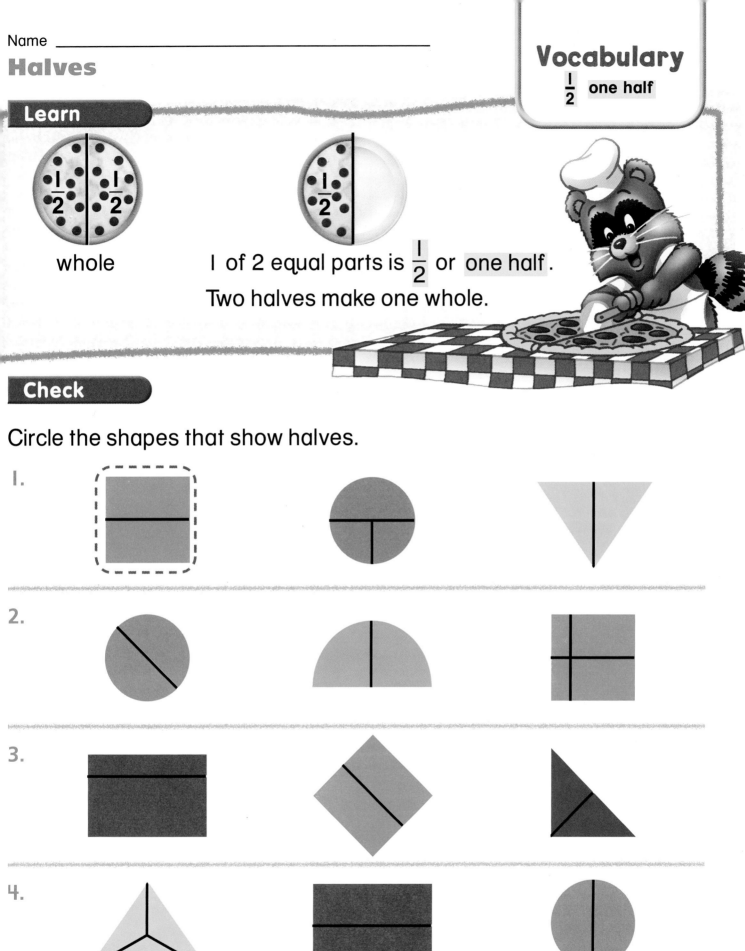

whole

1 of 2 equal parts is $\frac{1}{2}$ or one half.

Two halves make one whole.

Check

Circle the shapes that show halves.

1.

2.

3.

4.

Explain It • Daily Reasoning

Can one half of an object be larger
than the other half? Explain.

This has 2 equal parts.

Find the shapes that show halves.

Color $\frac{1}{2}$.

1.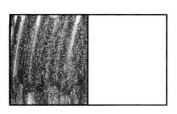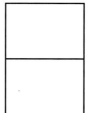

2.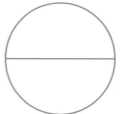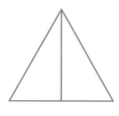

3.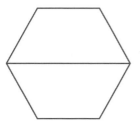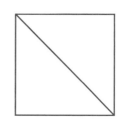

4.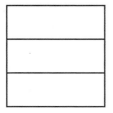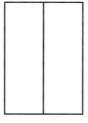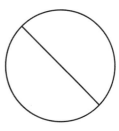

Problem Solving
Application

5. Draw a line on each cracker to show different ways to make halves.

 Write About It • Write a story about sharing a sandwich with a friend. Use **one half** in your story.

 HOME ACTIVITY • Give your child three sheets of paper, each a different size. Ask him or her to fold each sheet in half and to name each part as one half.

Name _____

Fourths

Learn

$\frac{1}{4}$ | $\frac{1}{4}$ | $\frac{1}{4}$ | $\frac{1}{4}$

whole

$\frac{1}{4}$

1 of 4 equal parts is $\frac{1}{4}$ or one fourth.

Four fourths make one whole.

Check

Find the shapes that show fourths. Color $\frac{1}{4}$.

1.
 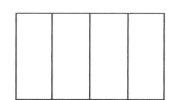 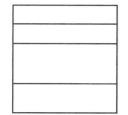

2.

3.
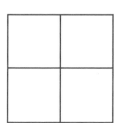 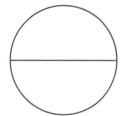 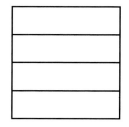

4.
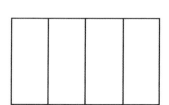 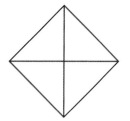 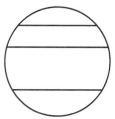

Explain It • Daily Reasoning

How could you find one fourth of a sheet of paper?
Use a sheet of paper to explain your answer.

Color one part. Circle the fraction.

1.

$\frac{1}{2}$ $\left(\frac{1}{4}\right)$

2.

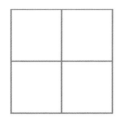

$\frac{1}{2}$ $\frac{1}{4}$

3.

$\frac{1}{2}$ $\frac{1}{4}$

4.

$\frac{1}{2}$ $\frac{1}{4}$

5.

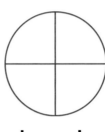

$\frac{1}{2}$ $\frac{1}{4}$

6.

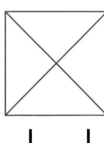

$\frac{1}{2}$ $\frac{1}{4}$

Problem Solving
Visual Thinking

7. Draw two different ways to make 4 equal parts.

Color 1 of the 4 equal parts.   Color 3 of the 4 equal parts.

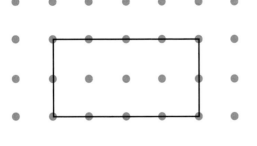

 Write About It • Look at Exercise 7.
Explain how the rectangles are the same.

HOME ACTIVITY • Invite your child to divide food items into fourths and to name each part as one fourth.

Name _____

Thirds

Learn

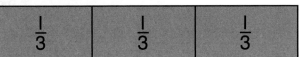

whole

I of 3 equal parts is $\frac{1}{3}$ or one third.

Three thirds make one whole.

Check

Find the shapes that show thirds. Color $\frac{1}{3}$.

1.

2.
  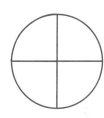

3.
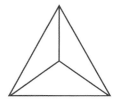 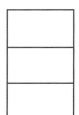 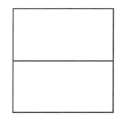

4.
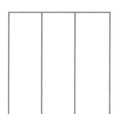 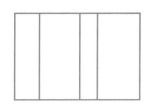 

Explain It • Daily Reasoning

Which is more, $\frac{1}{2}$ or $\frac{1}{3}$ of a glass of juice?

Use fraction strips to prove your answer.

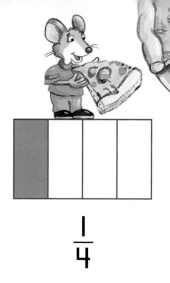

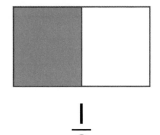

$\dfrac{1}{2}$

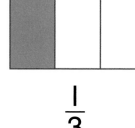

$\dfrac{1}{3}$

$\dfrac{1}{4}$

Color one part. Circle the fraction.

1.
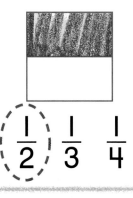

$\left(\dfrac{1}{2}\right)$ $\dfrac{1}{3}$ $\dfrac{1}{4}$

2.
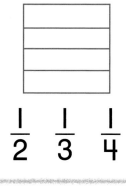

$\dfrac{1}{2}$ $\dfrac{1}{3}$ $\dfrac{1}{4}$

3.
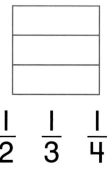

$\dfrac{1}{2}$ $\dfrac{1}{3}$ $\dfrac{1}{4}$

4.

$\dfrac{1}{2}$ $\dfrac{1}{3}$ $\dfrac{1}{4}$

5.
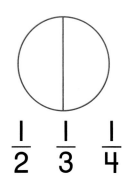

$\dfrac{1}{2}$ $\dfrac{1}{3}$ $\dfrac{1}{4}$

6.
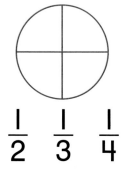

$\dfrac{1}{2}$ $\dfrac{1}{3}$ $\dfrac{1}{4}$

Problem Solving
Estimation

7. Circle the pizza pan that has about $\dfrac{1}{3}$ left.

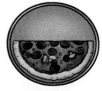  

 Write About It • Into how many pieces do you cut a whole pizza to make fourths? Tell how you know.

HOME ACTIVITY • Draw two squares that are the same size. Invite your child to show two ways to divide the squares into thirds.

Name _____

Problem Solving Strategy
Use Logical Reasoning

You can use clues to
solve problems.

Sharon cuts a pizza.

It has 3 parts.

The parts are not equal.

Which is Sharon's pizza?

UNDERSTAND

What do you want to find out?

Circle it.

PLAN

What are the clues in this problem?

Underline them.

SOLVE

Cross out pictures that
do not match the clues.
Circle the picture that
matches the clues.

CHECK

Does your answer make sense?

Use fraction circles to check. Explain.

Cross out pictures that do not match the
clues. Circle the picture that matches
the clues. Use fraction circles to check.

THINK:
Which picture matches
all the clues?

I. Matt and David
cut a pizza.
It has 2 equal parts.
Which is their pizza?

Problem Solving Practice

Cross out pictures that do not match the clues.
Circle the picture that matches the clues.
Use fraction circles to check.

1. 4 girls share a pizza.
   They will each eat 1 part.
   The parts are not equal.
   Which is their pizza?

  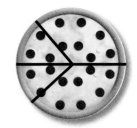

2. Sal and 2 other boys
   have a pizza.
   They share equal parts.
   Which is their pizza?

3. Janet cuts a pizza.
   It has 4 equal parts.
   Which is Janet's pizza?

4. Don cuts a pizza.
   It has 3 parts.
   They are equal.
   Which is Don's pizza?

5. Juan and Ellen
   share a pizza.
   They will each
   eat one half.
   Which is their pizza?

HOME ACTIVITY • Give your child a piece of bread (or a tortilla or muffin). Have your child divide it into 2 equal parts. Have your child then make 4 equal parts.

Name _____

Parts of Groups

1 of the 4 apples is red.

$\frac{1}{4}$ of the apples are red.

THINK:
$\frac{1}{4}$ is one of four equal parts.

Check

Color $\frac{1}{3}$.

1.

2.

Color $\frac{1}{4}$.

3.

4.

Explain It • Daily Reasoning

How do you know if you have an equal part of a group?

$\frac{1}{2}$ are red.　　$\frac{1}{3}$ are red.　　$\frac{1}{4}$ are red.

Color to show each fraction.

1. $\frac{1}{2}$

2. $\frac{1}{3}$

3. $\frac{1}{4}$

4. $\frac{1}{4}$

Problem Solving
Application

Color to show each fraction.

5. $\frac{1}{2}$

6. $\frac{1}{3}$

 Write About It ● Draw 4 cookies.
Color to show $\frac{1}{4}$.

HOME ACTIVITY ● Using objects that are the same, invite your child to point out $\frac{1}{2}$ of a group of 2 objects, $\frac{1}{3}$ of a group of 3 objects, and $\frac{1}{4}$ of a group of 4 objects.

Name _____

Extra Practice

1. Color $\frac{1}{2}$.

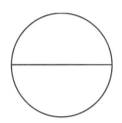

2. Color $\frac{1}{3}$.

3. Color $\frac{1}{4}$.

Color one part. Circle the fraction.

4.

$\frac{1}{2}$ $\frac{1}{3}$ $\frac{1}{4}$

5.

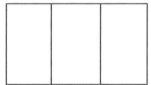

$\frac{1}{2}$ $\frac{1}{3}$ $\frac{1}{4}$

6.

$\frac{1}{2}$ $\frac{1}{3}$ $\frac{1}{4}$

7. Color $\frac{1}{4}$.

8. Color $\frac{1}{2}$.

9. Color $\frac{1}{3}$.

Problem Solving

Cross out pictures that do not match the clues.
Circle the picture that matches the clues.

10. Pat cuts a pizza.
It has 2 parts.
The parts are not equal.
Which is Pat's pizza?

✓ Review/Test

Concepts and Skills

1. Color $\frac{1}{2}$.

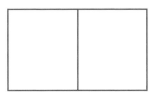

2. Color $\frac{1}{3}$.

3. Color $\frac{1}{4}$.

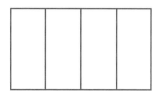

Color one part. Circle the fraction.

4.

$\frac{1}{2}$ $\frac{1}{3}$ $\frac{1}{4}$

5.

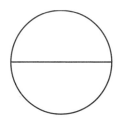

$\frac{1}{2}$ $\frac{1}{3}$ $\frac{1}{4}$

6.

$\frac{1}{2}$ $\frac{1}{3}$ $\frac{1}{4}$

7. Color $\frac{1}{3}$.

8. Color $\frac{1}{4}$.

9. Color $\frac{1}{2}$.

Problem Solving

Cross out pictures that do not match the clues.
Circle the picture that matches the clues.

10. 3 children share a pizza.
Each gets an equal part.
Which is their pizza?

Getting Ready for the EOG Test
Chapters 1–21

Choose the answer for questions 1– 5.

1. Which shape shows halves?

   ○
 ○

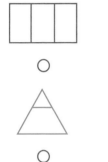 ○
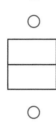 ○

2. Which shape has $\frac{1}{3}$ colored in?

 ○
 ○

 ○
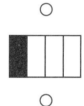 ○

3. Which shape shows fourths?

 ○
 ○

○   ○

4. What fraction does the colored part show?

$\frac{1}{4}$ $\frac{1}{2}$ $\frac{1}{3}$
○   ○   ○

5. Which is a way to make 20?

$10 + 10$ $10 + 4 + 4$ $10 + 6$ $10 + 4$
○   ○   ○   ○

Show What You Know

6. Explain how the children share the pizza. Draw a picture that matches the clues.

Ellen and Mara have a pizza. They share equal parts.

Color $\frac{1}{2}$ of the pizza.

MATH GAME

Pizza Party

Play with a partner.

1. Put your 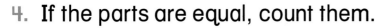 on START.

2. Spin the 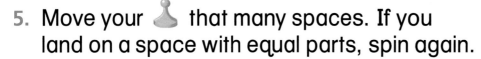.

3. If the parts in that circle are not equal, your turn is over.

4. If the parts are equal, count them.

5. Move your pawn that many spaces. If you land on a space with equal parts, spin again.

6. The first player to get to the party wins.

You will need

2 pawns

Counting Pennies, Nickels, and Dimes

SCIENCE

FUN FACTS

The face of a penny can hold about 30 drops of water.

✔ Check What You Know

Penny

Count the pennies.
Write how many cents.

1.   _____ ¢

2.

         _____ ¢

Nickel

Write how many cents.

3.   _____ ¢

4.   _____ ¢

5.   _____ ¢

Dime

Write how many cents.

6.   _____ ¢

7.   _____ ¢

Use this page to review important skills needed for this chapter.

Name _____

Pennies and Nickels

HANDS ON

Explore

A penny is worth I cent.
A nickel is worth 5 cents.

Vocabulary
penny
nickel

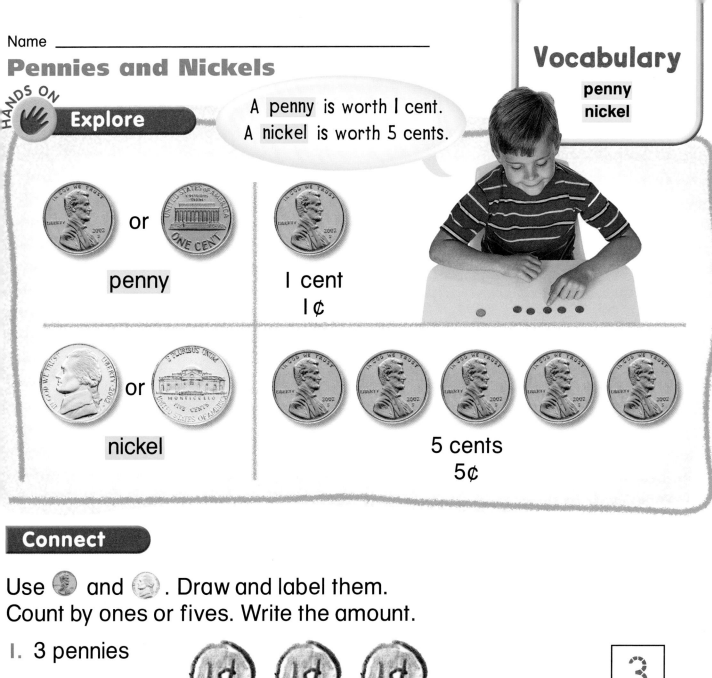

penny

or

I cent
I ¢

nickel

or

5 cents
5¢

Connect

Use and . Draw and label them.
Count by ones or fives. Write the amount.

I. 3 pennies

3 ¢

2. 4 pennies

☐ ¢

3. 2 nickels

☐ ¢

4. 3 nickels

☐ ¢

Explain It ● Daily Reasoning

Which is worth more, two pennies
or one nickel? Explain.

Count by ones or fives. Write the amount.

1.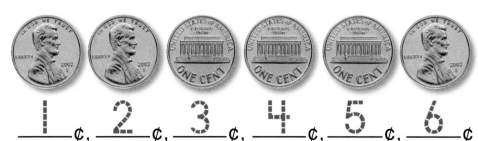

_____1_____¢, _____2_____¢, _____3_____¢, _____4_____¢, _____5_____¢, _____6_____¢

6 ¢

2.

_____¢, _____¢, _____¢, _____¢, _____¢, _____¢, _____¢

☐ ¢

3.

_____¢, _____¢, _____¢, _____¢

☐ ¢

4.

_____¢, _____¢, _____¢, _____¢, _____¢

☐ ¢

Problem Solving

Logical Reasoning

5. Mary has 2 nickels.
Sam has the same amount
of money in pennies.
How many pennies does Sam have?   _____ pennies

 Write About It • Look at Exercise 5.
What would Mary say to count her money? Explain.

🔺 **HOME ACTIVITY** • Set out a group of pennies or nickels. Have your child count by ones or fives to find the value of the group of coins.

Pennies and Dimes

Vocabulary
dime

HANDS ON Explore

or
penny

I cent
I ¢

A penny is worth I cent.
A dime is worth 10 cents.

or
dime

10 cents
10¢

Connect

Use 🪙. Draw and label them.
Count by tens. Write the amount.

1. 2 dimes

 20 ¢

2. 3 dimes

 ☐ ¢

3. 4 dimes

☐ ¢

4. 5 dimes

☐ ¢

Explain It • Daily Reasoning

How many pennies equal two dimes?
Explain how you know.

Count by tens. Write the amount.

1.

__10__ ¢, __20__ ¢, __30__ ¢

| 30 | ¢

2.

_____ ¢, _____ ¢, _____ ¢, _____ ¢, _____ ¢

 ¢

3.

_____ ¢, _____ ¢, _____ ¢, _____ ¢

 ¢

4.

_____ ¢, _____ ¢, _____ ¢, _____ ¢, _____ ¢, _____ ¢

¢

Problem Solving
Mental Math

5. Joanne has 9 dimes. How much money does she have? ¢

6. Paul has 7 dimes. How much money does he have? ¢

 Write About It • How much money would you have if you had 8 dimes? Explain.

 HOME ACTIVITY • Have your child count groups of dimes by tens and tell the value of each group.

Count Groups of Coins

Learn

Count by tens.

Then count on by ones.

10¢, 20¢, 30¢, 40¢, 41¢, 42¢, 43¢, 43¢

Check

Count by tens. Then count on by ones.
Write the amount.

1.

_____¢, _____¢, _____¢, _____¢, _____¢   ¢

2.

_____¢, _____¢, _____¢, _____¢, _____¢, _____¢   ¢

3.

_____¢, _____¢, _____¢, _____¢, _____¢, _____¢   ¢

Explain It • Daily Reasoning

You want to count this group of coins.
With which coin would you start? Why?

Count by fives.

Then count on by ones.

__5__¢, __10__¢, __15__¢, __20__¢, __25__¢, __26__¢, __27__ 27 ¢

Count. Write the amount.

1.

_____¢, _____¢, _____¢, _____¢, _____¢, _____¢, _____¢ ☐ ¢

2.

_____¢, _____¢, _____¢, _____¢, _____¢, _____¢, _____¢ ☐ ¢

Problem Solving

Application

3. Write the number. Draw and label dimes and pennies to show the same amount in cents. Write the amount.

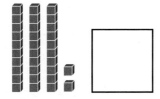 ☐

☐ ¢

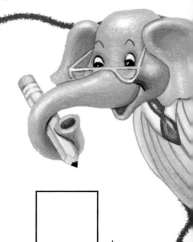

 Write About It • Look at Exercise 3. How many pennies would it take to show the same amount? Explain.

⬠ **HOME ACTIVITY** • Have your child count groups of dimes and pennies or groups of nickels and pennies and tell the value of each group.

Count Collections

Learn

Count by tens.   Count by fives.   Then count on by ones.

10 ¢, 20 ¢, 25 ¢, 30 ¢, 31 ¢, 32 ¢   [32] ¢

Check

Count. Write the amount.

1.

_____ ¢, _____ ¢, _____ ¢, _____ ¢, _____ ¢, _____ ¢   [ ] ¢

2.

_____ ¢, _____ ¢, _____ ¢, _____ ¢, _____ ¢, _____ ¢   [ ] ¢

3.

_____ ¢, _____ ¢, _____ ¢, _____ ¢, _____ ¢, _____ ¢   [ ] ¢

Explain It ● Daily Reasoning

What are three ways to show 16¢?
Use coins to prove your answer.

Start counting with the coins that have the greatest value.

Count. Write the amount.

1.

   36 ¢

2.

   ☐ ¢

3.

   ☐ ¢

4.

   ☐ ¢

5.

   ☐ ¢

6.

   ☐ ¢

Problem Solving

Logical Reasoning

Draw and label the coins.

7. You have 72¢.
   You have 9 coins.
   What coins do you have?

 Write About It • Look at Exercise 7. How many pennies would it take to show the same amount? Explain.

🏠 **HOME ACTIVITY** • Have your child count groups of dimes, nickels, and pennies. Ask your child to tell you the value of each group.

Problem Solving Strategy
Make a List

Earl wants to buy a yo-yo for 15¢.

In what ways can he use  and 🪙 to make 15¢?

UNDERSTAND

What do you need to find out?

Circle it.

PLAN

How can you solve the problem?

Make a list of the coins Earl can use.

SOLVE

Draw and label the coins that will make 15¢.

dimes	nickels
0	5¢ 5¢ 5¢

CHECK

Does each way equal 15¢?

Explain.

Tina wants to buy a toy for 20¢.
In what ways can she use 🪙 , 🪙 ,
and 🪙 to make 20¢?

List six ways to make 20¢.
Use 🪙 , 🪙 , and 🪙 .
Draw and label the coins.

Ways to Make 20¢		
dimes	nickels	pennies
10¢ 10¢	0	0
		0
0		

🔶 **HOME ACTIVITY** • Place pennies, nickels, and dimes on the table. Ask your child to show all the ways to make 20¢.

Name _____

Extra Practice

Count. Write the amount.

1.

_____¢, _____¢, _____¢, _____¢, _____¢

☐ ¢

2.

_____¢, _____¢, _____¢, _____¢

☐ ¢

3.

_____¢, _____¢, _____¢

☐ ¢

4.

_____¢, _____¢, _____¢, _____¢, _____¢

☐ ¢

Problem Solving

List two ways to make 25¢.
Use 🪙 and 🪙 .
Draw and label the coins.

5.

dimes	nickels

✓ Review/Test

Concepts and Skills
Count. Write the amount.

1.

_____ ¢, _____ ¢, _____ ¢, _____ ¢, _____ ¢, _____ ¢   ☐ ¢

2.

_____ ¢, _____ ¢, _____ ¢, _____ ¢, _____ ¢, _____ ¢, _____ ¢   ☐ ¢

3.

_____ ¢, _____ ¢, _____ ¢, _____ ¢, _____ ¢   ☐ ¢

4.

_____ ¢, _____ ¢, _____ ¢, _____ ¢, _____ ¢, _____ ¢, _____ ¢   ☐ ¢

Problem Solving

List two ways to make 30¢.
Use 🪙, 🪙, and 🪙.
Draw and label the coins.

5.

dimes	nickels	pennies

Name _____

Choose the answer for questions 1– 5.

1. Find the pattern. Which should come next?

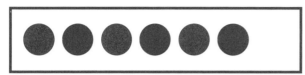

○   ○   ○   ○

2. How much money is shown?

   3¢   5¢   15¢   20¢
   ○   ○   ○   ○

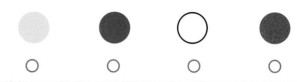

3. How much money is shown?

   4¢   6¢   10¢   12¢
   ○   ○   ○   ○

4. How much money is shown?

   10¢   20¢   40¢   50¢
   ○   ○   ○   ○

5. Which is the total amount?

   5¢, 10¢, 15¢, 16¢, _____¢

   13¢   15¢   17¢   20¢
   ○   ○   ○   ○

Show What You Know

6. Theo wants to buy a jump rope
   for 25¢. Which ways can he use
   🪙 and 🪙 to make 25¢?

   Explain different ways to make 25¢.
   Use 🪙 and 🪙 to list the ways.
   Draw to show what you choose.

Ways to Make 25¢	
dimes	nickels

EOG TEST PREP

MATH GAME

Finding Coins

Play with a partner.

1. Put your ♟ at START.

2. Toss the 🎲.

3. Move your ♟ that many spaces.

4. Take 🪙🪙🪙 to equal the amount you land on.

5. When both players get to the BANK, count 🪙🪙🪙.

6. The player with the greater amount wins.

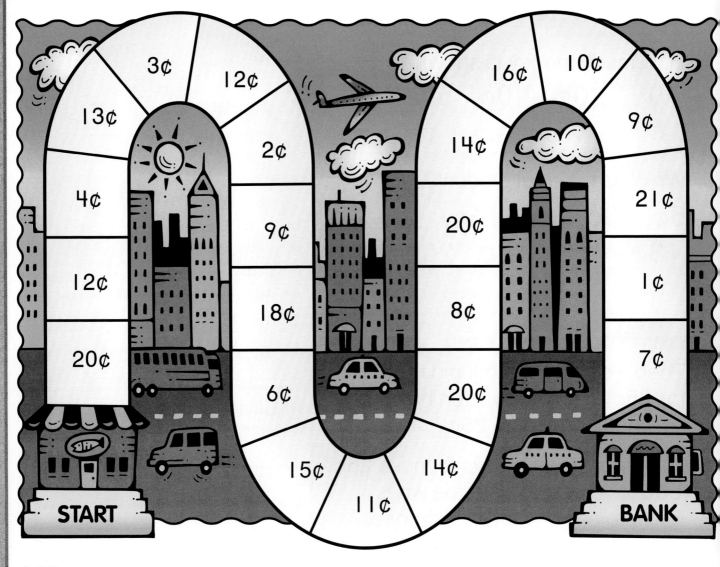

23 Using Money

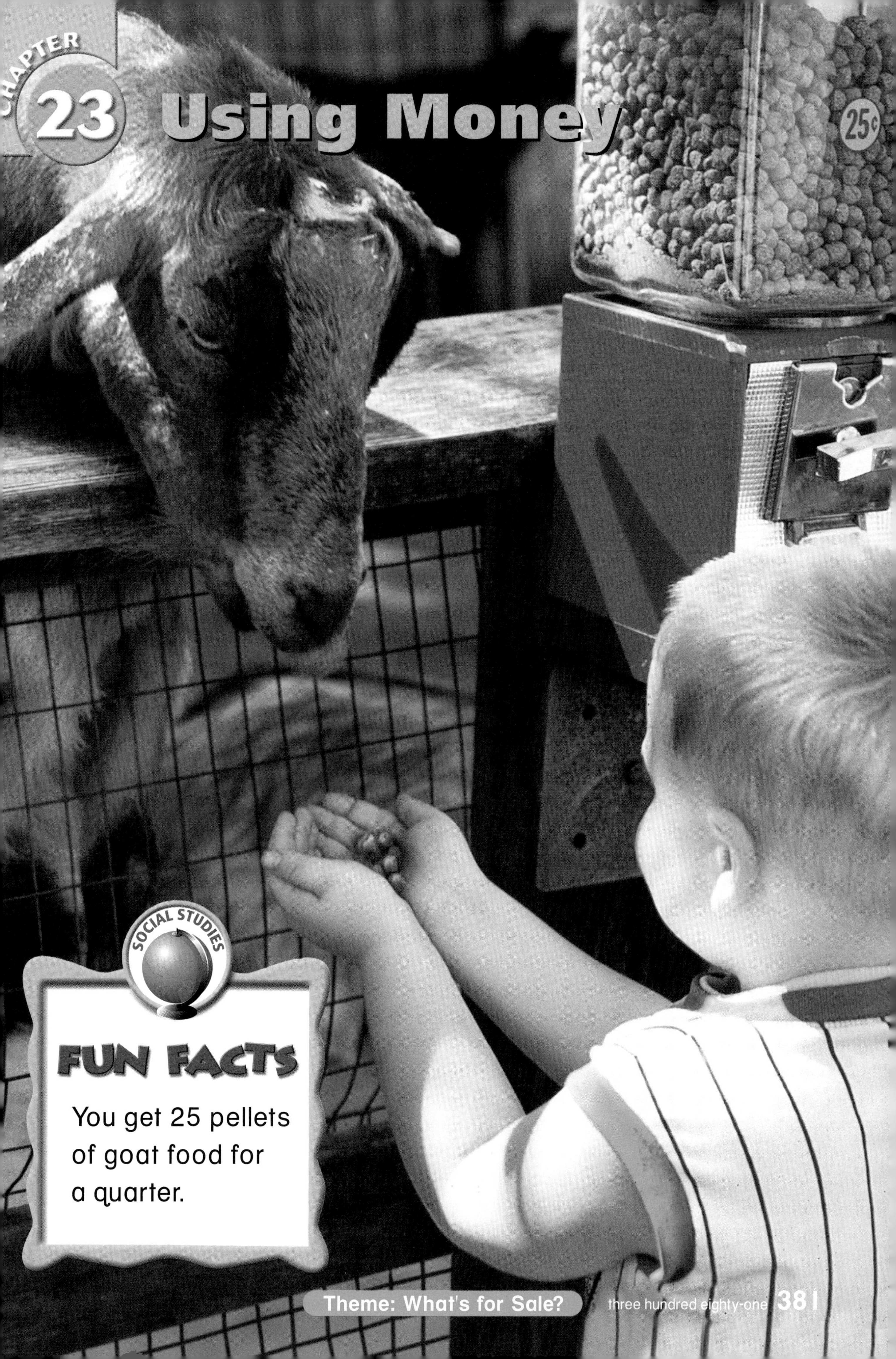

25¢

FUN FACTS

You get 25 pellets of goat food for a quarter.

SOCIAL STUDIES

Name _____

✅ Check What You Know

Pennies and Nickels

Count by ones or fives. Write the amount.

1.

_____ ¢, _____ ¢, _____ ¢, _____ ¢, _____ ¢, _____ ¢

☐ ¢

2.

_____ ¢, _____ ¢, _____ ¢, _____ ¢, _____ ¢

☐ ¢

Pennies and Dimes

Use . Draw and label them.
Count by tens. Write the amount.

3. 3 dimes

☐ ¢

Count by tens. Write the amount.

4.

_____ ¢, _____ ¢, _____ ¢, _____ ¢

☐ ¢

5.

_____ ¢, _____ ¢, _____ ¢, _____ ¢, _____ ¢, _____ ¢

☐ ¢

Use this page to review important skills needed for this chapter.

Trade Pennies, Nickels, and Dimes

Vocabulary

trade

Explore

You can trade pennies for nickels and dimes.

5 pennies
equal 1 nickel.

10 pennies
equal 1 dime.

15 pennies equal
1 dime and 1 nickel.

Connect

Use coins. Trade pennies for nickels and dimes.
Draw and label the coins.

1.

   5¢

2.

3.

4.

5.

6.

Explain It • Daily Reasoning

For what coins would you trade 20 pennies if you
wanted the fewest coins in your pocket? Explain.

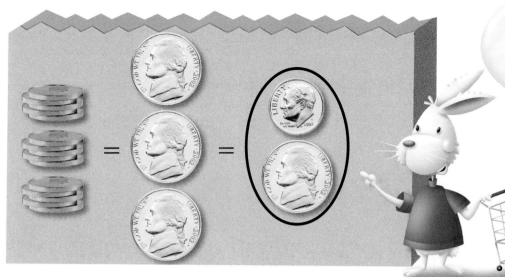

Each group shows 15¢, but this group has the fewest coins.

Use coins. Trade for nickels and dimes.
Use the fewest coins. Draw and label the coins.

1.

10¢   10¢

2.

3.

4.

Problem Solving

Application

Draw the same amount with the fewest coins.

5.

 Write About It ● Look at Exercise 5.
What are two other ways you could show 20¢?

🏠 **HOME ACTIVITY** • Have your child show you different groups of coins that equal the same amount of money as 20 pennies.

Name _____

Quarters

HANDS ON **Explore**

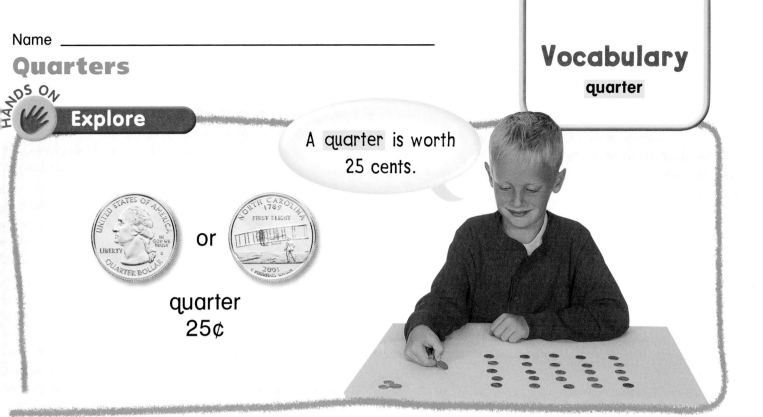

A quarter is worth 25 cents.

or

quarter
25¢

Connect

Show ways to make 25 cents.
Draw and label the coins.

Use only nickels.

1.

Use dimes and nickels.

Show two ways.

2.

3.

Explain It • Daily Reasoning

How many nickels would you need to equal
2 quarters? Explain how you know.

Say 25. Count on by tens. Count on by fives.

_25_ ¢, _35_ ¢, _45_ ¢, _50_ ¢, _55_ ¢ | 55 | ¢

Count on from the quarter. Write the total amount.

1.

_____ ¢, _____ ¢, _____ ¢, _____ ¢, _____ ¢ | | ¢

2.

_____ ¢, _____ ¢, _____ ¢, _____ ¢, _____ ¢ | | ¢

Problem Solving

Logical Reasoning

Use coins to solve.
Draw and label the coins.

3. Zoe has 4 coins that
   equal 50 cents in all.
   Which coins does she have?

 Write About It ● Explain the best
way to count the coins you drew.

HOME ACTIVITY • Show your child a quarter. Ask your child to show the same amount of money, using dimes, nickels, and pennies.

Half Dollar and Dollar

Vocabulary

 Explore

or

I dollar = 100¢

I half dollar = 50¢

Connect

Draw and label the coins. Write how many.

1. Show how many quarters equal I dollar.

___4___ quarters = I dollar

2. Show how many dimes equal I half dollar.

_____ dimes = I half dollar

Explain It ● Daily Reasoning

Explain how you could find out how many nickels equal I dollar.

THINK:
1 dollar = 100¢
1 half dollar = 50¢

Draw and label the coins. Write how many.

1. Show how many dimes equal 1 dollar.

_____ dimes = 1 dollar

2. Show how many quarters equal 1 half dollar.

_____ quarters = 1 half dollar

3. Show how many nickels equal 1 half dollar.

_____ nickels = 1 half dollar

Problem Solving
Mental Math

Solve. Write the amount.

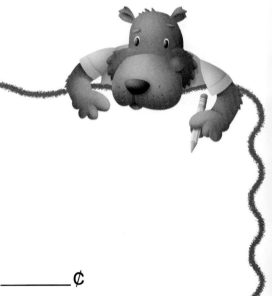

4. Kevin saved 4 dimes in one week. In the next week, he saved 1 half dollar. How much money did he have then?

_____¢

 Write About It • Look at Exercise 4. Kevin saves one dime this week. Draw a picture to show how much money Kevin has now.

🏠 HOME ACTIVITY • Show your child a dollar bill. Ask him or her to show the same amount of money, using quarters, dimes, and nickels.

Name _____

Compare Values

Learn

Write the value for each group.
Which amount is greater? Circle it.

$\left(\underline{50}\ ¢\right)$ $\underline{35}\ ¢$

Check

Write the value for each group.
Circle the amount that is greater.

1.

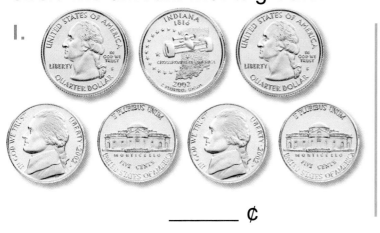

_____ ¢   _____ ¢

2.

_____ ¢   _____ ¢

Explain It • Daily Reasoning

Compare the values of 1 dollar, 1 quarter, and 1 half dollar.
Put them in order from least value to greatest value.

Write the amount for each group.
Circle the amount that is greater.

1.

_____ ¢

_____ ¢

2.

_____ ¢

_____ ¢

3.

_____ ¢

_____ ¢

Problem Solving

Application

4. Cary wants quarters.
   He has 6 dimes and 3 nickels.
   Draw quarters to show the
   same amount.

 **Write About It** ● Cary gets one more coin.
Now he has 1 dollar. Draw and label the coin.
Tell how you know.

⬠ **HOME ACTIVITY** • Show your child two groups of coins, each worth one dollar or less. Have your child tell you the amount for each group. Then ask which amount is greater.

Name _____

Same Amounts

Explore

I can show the amount in two ways. I can circle the way that uses fewer coins.

Connect

Use coins. Show the amount in two ways.
Draw and label the coins.
Circle the way that uses fewer coins.

1.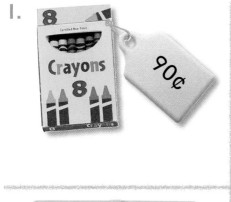

2.

Explain It • Daily Reasoning

How could you show this amount using fewer coins? Is there more than one way? Explain.

Use coins. Show the amount in two ways.
Draw the coins.
Circle the way that uses fewer coins.

1.

2.

3.

Problem Solving
Visual Thinking

4. Luis shows the same
amount in two ways.
One way has 1 quarter
and 2 dimes. One way
has 9 nickels.

Draw another way to show
the same amount.

 Write About It • Look at Exercise 4. Use
words to tell which group uses the fewest coins.

HOME ACTIVITY • Name an amount of money that is less than 50¢. Have your child use pennies,
nickels, and dimes to show the amount in different ways. Then have your child point to the way that
uses the fewest coins.

Name _____

Problem Solving Strategy
Act It Out

You want to buy these two things.
What coins could you use?

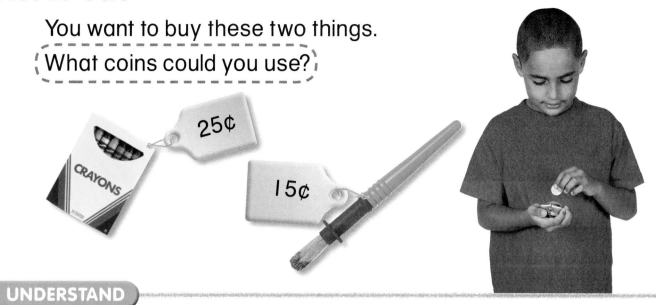

UNDERSTAND

What do you want to find out?

Circle it.

PLAN

How will you solve the problem?

Act it out. Use coins.

SOLVE

Show the coins you would use.
Draw and label the coins.

CHECK

Does your answer make sense?
Explain.

Show the coins you would use.
Draw and label the coins.

1.

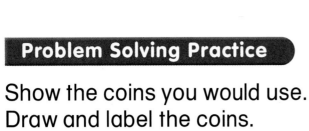

Show the coins you would use.
Draw and label the coins.

Keep in Mind!
Understand
Plan
Solve
Check

1.

25¢

10¢

2.

25¢

16¢

3.

35¢

20¢

4.

25¢

20¢

HOME ACTIVITY • Set out two items, and write a price under 30¢ for each item. Then have your child use coins to act out buying the items.

Extra Practice

Use coins. Show the amount
in two ways. Draw and label the coins.
Circle the way that uses fewer coins.

1.  | |

Count on from the quarter. Write the total amount.

2.

_____ ¢, _____ ¢, _____ ¢   ¢

Draw and label the coins. Write how many.

3. Show how many quarters
equal 1 half dollar.

_____ quarters = 1 half dollar

4. Show how many quarters
equal 1 dollar.

_____ quarters = 1 dollar

Problem Solving

Show the coins you
would use. Draw and
label the coins.

5.

Name _____

Name _____

✔ Review/Test

Concepts and Skills

Use coins. Show the amount
in two ways. Draw and label the coins.
Circle the way that uses fewer coins.

1.

Count on from the quarter. Write the total amount.

2.

_____¢, _____¢, _____¢, _____¢   ¢

Draw and label the coins. Write how many.

3. Show how many dimes equal
   I half dollar.

   _____ dimes = I half dollar

4. Show how many dimes equal
   I dollar.

   _____ dimes = I dollar

Problem Solving

Show the coins you would use. Draw
and label the coins.

5.  25¢    12¢

Getting Ready for the ★EOG Test
Chapters 1–23

Choose the answer for questions 1 – 4.

1. 5 + 3 = _____

2	4	8	9
○	○	○	○

2. How many  make  ?

2	4	5	8
○	○	○	○

3. Which is a way to make 25¢?

○

○

○

○

4. Which amount can you trade to equal the amount shown?

○

○

○

○

Show What You Know

5. Write a price on each toy that is less than 50¢. Draw coins to show each price. Explain which toy costs less. Circle it.

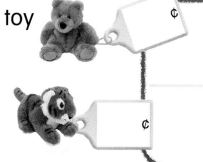

¢

¢

MATH GAME

Shopping Basket

Play with a partner.

1. Each player turns up 1 card.

2. Each player uses coins to show the total amount for the two cards.

3. The person who shows the correct amount with fewer coins keeps the two cards.

4. If both players use the same number of coins, each keeps one card.

5. Play until all the cards are used.

6. The player with more cards wins.

You will need

12 cards with prices

pile of

Stack the cards face down here.

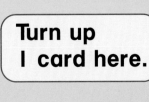

Turn up 1 card here.

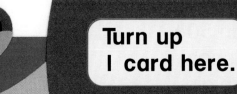

Turn up 1 card here.

CHAPTER 23 · MATH GAME

Telling Time

SOCIAL STUDIES

FUN FACTS

This clock has 2 hands like most clocks. It is special because it is made of foam material which does not break.

✔ Check What You Know

More Time, Less Time

Circle the activity that takes more time.

1.

Circle the activity that takes less time.

2.

Use a Clock

Write the number that tells the hour.
Circle the two clocks that show the same time.

3.

4.

5.

3:00

_____ o'clock   _____ o'clock   _____ o'clock

Name _____

Read a Clock

Explore

Vocabulary
minute hand
hour hand
o'clock

Write the missing numbers on the clock.

minute hand

hour hand

The time is 4 o'clock.

Connect

Use a 🕐. Show each time.
Trace the hour hand. Write the time.

1. _____9_____ o'clock

2. _____ o'clock

3. _____ o'clock

Explain It • Daily Reasoning

How are the minute hand and the hour hand different?

Use a . Show each time.
Trace the hour hand. Write the time.

1.

4 _____ o'clock

2.

_____ o'clock

3.

_____ o'clock

4.

_____ o'clock

5.

_____ o'clock

6.

_____ o'clock

Problem Solving
Visual Thinking

Write the time.

7.

_____ o'clock

8.

_____ o'clock

Write About It ● Write about what
you do at 2 o'clock on a school day.

HOME ACTIVITY • At times on the hour, have your child show you the minute hand and the hour
hand on a clock and tell what time it is.

Problem Solving Skill
Use Estimation

Vocabulary
minute

How long is a minute?
You can estimate it.

Close your eyes.

Estimate when 1 minute has passed. Raise your hand.

Was your estimate too long or too short?
Try again. Was your estimate closer this time?

About how long would it take?
Circle your estimate.
Then act it out to check.

1. snap your fingers

more than a minute

less than a minute

2. wave goodbye

more than a minute

less than a minute

3. write a story

more than a minute

less than a minute

PROBLEM SOLVING

About how long would it take?
Circle your estimate.
Then act it out to check.

1. write 1 to 50

(more than a minute)

less than a minute

2. clap your hands

more than a minute

less than a minute

3. draw a picture

more than a minute

less than a minute

4. say your name

more than a minute

less than a minute

5. read a book

more than a minute

less than a minute

6. write your name

more than a minute

less than a minute

⬠ **HOME ACTIVITY** • Have your child name an activity that he or she thinks will take about one minute. Time the activity to see if it takes about one minute, more than one minute, or less than one minute.

Time to the Hour

HANDS ON **Explore**

These clocks show time to the hour .

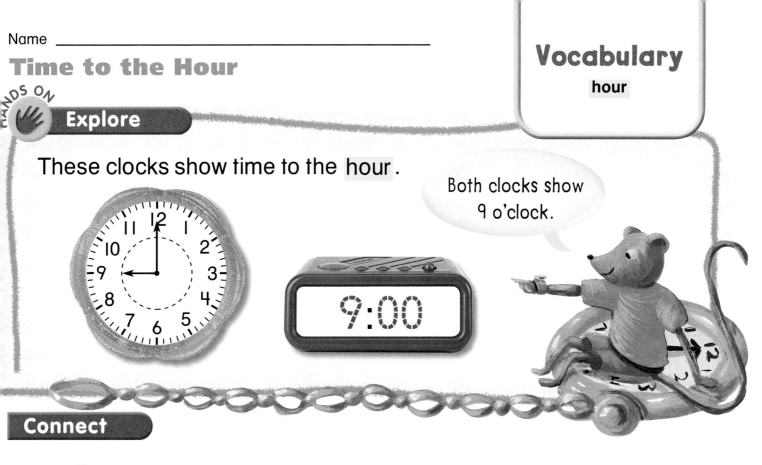

Both clocks show
9 o'clock.

9:00

Connect

Use a 🕐. Show each time. Write the time.

1.

12:00

2.

:

3.

:

4.

:

5.

:

6.

:

Explain It • Daily Reasoning

How far does each clock hand move in one hour?

Use a . Show each time. Write the time.

1.

11:00

2.

:

3.

:

4.

:

5.

:

6.

:

Problem Solving
Mental Math

Solve. Write the time.

7. Matt wakes up at 6 o'clock.
   Linda wakes up 1 hour later.
   What time does Linda wake up?

   _____ o'clock

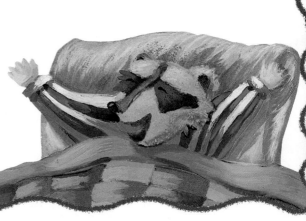

 Write About It • Look at Exercise 7.
You wake up 3 hours later than Matt.
What time is it? Tell how you know.

Name _____

Tell Time to the Half Hour

Vocabulary

half hour

HANDS ON Explore

There are 60 minutes in an hour.

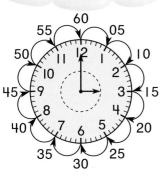

3:00 or
3 o'clock

There are 30 minutes in a half hour.

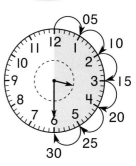

3:30 or
30 minutes after 3 o'clock

Connect

Use a 🕐 to show the time. Where are the hands?
Write the numbers. Write the time.

1. The hour hand is between __2__ and __3__.

   The minute hand is at __6__.

   __2:30__

2.

   The hour hand is between _____ and _____.

   The minute hand is at _____.

   ___:___

3.

   The hour hand is between _____ and _____.

   The minute hand is at _____.

   ___:___

Explain It ● Daily Reasoning

How far does each clock hand move in a half hour?

Use a to show the time.
Write the time.

1.

12:30

2.

___ : ___

3.

___ : ___

4.

___ : ___

5.

___ : ___

6.

___ : ___

Problem Solving

Estimation

Estimate. Circle **half hour** or **hour**.
Then measure with a clock.

	Activity	Estimate.	Measure.
7.	 **eat lunch**	half hour hour	_____
8.	**math class**	half hour hour	_____

Write About It • Write a list of things you can do in 30 minutes.

HOME ACTIVITY • At times on the half hour, have your child show you the minute hand and the hour hand on a clock and tell what time it is.

Practice Time to the Hour and Half Hour

Learn

3:00

The hour hand points to a number. The minute hand points to 12.

3:30

The hour hand points half way between numbers. The minute hand points to 6.

Check

Draw the hour hand and the minute hand.

1.

4:30

2.

9:00

3.

10:30

4.

8:00

5.

2:30

6.

11:00

Explain It • Daily Reasoning

At 1:30, where is the hour hand? Explain.

Draw the hour hand and the minute hand.

1.

1:30

2.

10:00

3.

8:30

4.

6:00

5.

12:30

6.

5:30

7.

9:30

8.

2:00

9.

11:30

Problem Solving

Algebra

10. Continue the pattern.
   Write the times that are missing.

   1:00, 1:30, 2:00, __:__, __:__, 3:30, __:__, __:__

 Write About It • Look at Exercise 10.
What is the pattern?

🔺 **HOME ACTIVITY** • At times on the hour, have your child read the time on a clock and then tell what time it will be in half an hour.

Extra Practice

Write the time.

1.

_____ o'clock

2.

_____ o'clock

3.

_____ o'clock

4.

5.

6.

7.

____ : ____

8.

____ : ____

9.

____ : ____

Problem Solving

10. About how long would it take to write the alphabet? Circle your estimate.

more than a minute

less than a minute

Name _____

✔Review/Test

Concepts and Skills
Write the time.

1.

_____ o'clock

2.

_____ o'clock

3.

_____ o'clock

4.

5.

6.

7.

: _____

8.

: _____

9.

: _____

Problem Solving

10. About how long would it take to write the numbers from 1 to 100? Circle your estimate.

more than a minute

less than a minute

Name _____

Choose the answer for questions 1–3.

1. Which object has 1 face?

   ○   ○   ○   ○

2. Which takes less than 1 minute?

   write your   write a story   eat lunch   read a book
   name

   ○   ○   ○   ○

3. Which clock shows the same time?

Show What You Know

4. Draw the hour hand and the minute hand on the clock.

   ○   ○

   ○   ○

Fill in the blanks to explain where the hands belong.

The hour hand is between

_____ and _____.

The minute hand is at _____.

MATH GAME

Clock Switch

Play with a partner.

You will need

25 ●   25 ○

1. One player uses ●. The other player uses ○.

2. Your partner picks any space.

3. You show that time on the other kind of clock.

4. If you are correct, put a counter there.

5. Play until all the spaces are covered.

6. The player with more counters wins.

25 Time and Calendar

FUN FACTS

Helper dogs begin training for 4 months at their school. Then they train 1 more month with their new owner.

Theme: All in My Day

Name _____

✔️ Check What You Know

Morning, Afternoon, and Evening

Identify the times of day.
Circle the time of day that is missing.

Use a Calendar: Identify Parts

DECEMBER						
Sunday	Monday	Tuesday	Wednesday	Thursday	Friday	Saturday
			1	2		4
5	6		8	9	10	11
12	13	14	15	16	17	
19	20	21	22	23	24	25
	27	28	29	30	31	

Fill in the missing numbers.
Circle the name of the month.
Color the first day of the month red.

Count the Mondays. _____   Count the Thursdays. _____

Use this page to review important skills needed for this chapter.

Name _____

Use a Calendar

Learn

These are the months
of the year in order.

This month is May.

Check

Use the calendar to answer the questions.

1. How many days are in a week?   _____ days

2. What day of the week is May 14?   _____

3. How many days are in May?   _____ days

4. What month comes before May?   _____

5. What is the first month of the year?   _____

Explain It • Daily Reasoning

How many months are left in the year after
the month of May? Tell how you know.

Fill in the calendar for next month.
Use the calendar to answer the questions.

Sunday	Monday	Tuesday	Wednesday	Thursday	Friday	Saturday

1. Color the Tuesdays 🖍 .

2. Color the Saturdays 🖍 .

3. What day of the week is the thirtieth? _____

4. On what day does the month end? _____

5. What is the date of the first Thursday? _____

6. How many days are in the month? _____ days

Problem Solving

Application

Look at the calendar above.
Suppose today is the twentieth.

7. What day of the week was yesterday? Circle it in 🖍 .

8. What day of the week is tomorrow? Circle it in 🖍 .

Write About It • Write about your favorite day of the week. Tell why it is your favorite.

 HOME ACTIVITY • Have your child draw pictures of special events in his or her life and label each with the month of the year in which it happens.

Name _____

Daily Events

Learn

I do this in the
morning.

I do this in the
afternoon.

I do this in the
evening.

Check

Draw pictures of things you do
in the morning, in the afternoon,
and in the evening.

Afternoon

Morning

Evening

Explain It • Daily Reasoning

How are the things you do in the morning
different from the things you do in the evening?

1. Today is Saturday. Draw something you could do at these times.

In the morning yesterday	In the afternoon today	In the evening tomorrow

Problem Solving

Visual Thinking   Write **day** or **night**.

2.

_____

3.

_____

 Write About It • Write about something you like to do in the afternoon.

HOME ACTIVITY • Have your child list activities from his or her school day in the order in which they happened.

Name _____

Problem Solving Strategy
Make a Graph

Which time of day is the favorite of the most classmates?

UNDERSTAND

What do you want to find out?

Circle it.

PLAN

How will you solve the problem?

SOLVE

Ask 10 classmates to choose their favorite time of day. Make a tally mark for each choice. Then make a picture graph.

Our Favorite Times		Total
☀ morning		
☀ afternoon		
🌙 evening		

CHECK

Which time of day is the favorite of the most classmates?

_____

Explain.

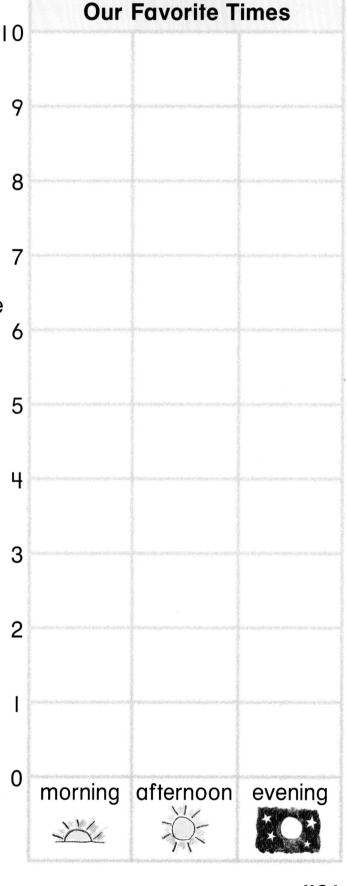

Our Favorite Times

10
9
8
7
6
5
4
3
2
1
0

morning   afternoon   evening

Ask 10 classmates to choose their favorite season. Make a tally mark for each choice. Then make a picture graph.

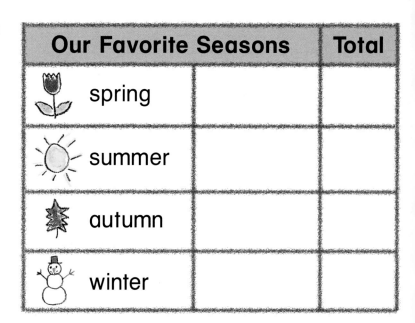

Our Favorite Seasons		Total
 spring		
summer		
autumn		
winter		

1. Draw a picture to show each person's choice.

Our Favorite Seasons

spring											
summer											
autumn											
winter											

0   1   2   3   4   5   6   7   8   9   10

2. Which season did the most classmates choose?

_____

3. Which season did the fewest classmates choose?

_____

4. How many classmates in all chose summer or winter?

_____ classmates

5. How many classmates in all chose spring or autumn?

_____ classmates

🏠 **HOME ACTIVITY** • Ask your child if there are any season totals that are greater than, less than, or equal to the total for spring.

422 four hundred twenty-two

Read a Schedule

Learn

The chart shows when each subject begins and ends.

Subject	Start	End
math		
language arts		
music		

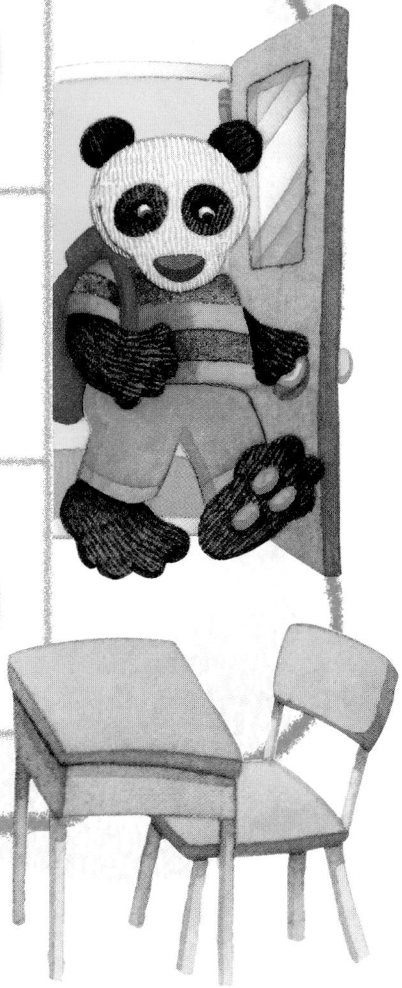

Check

Use the chart to answer the questions.

1. Which subject is before language arts?

2. Which subject is after language arts?

3. Which subject lasts the shortest time?

Explain It ● Daily Reasoning

How did you find out how long a subject lasts?

Activity	Start	End
games		
crafts		
lunch		

Use the chart to answer the questions.

1. Which activity is before crafts?

2. Which activity is after crafts?

3. Which activity lasts the longest time?

Problem Solving

Logical Reasoning Solve. You can use a 🕐 to help.

4. How long do the games
   and crafts last altogether? _____ hours

 Write About It • Look at Exercise 4.
Explain how you got your answer.

◆ **HOME ACTIVITY** • Help your child make a chart to show what he or she does on Saturday
mornings. Use times to the hour or half hour.

Problem Solving Skill
Make Reasonable Estimates

Circle the best estimate
for each activity.

1. tie a shoe

about one minute

about one hour

about one week

2. play a game of baseball

about one minute

about one hour

about one week

3. plant a seed

about one minute

about one hour

about one week

4. measure a plant

about one minute

about one hour

about one week

PROBLEM SOLVING

Problem Solving Practice

Circle the best estimate
for each activity.

1. wash your hands

(about one minute)

about one hour

about one week

2. take a vacation

about one minute

about one hour

about one week

3. put a puzzle together

about one minute

about one hour

about one week

4. eat a cracker

about one minute

about one hour

about one week

5. clean up your room

about one minute

about one hour

about one week

HOME ACTIVITY • Name an activity, such as brushing teeth. Ask your child to choose the best estimate for the amount of time that activity takes: about one minute, about one hour, or about one week.

Extra Practice

March

Sunday	Monday	Tuesday	Wednesday	Thursday	Friday	Saturday
	1	2	3	4	5	6
7	8	9	10	11	12	13

Use the calendar to answer the questions.

1. What day of the week is March 4?

2. How many Tuesdays are shown?

Use the chart to answer the question.

3. Which activity lasts the shortest time?

Activity	Start	End
storytime	(clock)	(clock)
swimming	(clock)	(clock)

Problem Solving

Circle the best estimate for the activity.

4. go for a bike ride

about one minute

about one hour

about one week

Name _____

✅ Review/Test

Concepts and Skills

April						
Sunday	Monday	Tuesday	Wednesday	Thursday	Friday	Saturday
				1	2	3
4	5	6	7	8	9	10

Use the calendar to answer the questions.

1. On what day does the month begin?

_____

2. What day of the week is April 5?

_____

Use the chart to answer the question.

3. Which subject lasts the longest time?

_____

Subject	Start	End
math	12:00	12:00
science	11:55	12:30

Problem Solving

Circle the best estimate for the activity.

4. paint a picture

about one minute

about one hour

about one week

Name _____

Getting Ready for the EOG Test
Chapters 1-25

Choose the answer for questions 1 – 4.

1. 4 children share a muffin. Each gets an equal part. Which shows how the muffin is cut?

 ○    ○   ○   ○

2. Which day comes after Friday?

Monday	Tuesday	Friday	Saturday
○	○	○	○

3. Which is the best estimate?
   About how long does it take to play a soccer game?

about 1 minute	about 1 hour	about 1 week
○	○	○

4. Which subject lasts the shortest amount of time?

   math ○   music ○

Subject	Start	End
music		
math		

Show What You Know

5. Draw pictures to explain something you do in the morning, in the afternoon, and in the evening.

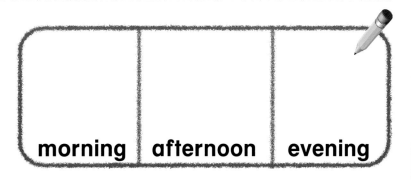

| morning | afternoon | evening |

IT'S IN THE BAG
Brown-Bag Grandfather Clock

PROJECT You will make a grandfather clock to practice telling time.

You Will Need

- Brown paper bag
- Crayons
- Glue
- Scissors
- Brass fastener
- Pattern tracer
- Blackline patterns

Directions

1 Trace around the clock outline. Then trace over your lines and add details.

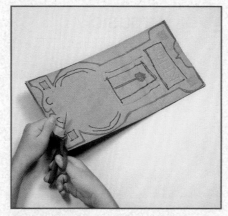

2 Cut out the top part of the clock, the clock face, and the hands.

3 Glue on the face.

4 Use a fastener to attach the hands.

5 Practice telling the time with your clock.

Is It Time?

written by Lucy Floyd
illustrated by Liz Conrad

🔷 This book will help me review telling time.

This book belongs to _____.

It can't be time so soon!
Tick-tock. Tick-tock. Tick-tock.
Do I need to get up now?

Yes! It's _____ o'clock!

_____ : _____

A half hour later . . .

I like to walk to school.
I walk just one short block.
Is it time for school to start?

Yes! It's _____ o'clock!

A half hour later . . .

We do our math in school
until we hear a knock.
Is it time to go to art?

Yes! It's ____ o'clock!

A half hour later . . .

When school is out, we play.
I show a friend my rock.
Is it time for me to go?

Yes! It's _____ o'clock!

_____ : _____

A half hour later . . .

Dad cooks some beans for us.
He stirs them in a wok.
Is it time for supper now?

Yes! It's _____ o'clock!

A half hour later . . .

I sit with Mom at night.
We like to sing and rock.
Is it time to read a book?

Yes! It's _____ o'clock!

A half hour later . . .

**Now it's time to
go to sleep . . .**

Tick-tock. Tick-tock.

Name —————————————————————————

PROBLEM SOLVING IN NORTH CAROLINA

Raleigh, NC

At the State Fair

The North Carolina State Fair takes place in Raleigh. You can see arts and crafts, animals, and shows.

You use tickets to go on rides or see shows.

Use ● to solve.

Draw a picture to show the answer.

Write the numbers.

1 Kyle and Viv have 8 tickets. What is each friend's fair share?

Kyle   Viv

_____ tickets   _____ tickets

2 Mr. Casson has 12 tickets. He gives 3 tickets to each child. How many children will get tickets?

_____ children

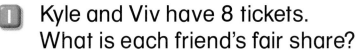

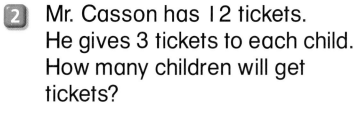

CHALLENGE

Writing Fractions

What fraction is shaded?

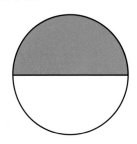 **1** part is shaded out of **2** equal parts.

 **1** part **3** equal parts

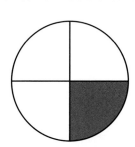 **1** part **4** equal parts

Is the shaded part $\frac{1}{2}$, $\frac{1}{4}$, or $\frac{1}{3}$?
Write the fraction.

1.
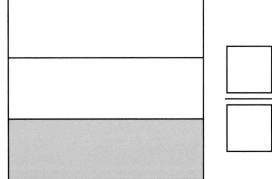

2.
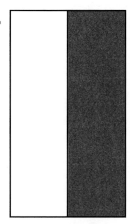

3.
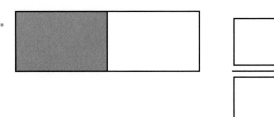

4.
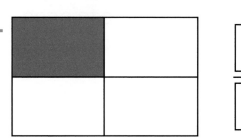

✅ Study Guide and Review

Vocabulary

Circle the **penny** . Circle the **dime** .
Circle the **quarter** . Circle the **nickel** .

1.

Skills and Concepts

Count the coins. Write the amount.

2.

_____ ¢, _____ ¢, _____ ¢, _____ ¢, _____ ¢   ¢

3.

_____ ¢, _____ ¢, _____ ¢, _____ ¢, _____ ¢   ¢

Use coins. Show the amount in two ways. Draw and label
the coins. Circle the way that uses fewer coins.

4.

55¢

Draw and label the coins. Write how many.

5. Show how many dimes equal 1 dollar.

_____ dimes = 1 dollar

Write the time.

6.

7.

8.

Color one part. Circle the fraction for the shaded part.

9.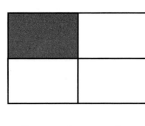

$\dfrac{1}{2}$ $\dfrac{1}{3}$ $\dfrac{1}{4}$

10.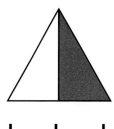

$\dfrac{1}{2}$ $\dfrac{1}{3}$ $\dfrac{1}{4}$

11.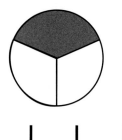

$\dfrac{1}{2}$ $\dfrac{1}{3}$ $\dfrac{1}{4}$

Problem Solving

Circle the best estimate for the activity.

12. take a walk in the park.

about one minute

about one hour

about one week

Performance Assessment

Party Favors

Ed had these hats and blowers to give to friends at his party.

Choose one of the objects in the picture.

Use a fraction to tell what part of a group the object is.

Show your work.

Draw a picture to show the group.
Color the object you chose.

What part of the group does your fraction show?

PERFORMANCE ASSESSMENT

TECHNOLOGY

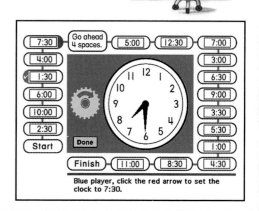

The Learning Site •
Willy the Watchdog

1. Go to **www.harcourtschool.com**.

2. Click on 🐶 .

3. Play with a friend. **Begin ▶**

4. Set the clock to match each time.

5. Play again.

Practice and Problem Solving

Write the time.

1.

3:00

2.

_____:_____

3.

_____:_____

Draw the hour hand and the minute hand.

4.

`11:00`

5.

`2:30`

6.

`6:30`

---

7. Draw the hands on the clock to show
   30 minutes later than 5:00.

Dear Family,

In Unit 5 we learned about money, time, and fractions. Here is a game for us to play together. This game will give me a chance to share what I have learned.

Love,

_____

Directions

1. Put your game piece at START.
2. Your partner hides 3 pennies in one hand and 2 pennies in the other.
3. Tap on one of your partner's hands. Your partner opens that hand.
4. Count the pennies. Move forward that many spaces.
5. Tell about the picture you land on.
   - Show the value with coins.
   - Tell what fraction is shown.
   - Tell what time the clock shows.
6. Take turns.
7. The first person to get to END wins.

Materials

- pile of pennies, nickels, dimes, and quarters
- 2 game pieces or 2 rocks

Tell About It

LOOKING FORWARD
SCHOOL HOME CONNECTION

Dear Family,

During the next few weeks, we will learn about measurement. We will also learn about adding and subtracting 2-digit numbers. Here is important math vocabulary and a list of books to share.

Love,

_____

Vocabulary Power

An inch is a customary unit for measuring short lengths.

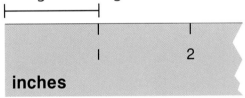

inches

A foot is a customary unit for measuring longer lengths.

This bag of sugar weighs 1 pound.

A cup is a customary unit for measuring how much an object holds.

BOOKS TO SHARE

To read about measurement and about 2-digit numbers with your child, look for these books in your library.

Koala Lou,
by Mem Fox,
Harcourt, 1994.

Stone Soup,
by Ann McGovern,
Scholastic, 1986.

Lulu's Lemonade,
by Barbara deRubertis,
Kane Press, 2000.

One Hundred Hungry Ants,
by Elinor J. Pinczes,
Houghton Mifflin, 1999.

Visit *The Learning Site* **for additional ideas and activities. www.harcourtschool.com**

Length

FUN FACTS

You can make a 100 day paper chain by cutting 10 strips of paper all 1 inch by 9 inches in 10 different colors.

✓ Check What You Know

Compare Length

Circle the longer object.
Draw a line under the shorter object.

1.
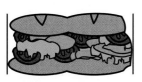
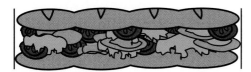

2.

3.

4.

Order Length

Circle the objects that are in order from shortest to longest, starting at the top.

5.
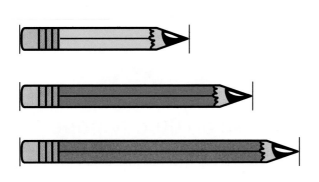

6.
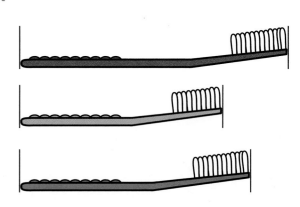

Name _____

Compare Lengths

HANDS ON ✋ Explore

These paper strips are in order
from shortest to longest.

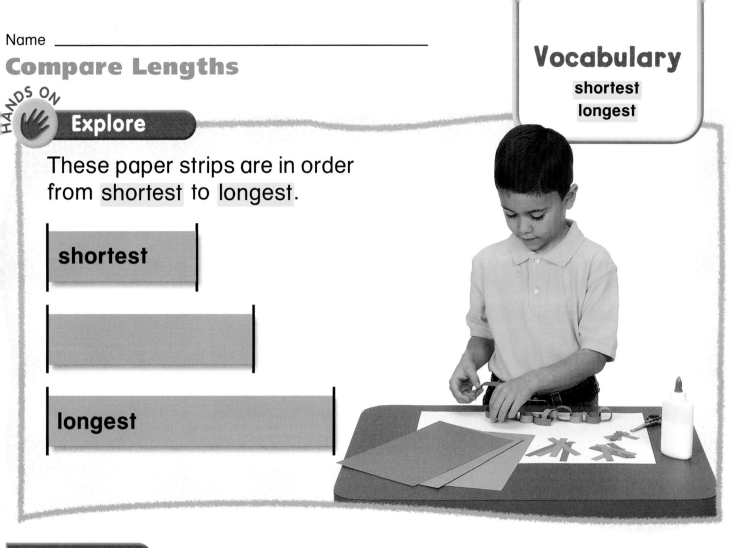

| shortest |
| longest |

Connect

Put three paper strips in order from shortest to longest.
Draw them.

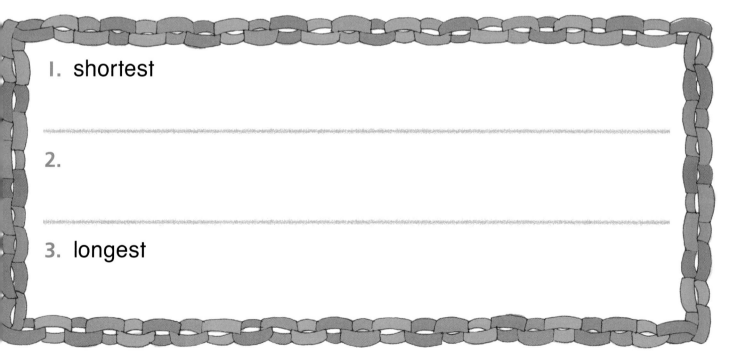

1. shortest

2.

3. longest

Explain It ● Daily Reasoning

In what other way could you put the paper
strips in order?

Use real objects. Cut yarn to show each length. Use different colors. Then compare the pieces of yarn. Tell which object is the longest and which is the shortest.

Circle the object to answer the question.

1. Which is longer?

2. Which is shorter?

3. Which is longer?

4. Which is the longest?

Problem Solving
Visual Thinking

5. Circle the string that is longer. Use real string to check.

Write About It • Look at Exercise 5. Explain your answer.

 HOME ACTIVITY • Give your child three small objects of different lengths. Ask him or her to put them in order from shortest to longest.

Name _____

Use Nonstandard Units

Explore

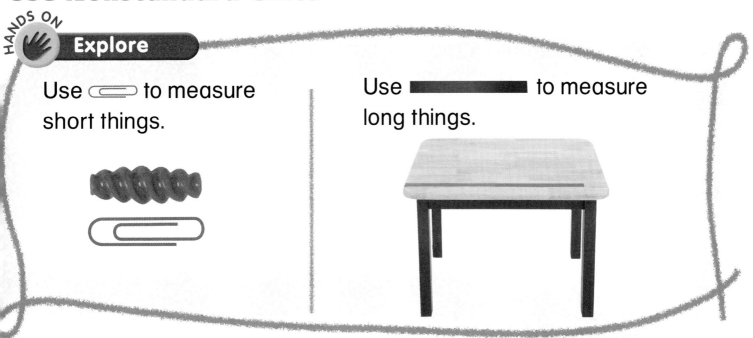

Use ⬭ to measure short things.

Use ▬▬▬ to measure long things.

Connect

Use real objects. Circle the unit you would use to measure. Then measure.

	Object	Unit	Measurement
1.	(desk)	⬭ ▬▬▬	about _____
2.	(scissors)	⬭ ▬▬▬	about _____
3.	(bookshelf)	⬭ ▬▬▬	about _____
4.	(pencil)	⬭ ▬▬▬	about _____

Explain It ● Daily Reasoning

How do you decide which unit to choose?

Use real objects and ⬭ .
Estimate. Then measure.
Circle the shortest object with 🖍 .
Circle the longest object with 🖍 .

	Object	Estimate	Measurement
1.		about _____ ⬭	about _____ ⬭
2.		about _____ ⬭	about _____ ⬭
3.		about _____ ⬭	about _____ ⬭
4.		about _____ ⬭	about _____ ⬭

Problem Solving

Logical Reasoning

5. Circle your answer.

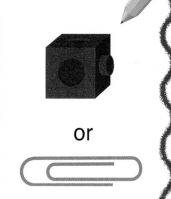

Carol measured with ⬭ .
Then she measured with ⬛ .
Did she use more ⬭ or ⬛ ?

or

⬭

 Write About It • Look at Exercise 5.
Draw an object that is longer. Draw an object
that is shorter.

⬠ **HOME ACTIVITY** • Give your child some paper clips or other small objects that are all the same
length. Have him or her use them to measure things around the house.

Name _____

Inches

HANDS ON
Explore

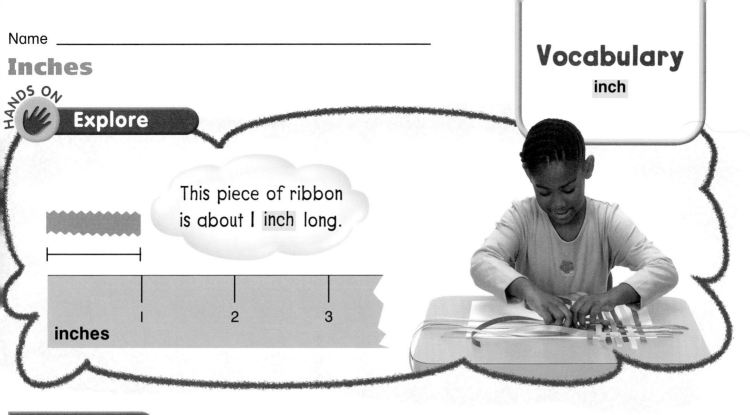

This piece of ribbon is about 1 inch long.

inches

Connect

Use an inch ruler to measure.
Circle the longest ribbon.
Underline the shortest ribbon.

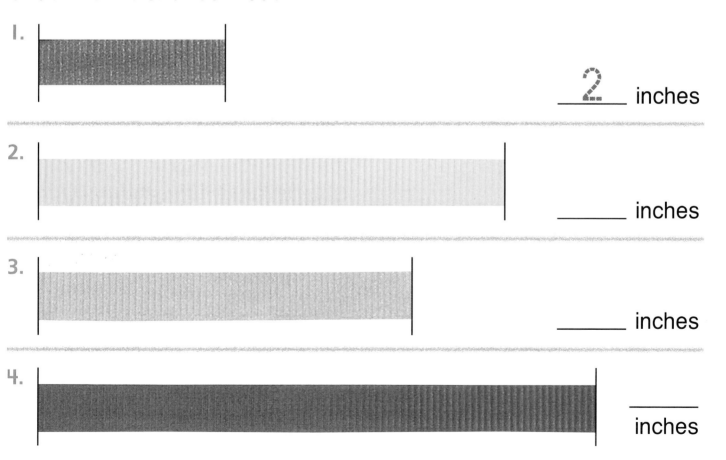

1. ___2___ inches

2. _____ inches

3. _____ inches

4. _____ inches

Explain It • Daily Reasoning

How did you know which ribbons were
the longest and the shortest?

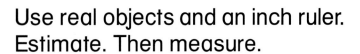

Practice and Problem Solving

Use real objects and an inch ruler.
Estimate. Then measure.

	Object	Estimate	Measurement
1.		about _____ inches	about _____ inches
2.		about _____ inches	about _____ inches
3.		about _____ inches	about _____ inches
4.		about _____ inches	about _____ inches

Problem Solving

Estimation

5. Rita's pencil is 6 inches long.
   About how long is Ben's pencil?

Rita's pencil

Ben's pencil   about _____ inches

 Write About It • Look at Exercise 5.
Explain your estimate.

HOME ACTIVITY • Have your child estimate the lengths in inches of some small objects. Together, use a ruler to check.

Inches and Feet

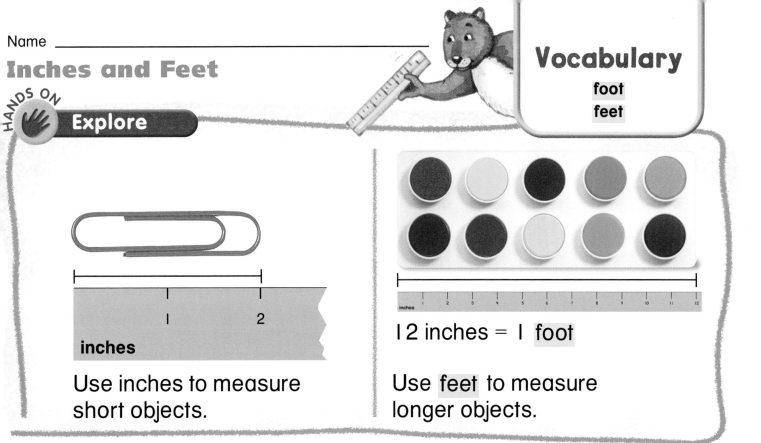

Vocabulary

foot
feet

HANDS ON
Explore

Use inches to measure short objects.

inches

12 inches = 1 **foot**

Use **feet** to measure longer objects.

Connect

Use real objects. Circle the units you would use to measure.

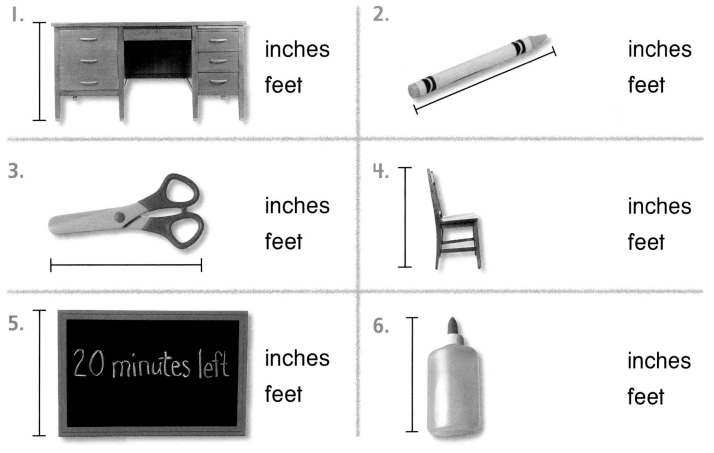

1. inches
    feet

2. inches
    feet

3. inches
    feet

4. inches
    feet

5. inches
    feet

6. inches
    feet

Explain It • Daily Reasoning

Estimate the measurements of the door. How could you check?

About how long is the real object?
Circle the answer that makes sense.

THINK:
A paper clip is about 1 inch. Your math book is about 1 foot.

1.

6 inches

6 feet

2.

1 inch

1 foot

3.

12 inches

12 feet

4.

4 inches

4 feet

5.

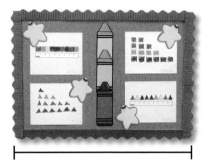

3 inches

3 feet

6.

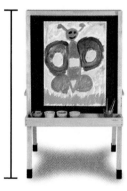

5 inches

5 feet

Problem Solving
Application

7. Look around your classroom. Draw one object you can measure in feet. Draw one object you can measure in inches.

 Write About It • Look at Exercise 7. Write a sentence about each of the objects you drew. Use the words **feet** and **inches**.

 HOME ACTIVITY • Gather some objects of different lengths. Have your child choose the objects that can be measured in feet.

Name _____

Centimeters

HANDS ON **Explore**

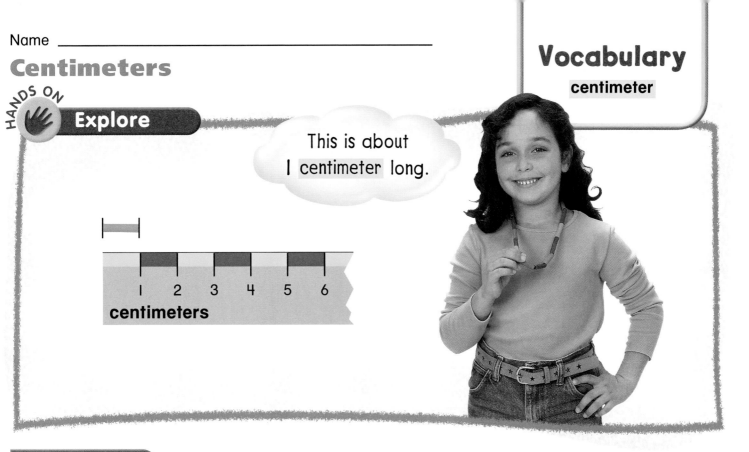

This is about
I centimeter long.

Connect

Use a centimeter ruler to measure.
Circle the longest object. Underline the shortest object.

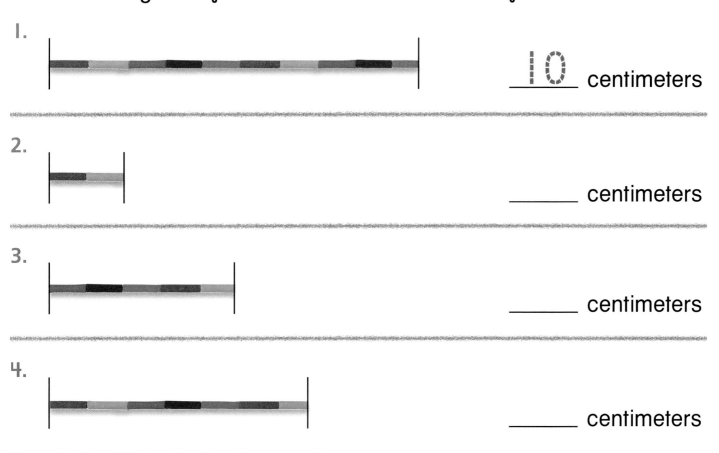

1. _____10_____ centimeters

2. _____ centimeters

3. _____ centimeters

4. _____ centimeters

Explain It • Daily Reasoning

How did you know which objects were the
longest and the shortest?

Use real objects and a centimeter ruler.
Estimate. Then measure.

Object	Estimate	Measurement
1.	about _____ centimeters	about _____ centimeters
2.	about _____ centimeters	about _____ centimeters
3.	about _____ centimeters	about _____ centimeters
4.	about _____ centimeters	about _____ centimeters

Problem Solving

Estimation

5. Anna's string of beads is 10 centimeters long.
   About how long is Tia's string of beads?

Anna's string

Tia's string

about _____ centimeters

 Write About It • Look at Exercise 5.
How did you decide how long Tia's string
of beads is?

HOME ACTIVITY • Give your child two objects of different lengths. Tell him or her how long in
centimeters one of them is. Have your child tell you which object he or she thinks is that length.

Problem Solving Skill
Make Reasonable Estimates

Lydia makes necklaces.
About how many beads long is the string?

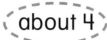

about 2	about 4	about 6
2 beads long is too short.	4 beads long is about right.	6 beads long is too long.

About how many beads long is the string?
Circle the answer that makes sense.

1.

about 5   about 8   about 10

2.

about 2   about 6   about 10

3.

about 3   about 10   about 15

4.

about 3   about 5   about 10

PROBLEM SOLVING

THINK:
Look at the choices to help you decide.

About how many beads long is the string?
Circle the answer that makes sense.

1.

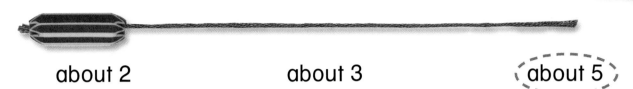

about 2   about 3   (about 5)

2.

about 5   about 10   about 15

3.

about 2   about 3   about 7

4.

about 3   about 10   about 15

5.

about 2   about 4   about 6

 HOME ACTIVITY • Ask your child to explain how he or she chose each answer.

Name _____

Extra Practice

Circle the string that is the shortest.

1.

Use the real object and . Estimate. Then measure.

2.

Estimate

about _____ 🖇

Measurement

about _____ 🖇

Use the real object and an inch ruler. Estimate. Then measure.

3.

Estimate

about _____ inches

Measurement

about _____ inches

Use the real object and a centimeter ruler. Estimate. Then measure.

4.

Estimate   about _____ centimeters

Measurement   about _____ centimeters

Problem Solving

About how many beads long is the string?
Circle the answer that makes sense.

5.

about 2   about 6   about 10

Name _____

✓Review/Test

Concepts and Skills
Circle the string that is the longest.

1.

Use the real object and ⌒. Estimate. Then measure.

2.

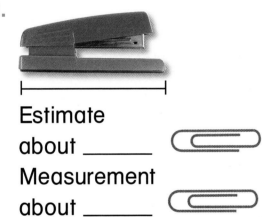

Estimate
about _____ ⌒

Measurement
about _____ ⌒

Use the real object and an inch ruler. Estimate. Then measure.

3.

Estimate
about _____ inches

Measurement
about _____ inches

Use the real object and a centimeter ruler. Estimate. Then measure.

4.

Estimate   about _____ centimeters

Measurement   about _____ centimeters

Problem Solving
About how many beads long is the string?
Circle the answer that makes sense.

5.

about 3   about 5   about 7

Getting Ready for the ★EOG Test
Chapters 1–26

Choose the answer for questions 1– 5.

1. Which crayon is the shortest?

○   ○
○   ○

2. Use a ⊂⊃ to measure.
About how long is the paint brush?

2	3	4	8
○	○	○	○

3. What fraction does the green part show?

$\dfrac{1}{2}$ $\dfrac{1}{3}$ $\dfrac{1}{4}$ $\dfrac{1}{5}$
○   ○   ○   ○

4. Which unit would you use to measure ⬤ RED ▷ ?

○ inch

○ centimeter

○ foot

5. Which is the best estimate?
About how many beads long is the string?

4	5	6	7
○	○	○	○

Show What You Know

6. Draw a ruler that is 3 inches
long. Mark each inch. Use your
ruler to measure your thumb.
Draw a line to show how long it is.

Is your thumb longer or shorter
than your ruler? Circle to explain.

EOG TEST PREP

MATH GAME

Ruler Race

Play with a partner.

1. Put your  at START.

2. Spin the .

3. Use a ruler to find an object that many inches long.

4. Move your that many spaces.

5. The first player to get to END wins.

You will need

2

inch ruler

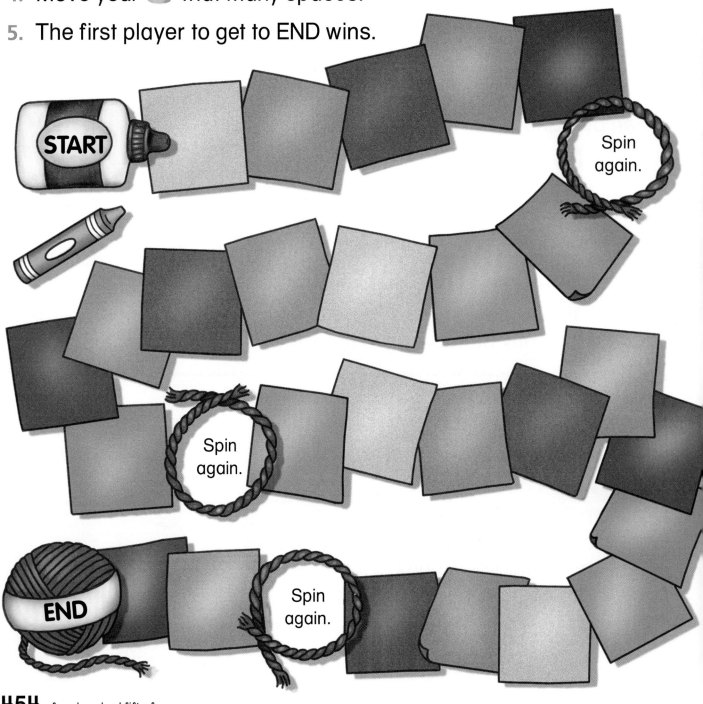

Weight

FUN FACTS

Baby chicks weigh about 1 pound, which is about the same as 2 large apples.

Name _____

✅ Check What You Know

Compare Weight

Circle the object that is heavier.
Mark an X on the object that is lighter.

1.

2.

3.

4.

5.

6.

Use this page to review important skills needed for this chapter.

Name _____

Use a Balance

Vocabulary
balance

HANDS ON Explore

It takes 6 bears to **balance** the crayons.

It takes a lot of paper clips to balance the crayons.

Connect

Use a  and real objects.
Circle the unit you would use to measure.
Then measure.

Object	Unit	Measurement
1. ✂	▭ 🧸	about _____
2. 🪙	▭ 🧸	about _____
3. ▪	▭ 🧸	about _____
4. glue	▭ 🧸	about _____

Explain It • Daily Reasoning

How did you decide which unit to use?

About how many ⬭ does it take to balance?
Use real objects, a ⚖, and ⬭.
Estimate. Then measure.

	Object	Estimate	Measurement
1.		about _____ ⬭	about _____ ⬭
2.		about _____ ⬭	about _____ ⬭
3.		about _____ ⬭	about _____ ⬭
4.		about _____ ⬭	about _____ ⬭

5. Circle the heaviest object in blue.
6. Circle the lightest object in red.

Problem Solving

Logical Reasoning

7. 2 boxes of ⬭ balance a 🦆.

6 boxes of ⬭ balance a 📖.

How many 🦆 will balance the 📖? _____ 🦆

 Write About It • Look at Exercise 5.
Draw a picture to show your work.

⬠ HOME ACTIVITY • Give your child some cans or boxes. Ask him or her to put them in order from heaviest to lightest.

Name _____

Pounds

Explore

This bag of sugar weighs about one pound.

This bag of flour weighs about 5 pounds.

Vocabulary

pound

Connect

Look at each object.
Circle the better estimate.

1.

about 1 pound

about 10 pounds

2.

about 1 pound

about 10 pounds

3.

about 1 pound

about 10 pounds

4.

about 1 pound

about 10 pounds

Explain It • Daily Reasoning

Explain how you estimated what the objects would weigh.

Find three items to weigh.
Draw them. Estimate how much
each object weighs. Then measure.

	Object	Estimate	Measurement
1.		about _____ pounds	about _____ pounds
2.		about _____ pounds	about _____ pounds
3.		about _____ pounds	about _____ pounds

4. Circle the heaviest item in blue.

5. Circle the lightest item in red.

Problem Solving
Visual Thinking

Does each object weigh more than or less than 1 pound?
Circle the better estimate.

6.

more than 1 pound	more than 1 pound	more than 1 pound
less than 1 pound	less than 1 pound	less than 1 pound

 Write About It • Draw three things that
weigh less than a pound. Tell how you know.

🏠 **HOME ACTIVITY** • Ask your child to read you the weights, in pounds, of some grocery items.

Name _____

Kilograms

Explore

This large book is about 1 kilogram.

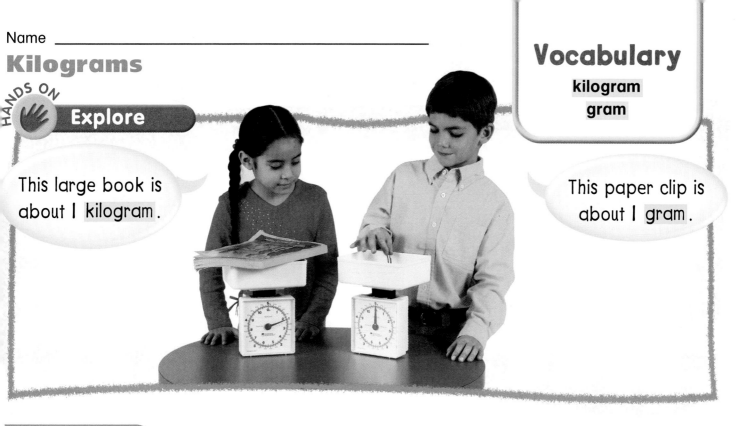

Vocabulary

kilogram
gram

This paper clip is about 1 gram.

Connect

Circle the unit you would use to measure the real object.

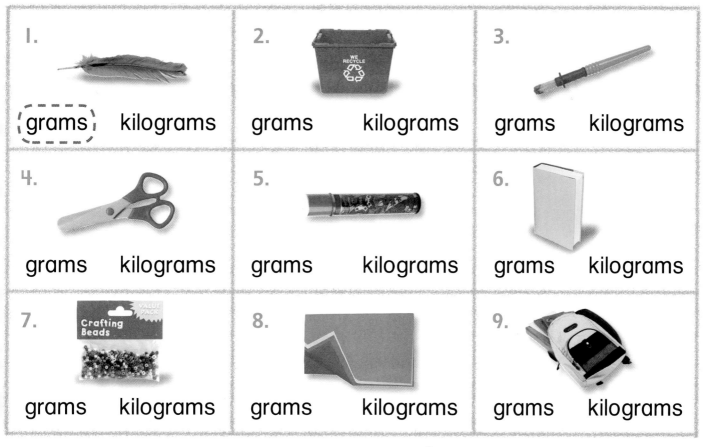

1. grams   kilograms

2. grams   kilograms

3. grams   kilograms

4. grams   kilograms

5. grams   kilograms

6. grams   kilograms

7. grams   kilograms

8. grams   kilograms

9. grams   kilograms

Explain It • Daily Reasoning

What kind of objects did you choose to measure in grams? Why?

Estimate how much the real object will measure.
Use grams or kilograms. Then measure.

	Object	Estimate	Measurement
1.		about _____ kilograms	about _____ kilograms
2.		about _____ grams	about _____ grams
3.		about _____ kilograms	about _____ kilograms
4.		about _____ grams	about _____ grams

Problem Solving

Visual Thinking

Think about the real objects. Which would you
measure in grams? Circle in .

5.

 |  |

 Write About It • Draw three things
that weigh more than 1 kilogram.
Tell how you know.

⬟ **HOME ACTIVITY** • Ask your child to read you the weights, in grams, of some grocery items.

Name _____

Problem Solving Strategy
Predict and Test

How many grams is this marker?

UNDERSTAND

What do you want to find out?
How many grams is the marker?

PLAN

How will you solve the problem?
I will predict how many grams it is.
To test, I will use the balance to measure.

SOLVE

Predict.
Then use large ⟨⟩ as grams
to balance.

THINK:
A large paper clip is
about 1 gram.

Predict _____ grams   Test __9__ grams

CHECK

Was your prediction close?
Explain.

How many grams is the object?
Use the real object and ⟨⟩.

Predict. Then test.

1.

  Predict _____ grams   Test _____ grams

PROBLEM SOLVING

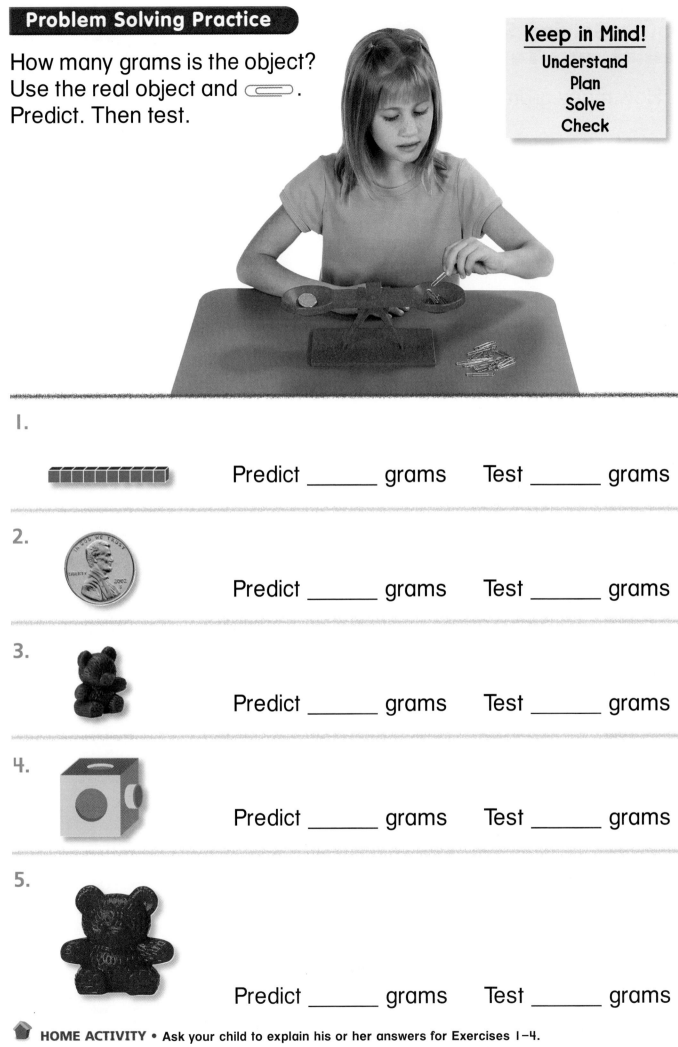

Problem Solving Practice

How many grams is the object?
Use the real object and ⊂▭▭ .
Predict. Then test.

Keep in Mind!
Understand
Plan
Solve
Check

1.

Predict _____ grams   Test _____ grams

2.

Predict _____ grams   Test _____ grams

3.

Predict _____ grams   Test _____ grams

4.

Predict _____ grams   Test _____ grams

5.

Predict _____ grams   Test _____ grams

🏠 **HOME ACTIVITY** • Ask your child to explain his or her answers for Exercises 1–4.

Name _____

Extra Practice

1. Choose the unit you would use to measure.
   Circle 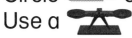 or 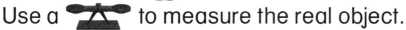.
   Use a ⚖ to measure the real object.

Object	Unit	Measurement
	📎 🧸	about _____

2. Find an object to weigh. Draw it.
   Estimate how much the object weighs.
   Then measure.

Object	Estimate	Measurement
	about _____ pounds	about _____ pounds

3. Estimate how much the real object will measure.
   Then measure.

Object	Estimate	Measurement
	about _____ kilograms	about _____ kilograms

Problem Solving

4. How many grams is the object?
   Use the real object and 📎.
   Predict. Then test.

Predict _____ grams   Test _____ grams

Review/Test

Concepts and Skills

1. Choose the unit you would use to measure.
   Circle or 🧸 .
   Use a ⚖ to measure the real object.

Object	Unit	Measurement
👟	⊂⊃ 🧸	about _____

2. Find an object to weigh. Draw it.
   Estimate how much the object weighs.
   Then measure.

Object	Estimate	Measurement
	about _____ pounds	about _____ pounds

3. Estimate how much the object measures.
   Then measure.

Object	Estimate	Measurement
📒	about _____ kilograms	about _____ kilograms

Problem Solving

4. How many grams is the object?
   Use the real object and ⊂⊃ .
   Predict. Then test.

   Predict _____ grams   Test _____ grams

Name _____

Choose the answer for questions 1– 4.

1.
$$20$$
$$-10$$

9   10   11   29
○   ○   ○   ○

2. Which object weighs about 1 kilogram?

○   ○   ○   ○

3. Which object weighs about 1 pound?

○   ○   ○   ○

4. Which is the heaviest?

1 gram   5 grams   5 grams   10 grams
○   ○   ○   ○

Show What You Know

5. How many grams is the object?
   Predict. Then test.

Predict _____ grams

Test _____ grams

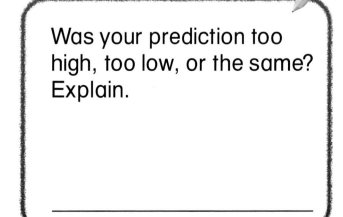

Was your prediction too high, too low, or the same? Explain.

_____

EOG TEST PREP

MATH GAME

Gram Grab

Play with a partner.

1. Put your 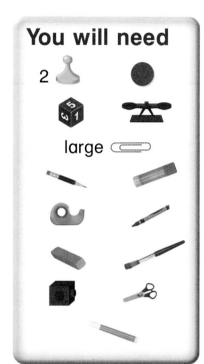 at START.

2. Toss the 🎲.

3. Move your ♟ that many spaces.

4. Measure the object shown on that space in grams.

5. Take that many ●.

6. When both players get to END, count ●.

7. The player with more ● wins.

You will need

2 ♟ ●

🎲 ⚖

large ⊂⊃

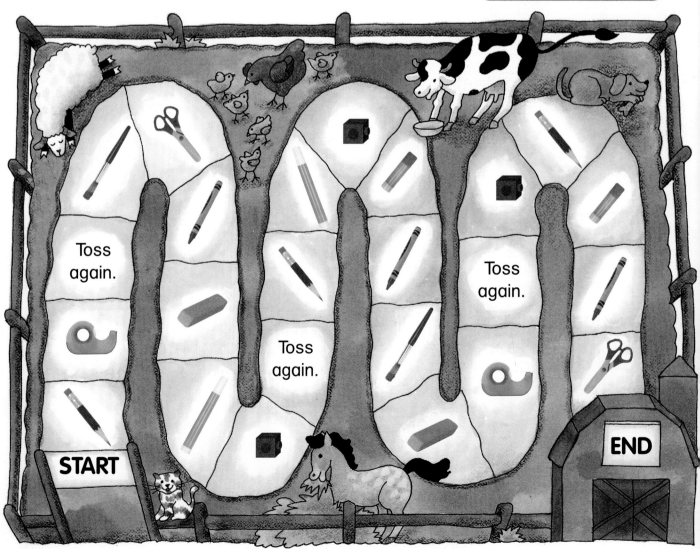

Toss again.

Toss again.

Toss again.

Toss again.

START

END

28 Capacity

FUN FACTS

Each starfish needs 30 liters of water to live in.

✓ Check What You Know

Compare Capacity

Circle the container that holds more.
Mark an X on the container that holds less.

1.

2.

3.

4.

5.

6.

Use this page to review important skills needed for this chapter.

Nonstandard Units

Explore

It took 3 of these scoops to fill the container.

It took 6 of these cups to fill the container.

Connect

Choose the unit you would use to measure.
Circle ⬤ or ⬤ . Measure.

Container	Unit	Measurement
1. Yogurt		about _____
2. ORGANIC WHOLE MILK		about _____
3. Large Curd Cottage Cheese		about _____
4.		about _____

Explain It ● Daily Reasoning

How did you decide which units to use?

Use the real container and a 🥄.
Estimate. Then measure.

	Container	Estimate	Measurement
1.		about _____ 🥄	about _____ 🥄
2.	*Margarine*	about _____ 🥄	about _____ 🥄
3.		about _____ 🥄	about _____ 🥄
4.		about _____ 🥄	about _____ 🥄

Problem Solving

Estimation

Circle your answer.

5. Which container do you think will hold the most 🥄 of rice?

 Write About It • Look at Exercise 5.
Explain how you chose your answer.

⬠ **HOME ACTIVITY •** Show your child three containers. Ask him or her to estimate which will hold the most water. Together, use a small cup or scoop to find out.

Name _____

Cups, Pints, and Quarts

HANDS ON
Explore

You can use a cup to measure how much a container holds.

This pint container will hold 2 cups.

This quart container will hold 4 cups.

Vocabulary
cup
pint
quart

Connect

Use a ⌣ and containers.
Estimate. Then measure.

	Container	Estimate	Measurement
1.		about _____ cups	about _____ cups
2.		about _____ cups	about _____ cups
3.		about _____ cups	about _____ cups
4.		about _____ cups	about _____ cups

Explain It • Daily Reasoning

Which container holds about 2 cups?
Which containers hold about 4 cups?

Estimate. Then measure.
Trace to name the size of the container.

Container	Estimate	Measurement	Size
1. MILK	about _____ cups	about _____ cups	‾‾‾‾‾‾‾ pint
2. WATER	about _____ cups	about _____ cups	‾‾‾‾‾‾‾ pint
3. Milk	about _____ cups	about _____ cups	‾‾‾‾‾‾‾ quart

Problem Solving

Logical Reasoning

4. Circle what you would use to measure a quart of milk.

5. Circle what you would use to measure a cup of juice.

Write About It • Look at Exercises 4 and 5. Explain how you decided which unit to use to measure.

 HOME ACTIVITY • Show your child three containers, and ask him or her to estimate which will hold more than a pint. Together, use a cup measure to find out.

Liters

HANDS ON Explore

This liter bottle will hold a little more than 4 cups.

This liter bottle will hold a little more than 1 quart.

Connect

Estimate whether the container holds less than or more than a liter. Then use a liter bottle to measure.

	Container	Estimate	Measurement
1.		less than a liter more than a liter	less than a liter more than a liter
2.		less than a liter more than a liter	less than a liter more than a liter
3.		less than a liter more than a liter	less than a liter more than a liter
4.		less than a liter more than a liter	less than a liter more than a liter

Explain It • Daily Reasoning

Would you use a liter bottle to fill a fish tank with water? Why or why not?

Does the container hold
less than or more than 2 liters?
Estimate. Then measure.

2 liters

a liter

	Container	Estimate	Measurement
1.		less than 2 liters more than 2 liters	less than 2 liters more than 2 liters
2.		less than 2 liters more than 2 liters	less than 2 liters more than 2 liters
3.		less than 2 liters more than 2 liters	less than 2 liters more than 2 liters

Problem Solving

Logical Reasoning

4. A liter bottle holds a little more than 4 cups.
   About how many cups will there be in
   2 liter bottles?

   about _____ cups

 Write About It • Look at Exercise 4.
Explain how you got your answer.

HOME ACTIVITY • Help your child find a 1-liter container and a 1-quart container. Ask him or her to tell you if a liter is less than or more than a quart. Then use water to check.

Temperature

Learn

A thermometer measures temperature.

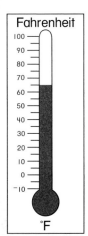

The temperature is 65 degrees.

It is __85__ °F.

It is __50__ °F.

Check

Read the thermometer.
Write the temperature.

1.
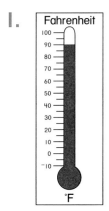

_____ °F

2.
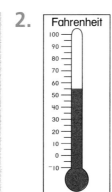

_____ °F

3.
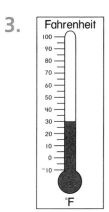

_____ °F

4.
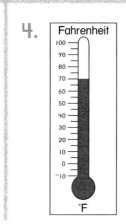

_____ °F

Explain It • Daily Reasoning

What happens to a thermometer
when the temperature gets warmer?

Read the temperature.
Color the thermometer to show the temperature.

1. **60°F**
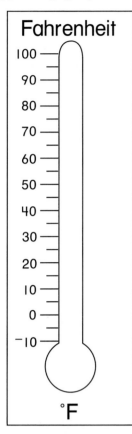

2. **20°F**
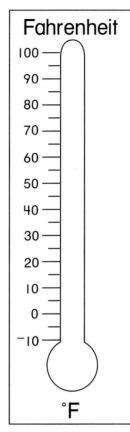

3. **75°F**
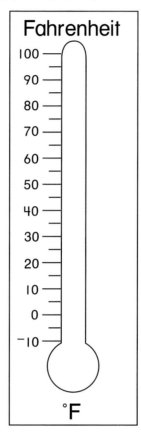

4. **95°F**
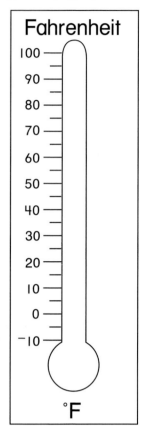

Problem Solving
Visual Thinking

5. The thermometer shows the temperature is 80 degrees. The sun goes down, and the temperature gets cooler. Circle the thermometer that shows what the temperature might be now.

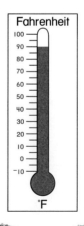
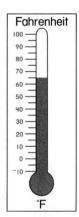

 Write About It • Tell what you would wear if the temperature was 85 degrees and what you would wear if it was 40 degrees.

HOME ACTIVITY • With your child, look at an outdoor thermometer or a weather report. Talk together about what the temperature is today.

Name _____

Problem Solving Skill
Choose the
Measuring Tool

I use different tools to measure in different ways.

Find five objects to measure in different ways.
Choose the correct tool to measure in each way.
Draw and write to complete the chart.

	What to Find Out	Object	Tool	Measurement
1.	How tall is it?			
2.	How wide is it?			
3.	How much does it hold?			
4.	How much does it weigh?			
5.	How hot or cold is it?			

Circle the correct tool to measure.

1. How tall is the plant?

2. Which book is heavier?

3. How much will the jar hold?

4. How wide is the chair?

5. Which container holds more?

6. How cold is the water?

🔶 **HOME ACTIVITY** • Give your child an object, such as a book, and ask him or her to tell about all the different ways to measure it.

Name _____

Extra Practice

1. Use the real container and a 🥄.
Estimate. Then measure.

Container	Estimate	Measurement
[cottage cheese container]	about _____ 🥄	about _____ 🥄

2. Estimate how many cups it will take to fill
the container. Then measure.

Container	Estimate	Measurement
[glass]	about _____ cups	about _____ cups

3. Estimate whether the container holds less than or
more than a liter. Then use a liter bottle to measure.

Container	Estimate	Measurement
[thermos]	less than a liter more than a liter	less than a liter more than a liter

Read the temperature.
Color the thermometer
to show the temperature.

4. 80°F

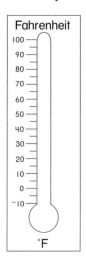

Problem Solving

5. Circle the correct tool to measure
how hot the water is.

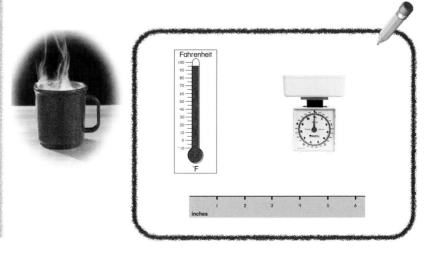

Name _____

✓ Review/Test

Concepts and Skills

1. Use the real container and a 🥄 .
   Estimate. Then measure.

Container	Estimate	Measurement
OATS	about _____ 🥄	about _____ 🥄

2. Estimate how many cups it will take to fill
   the container. Then measure.

Container	Estimate	Measurement
HALF & HALF	about _____ cups	about _____ cups

3. Estimate whether the container holds less than or
   more than a liter. Then use a liter bottle to measure.

Container	Estimate	Measurement
	less than a liter more than a liter	less than a liter more than a liter

Read the temperature.
Color the thermometer
to show the temperature.

4. 45°F

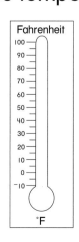

Problem Solving

5. Circle the correct tool to measure how
   tall the notebook is.

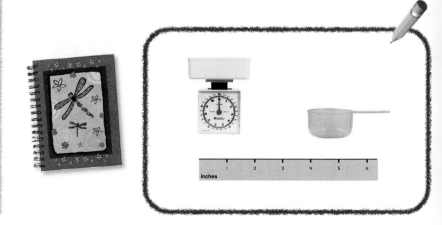

Getting Ready for the ★EOG Test
Chapters 1–28

Choose the answer for questions 1 – 5.

1. 15 − 8 = _____

    6   7   8   9
    ○   ○   ○   ○

2. Which one would you use a small  to measure?

    ○   ○   ○   ○

3. Which container holds about 1 cup?

    ○   ○   ○   ○

4. Which container holds more than 1 quart?

    ○   ○   ○   ○

5. What is the temperature?

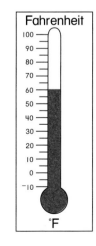

    20°F   32°F
    ⊙   ○

    60°F   90°F
    ○   ○

Show What You Know

6. How much will the glass hold? Circle the correct tool to explain how you would measure.

MATH GAME

How Many Cups?

Play with a partner.

1. Put your ♟ at START.

2. Spin the ◓.

3. Move your ♟ to the next space that matches that color.

4. Measure to find how many cups that container holds.

5. Take 1 ⬤ for each cup it holds.

6. Take turns until both players get to END.

7. The player with more counters wins.

You will need

2 ♟   70 ⬤

START

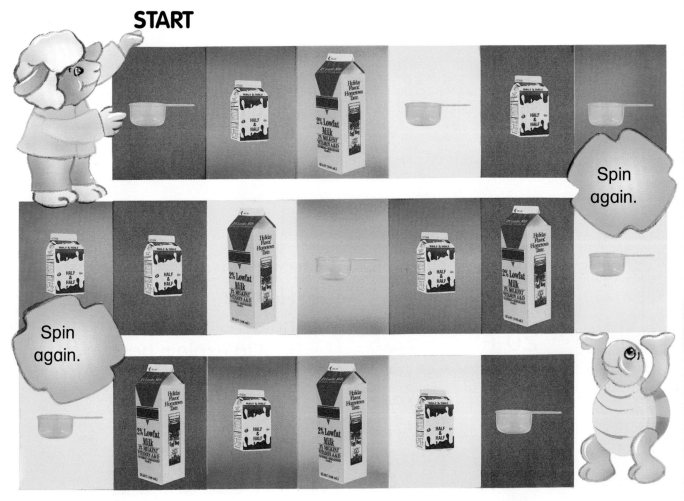

END

Adding and Subtracting 2-Digit Numbers

FUN FACTS

A toucan's huge beak is almost the length of its body which is from 13 to 25 inches long.

✅ Check What You Know

Tens and Ones to 100

Write how many tens and ones.
Write the number.

1.

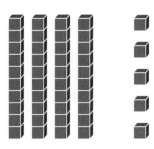

____ tens ____ ones = ____

2.

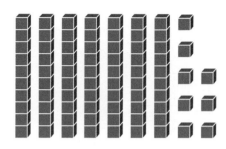

____ tens ____ ones = ____

Addition and Subtraction Facts to 20

Add or subtract.

3. $\begin{array}{r} 7 \\ +8 \\ \hline \end{array}$ 4. $\begin{array}{r} 9 \\ +7 \\ \hline \end{array}$ 5. $\begin{array}{r} 20 \\ -10 \\ \hline \end{array}$ 6. $\begin{array}{r} 18 \\ -9 \\ \hline \end{array}$ 7. $\begin{array}{r} 10 \\ +9 \\ \hline \end{array}$ 8. $\begin{array}{r} 17 \\ -9 \\ \hline \end{array}$

Fact Families to 20

Write the sum or difference. Circle the two
facts if they are in the same fact family.

9. $6 + 9 =$ _____

$16 - 9 =$ _____

10. $15 - 8 =$ _____

$15 - 7 =$ _____

11. $9 + 8 =$ _____

$17 - 9 =$ _____

12. $7 + 6 =$ _____

$14 - 7 =$ _____

Use Mental Math to Add Tens

Learn

A red panda eats 20 leaves.
Then it eats 10 more leaves.
How many leaves does it eat in all?

Start with two tens
and add one more ten.

THINK

| 2 | tens |

$$
\begin{array}{r}
20 \\
+10 \\
\hline
30
\end{array}
$$

$+$ | 1 | ten

| 3 | tens |

It eats __30__ leaves in all.

Check

Write how many tens. Then add.

1.
$$
\begin{array}{r}
30 \\
+40
\end{array}
$$

THINK
☐ tens
$+$ ☐ tens
☐ tens

2.
$$
\begin{array}{r}
50 \\
+10
\end{array}
$$

THINK
☐ tens
$+$ ☐ ten
☐ tens

3.
$$
\begin{array}{r}
20 \\
+70
\end{array}
$$

THINK
☐ tens
$+$ ☐ tens
☐ tens

4.
$$
\begin{array}{r}
40 \\
+40
\end{array}
$$

THINK
☐ tens
$+$ ☐ tens
☐ tens

Explain It • Daily Reasoning

How does knowing $7 + 2 = 9$ help
you find the sum for $70 + 20$?

$7 + 2 = 9$

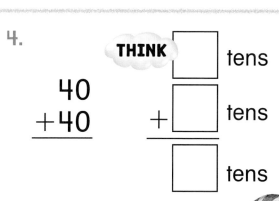

40 + 30 means
4 tens + 3 tens.

THINK

```
  40        4 tens
+ 30      + 3 tens
─────      ────────
  70        7 tens
```

Add.

1. 50 +40	2. 30 +30	3. 50 +30	4. 10 +30	5. 20 +60
6. 10 +70	7. 20 +20	8. 80 +10	9. 10 +10	10. 70 +20
11. 10 +50	12. 20 +30	13. 40 +10	14. 30 +50	15. 60 +10

Problem Solving

Visual Thinking

Draw what was added.
Complete the number sentence.

16. + =

_____ + _____ = _____

 Write About It • Look at Exercise 16.
Explain how you figured out how many tens
to add.

 HOME ACTIVITY • Ask your child to explain how to find the sum for 30 + 20.

Name _____

Add Tens and Ones

Explore

Add.   32
      + 4

	STEP 1	STEP 2	STEP 3

STEP 1

Show 32. Show 4.

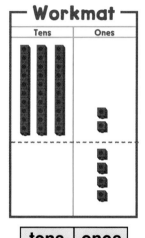

tens	ones
3	2
+	4

STEP 2

Add the ones.

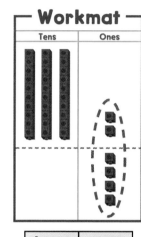

tens	ones
3	2
+	4
	6

STEP 3

Add the tens.

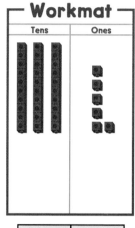

tens	ones
3	2
+	4
3	6

Connect

Use Workmat 3 and 🎲 to add. Write the sum.

1.
tens	ones
2	5
+	3

tens	ones

2.
tens	ones
4	5
+	2

tens	ones

Explain It • Daily Reasoning

How could you find the sum for
64 + 3 without using blocks?

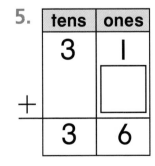

Practice and Problem Solving

Use Workmat 3 and ▪ to add.
Write the sum.

1.

tens	ones
4	1
+	4
4	5

tens	ones
‖‖‖‖	
	▪

2.

tens	ones
1	6
+	3

tens	ones
❘	▪

3.

tens	ones
3	5
+	2

tens	ones
‖‖‖	▪

4.

tens	ones
2	3
+	3

tens	ones
‖‖	▪

Problem Solving
Algebra

Write the missing numbers.

5.

tens	ones
3	1
+	□
3	6

6.

tens	ones
5	3
+	□
5	9

7.

tens	ones
2	2
+	□
2	5

8.

tens	ones
6	4
+	□
6	8

Write About It ● What are two ways you could show 19 + 1 with blocks?

HOME ACTIVITY • Ask your child to draw pictures to show how to find the sum for 24 + 5.

Name _____

Add Money

Learn

Add money amounts
the same way you add
other numbers.

Add the ones. Then add the tens.

Add numbers.   Add money.

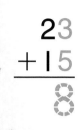

$$\begin{array}{r} 23 \\ +15 \\ \hline 8 \end{array} \qquad \begin{array}{r} 23 \\ +15 \\ \hline 38 \end{array} \qquad \begin{array}{r} 23¢ \\ +15¢ \\ \hline 8¢ \end{array} \qquad \begin{array}{r} 23¢ \\ +15¢ \\ \hline 38¢ \end{array}$$

Check

Add.

1.
$$\begin{array}{r} 32¢ \\ +27¢ \\ \hline ¢ \end{array}$$

2.
$$\begin{array}{r} 17¢ \\ +10¢ \\ \hline ¢ \end{array}$$

3.
$$\begin{array}{r} 75¢ \\ +22¢ \\ \hline ¢ \end{array}$$

4.
$$\begin{array}{r} 43¢ \\ +16¢ \\ \hline ¢ \end{array}$$

5.
$$\begin{array}{r} 55¢ \\ +31¢ \\ \hline ¢ \end{array}$$

6.
$$\begin{array}{r} 61¢ \\ +18¢ \\ \hline ¢ \end{array}$$

7.
$$\begin{array}{r} 24¢ \\ +33¢ \\ \hline ¢ \end{array}$$

8.
$$\begin{array}{r} 82¢ \\ + 6¢ \\ \hline ¢ \end{array}$$

9.
$$\begin{array}{r} 10¢ \\ +29¢ \\ \hline ¢ \end{array}$$

10.
$$\begin{array}{r} 52¢ \\ + 7¢ \\ \hline ¢ \end{array}$$

11.
$$\begin{array}{r} 53¢ \\ +15¢ \\ \hline ¢ \end{array}$$

12.
$$\begin{array}{r} 36¢ \\ +41¢ \\ \hline ¢ \end{array}$$

13.
$$\begin{array}{r} 65¢ \\ +23¢ \\ \hline ¢ \end{array}$$

14.
$$\begin{array}{r} 24¢ \\ +50¢ \\ \hline ¢ \end{array}$$

15.
$$\begin{array}{r} 32¢ \\ +47¢ \\ \hline ¢ \end{array}$$

Explain It • Daily Reasoning

How are pennies like ones?
How are dimes like tens?

Add.

1. 40¢
+50¢
90¢

2. 72¢
+23¢
___¢

3. 25¢
+24¢
___¢

4. 35¢
+ 4¢
___¢

5. 19¢
+20¢
___¢

6. 53¢
+46¢
___¢

7. 64¢
+14¢
___¢

8. 75¢
+ 3¢
___¢

9. 39¢
+50¢
___¢

10. 81¢
+17¢
___¢

11. 44¢
+33¢
___¢

12. 24¢
+42¢
___¢

13. 10¢
+ 5¢
___¢

14. 61¢
+ 8¢
___¢

15. 50¢
+25¢
___¢

Problem Solving

Algebra

Write the missing numbers.

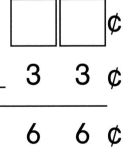

16.
  4 2 ¢
+ ☐ ☐ ¢
  6 4 ¢

17.
  ☐ ☐ ¢
+ 3 3 ¢
  6 6 ¢

18.
  3 5 ¢
+ ☐ ¢
  3 9 ¢

 Write About It • Look at Exercise 18. Tell how you can subtract to find the missing number.

 HOME ACTIVITY • Have your child add a group of 9 or fewer pennies and a group of 9 or fewer dimes.

Use Mental Math to Subtract Tens

Learn

A bird finds 40 seeds.
It eats 30 of them.
How many seeds are left?

Start with 4 tens and subtract 3 tens.

```
  40        THINK   4  tens
 -30            -   3  tens
 ──             ─────
  10                1  ten
```

There are __10__ seeds left.

Check

Write how many tens. Then subtract.

1.
```
  90     THINK    ☐  tens
 -30         -   ☐  tens
               ──────
                 ☐  tens
```

2.
```
  30     THINK    ☐  tens
 -10         -   ☐  ten
               ──────
                 ☐  tens
```

3.
```
  80     THINK    ☐  tens
 -40         +   ☐  tens
               ──────
                 ☐  tens
```

4.
```
  70     THINK    ☐  tens
 -20         -   ☐  tens
               ──────
                 ☐  tens
```

Explain It ● Daily Reasoning

How does knowing 6 − 4 = 2 help you
find the difference for 60 − 40?

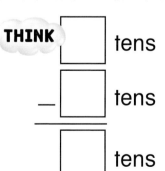

6 − 4   60 − 40

50 − 20 means
5 tens − 2 tens.

THINK

50	5 tens
−20	−2 tens
30	3 tens

Subtract.

1.	2.	3.	4.	5.
70	40	60	80	40
−50	−40	−30	−70	−10

6.	7.	8.	9.	10.
90	50	20	60	70
−20	−30	−10	−20	−40

11.	12.	13.	14.	15.
80	30	90	50	40
−50	−20	−60	−10	−20

Problem Solving

Visual Thinking

Write the number sentence
that tells about the picture.

16.

_____ ◯ _____ ◯ _____

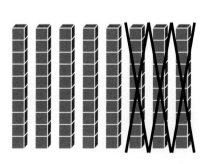

 Write About It • Look at Exercise 16.
Write a math story to go with
your number sentence.

 HOME ACTIVITY • Ask your child to explain how to find the difference for 70 − 40.

Name _____

Subtract Tens and Ones

Explore

Subtract.   28
           − 5
           ‾‾‾‾

STEP 1	STEP 2	STEP 3
Show 28.	Subtract the ones.	Subtract the tens.

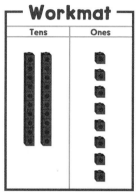

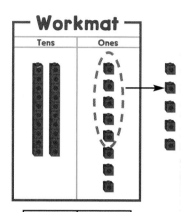

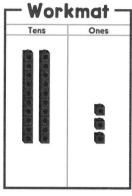

tens	ones
2	8
−	5

tens	ones
2	8
−	5
	3

tens	ones
2	8
−	5
2	3

Connect

Use Workmat 3 and to subtract.
Write the difference.

1.

tens	ones
4	7
	5

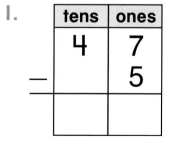

2.

tens	ones
1	9
	4

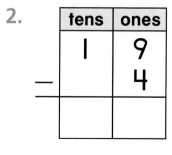

Explain It • Daily Reasoning

How could you find the difference for
27 − 4 without using blocks?

Use Workmat 3 and to subtract.
Write the difference.

1.

tens	ones
3	9
−	2
3	7

tens	ones

2.

tens	ones
4	5
−	2

tens	ones

3.

tens	ones
2	6
−	5

tens	ones

4.

tens	ones
1	7
−	3

tens	ones

Problem Solving

Algebra

Write the missing numbers.

5.

tens	ones
4	9
−	
4	1

6.

tens	ones
8	6
−	
8	0

7.

tens	ones
1	8
−	
1	4

8.

tens	ones
7	5
−	
7	2

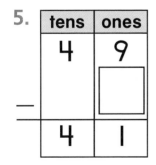

Write About It • Look at Exercise 5. How
could you draw to prove your answer?

HOME ACTIVITY • Ask your child to explain how to find the difference for 48 − 3.

Subtract Money

Learn

Subtract the ones. Then subtract the tens.

Add numbers.

$$\begin{array}{r} 34 \\ -13 \\ \hline 1 \end{array} \qquad \begin{array}{r} 34 \\ -13 \\ \hline 21 \end{array}$$

Add money.

$$\begin{array}{r} 34¢ \\ -13¢ \\ \hline 1¢ \end{array} \qquad \begin{array}{r} 34¢ \\ -13¢ \\ \hline 21¢ \end{array}$$

Subtract money amounts the same way you subtract other numbers.

Check

Subtract.

1. $\begin{array}{r} 26¢ \\ -13¢ \\ \hline ¢ \end{array}$
2. $\begin{array}{r} 39¢ \\ -22¢ \\ \hline ¢ \end{array}$
3. $\begin{array}{r} 68¢ \\ -32¢ \\ \hline ¢ \end{array}$
4. $\begin{array}{r} 54¢ \\ -30¢ \\ \hline ¢ \end{array}$
5. $\begin{array}{r} 93¢ \\ -62¢ \\ \hline ¢ \end{array}$

6. $\begin{array}{r} 69¢ \\ -\ 7¢ \\ \hline ¢ \end{array}$
7. $\begin{array}{r} 77¢ \\ -33¢ \\ \hline ¢ \end{array}$
8. $\begin{array}{r} 97¢ \\ -76¢ \\ \hline ¢ \end{array}$
9. $\begin{array}{r} 29¢ \\ -19¢ \\ \hline ¢ \end{array}$
10. $\begin{array}{r} 48¢ \\ -18¢ \\ \hline ¢ \end{array}$

11. $\begin{array}{r} 86¢ \\ -23¢ \\ \hline ¢ \end{array}$
12. $\begin{array}{r} 56¢ \\ -25¢ \\ \hline ¢ \end{array}$
13. $\begin{array}{r} 45¢ \\ -12¢ \\ \hline ¢ \end{array}$
14. $\begin{array}{r} 69¢ \\ -45¢ \\ \hline ¢ \end{array}$
15. $\begin{array}{r} 39¢ \\ -22¢ \\ \hline ¢ \end{array}$

Explain It • Daily Reasoning

What happens when both numbers have the same ones and tens? Why?

Subtract.

1.   68¢
    −25¢
    ___¢

2.   75¢
    −50¢
    ___¢

3.   89¢
    −64¢
    ___¢

4.   45¢
    −44¢
    ___¢

5.   35¢
    −12¢
    ___¢

6.   56¢
    −36¢
    ___¢

7.   64¢
    −14¢
    ___¢

8.   90¢
    −40¢
    ___¢

9.   28¢
    −24¢
    ___¢

10.   65¢
    −20¢
    ___¢

11.   95¢
    −70¢
    ___¢

12.   83¢
    −22¢
    ___¢

13.   17¢
    − 6¢
    ___¢

14.   75¢
    −25¢
    ___¢

15.   88¢
    −28¢
    ___¢

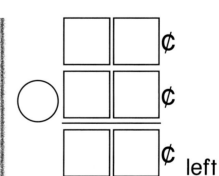

Problem Solving
Application

Write the problem. Solve it.

16. Greg has 49¢.
    He spends 24¢ for bird food.
    How much does he have left?

___¢

○   ___¢

___¢ left

 Write About It • Suppose Greg has 68¢ and buys something different. Write your own story problem and solve it.

 HOME ACTIVITY • Write a two-digit subtraction problem. Have your child show it with pennies and dimes and solve it.

Name _____

Problem Solving Skill
Make Reasonable Estimates

THINK:
Using tens can
help me estimate.

Without adding or subtracting,
circle the best estimate.

1. Jon picks 14 flowers.
   Sam picks 5 flowers.
   About how many do
   they pick in all?

   Too few.   about 2 flowers

   (about 20 flowers)

   Too many.   about 200 flowers

2. The school has 30 books
   about animals.
   Kim takes out 13 books.
   About how many are left?

   about 2 books

   about 20 books

   about 200 books

3. Aman saw 10 monkeys.
   Carla counted 10 more.
   Logan saw 6 other monkeys.
   About how many did
   they see in all?

   about 10 monkeys

   about 30 monkeys

   about 100 monkeys

4. 40 birds are in the forest.
   12 fly away.
   About how many birds
   are left in the forest?

   about 5 birds

   about 30 birds

   about 100 birds

PROBLEM SOLVING

Problem Solving Practice

THINK: I do not need an exact answer.

Without adding or subtracting, circle the best estimate.

1. Lana's bird eats 5 seeds for breakfast.
   It eats 5 seeds for lunch.
   It eats 7 more seeds for dinner.
   About how many seeds does it eat in one day?

   about 5 seeds

   about 20 seeds

   about 100 seeds

2. Cam walks 22 steps in the forest.
   She walks 26 more.
   About how many steps does she walk in all?

   about 5 steps

   about 50 steps

   about 500 steps

3. Connor has 50¢.
   He buys a banana for 26¢.
   About how much money does he still have?

   about 5¢

   about 25¢

   about 100¢

4. 100 people are at the park.
   52 of them leave.
   About how many people are still at the park?

   about 5 people

   about 50 people

   about 100 people

HOME ACTIVITY • Ask your child how he or she chose the answer for each problem.

Name _____

Extra Practice

Add or subtract.

1.	2.	3.	4.	5.
30 +50	70 +10	20 +50	90 −30	60 −10

Use Workmat 3 and to add or subtract.

6.

tens	ones
1	5
+	4

tens	ones

7.

tens	ones
1	9
−	7

tens	ones

Add or subtract.

8.	9.	10.	11.	12.
13¢ +35¢ ¢	20¢ +47¢ ¢	83¢ −21¢ ¢	65¢ − 3¢ ¢	52¢ −11¢ ¢

Problem Solving

Without adding or subtracting,
circle the best estimate.

13. Juan sees 12 frogs.
Elsa sees 11 more frogs.
About how many frogs
do they see in all?

about 5 frogs

about 20 frogs

about 100 frogs

Name _____

✓ Review/Test

Concepts and Skills

Add or subtract.

1.	2.	3.	4.	5.
70 +20	40 +30	50 +40	80 −10	60 −20

Use Workmat 3 and  to add or subtract.

6.

tens	ones
2	4
+	5

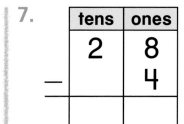

7.

tens	ones
2	8
−	4

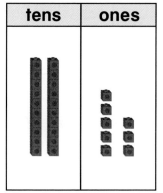

Add or subtract.

8.	9.	10.	11.	12.
31¢ +26¢ ____¢	15¢ +32¢ ____¢	65¢ −43¢ ____¢	58¢ −27¢ ____¢	26¢ − 4¢ ____¢

Problem Solving

Without adding or subtracting,
circle the best estimate.

13. Sam sees 25 lizards.
Then he sees 12 more.
About how many
lizards does Sam see?

about 10 lizards

about 40 lizards

about 100 lizards

Name _____

Choose the answer for questions 1– 4.

1.   53
    + 4

   35 ○   57 ○

   45 ○   81 ○

2.   85¢
    −63¢

   15¢ ○   21¢ ○

   22¢ ○   34¢ ○

3. Which shows 50¢?

 ○    ○    ○    ○

4. Which is the best estimate?

Rachel jumps rope 23 times. She jumps rope 33 more times. About how many times does she jump rope in all?

about 5 ○   about 55 ○

about 15 ○   about 500 ○

Show What You Know

5. Use . Explain two ways to make 90. Write the numbers.

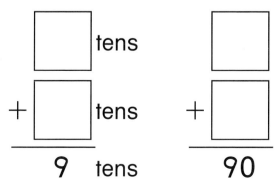

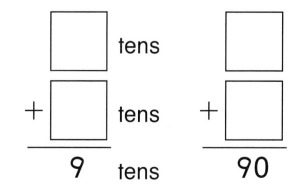

Name _____

MATH GAME

Math Path

Play with a partner.

1. Stack the number cards face down.

2. Put your  on START. Toss the 🎲.
   Move your that many spaces.

3. Take 2 cards. Use the numbers to make a two digit number to complete the problem.

4. Write the problem on paper.

5. Solve. Your partner will check your answer.

6. If you are not correct, lose a turn.

7. The first player to get to END wins.

You will need

2 ♟ 🎲

2 sets of 0–6 [0]

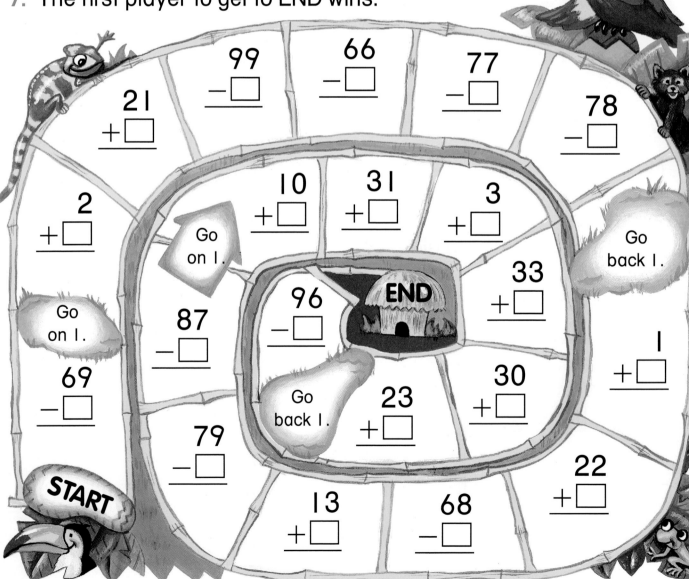

30 Probability

FUN FACTS

These puppies are red, and black and tan. For every 3 puppies born, 2 are red, and 1 is black and tan.

Name

✅ Check What You Know

Could It Happen?

1. Circle the picture that shows which is more likely to happen.

2. Circle the picture that shows which is less likely to happen.

Chance

Use a paper clip and a pencil to make a spinner.
Spin 10 times.
Mark a tally mark in the table after each spin.
Circle the color the paper clip landed on more often.

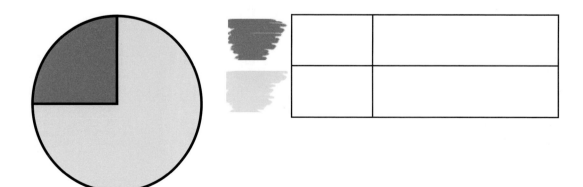

Use this page to review important skills needed for this chapter.

Certain or Impossible

Vocabulary
certain
impossible

Learn

Pulling a green 🟩 is certain.

Pulling a red 🟥 is impossible.

Check

Mark an X to tell if pulling the cube
from the bowl is certain or impossible.

			Certain	Impossible
1.	🟦 blue		X	
2.	🟥 red			
3.	🟨 yellow			
4.	🟩 green			

Explain It • Daily Reasoning

Suppose a bowl had only yellow cubes in it. What
color would be certain to be pulled? Explain.

Mark an X to tell if pulling the cube from the bowl is certain or impossible.

		Certain	Impossible
1.	yellow		
2.	red		
3.	green		
4.	blue		

Problem Solving

Application

5. Circle the bowl from which pulling a ■ is certain.

 Write About It ● Draw a bowl from which pulling a ▣ is certain. Then draw a bowl from which pulling a ▣ is impossible. Write **certain** or **impossible** under each bowl.

⬠ **HOME ACTIVITY** • Put some pennies in a bowl. Ask your child if pulling a dime from the bowl is certain or impossible. Have him or her explain.

More Likely, Less Likely

Vocabulary

more likely

less likely

Learn

Pulling yellow is more likely than pulling green.

Pulling green is less likely than pulling yellow.

Check

Write **more** or **less** to tell how likely each color is to be pulled from the bowl.

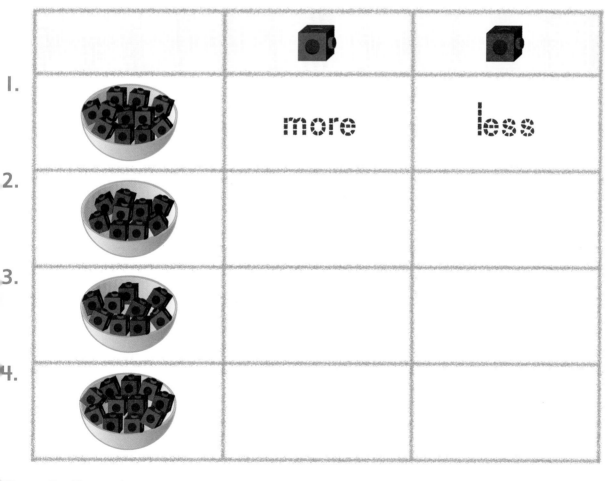

1.	more	less
2.		
3.		
4.		

Explain It • Daily Reasoning

How can you tell which color is more likely to be pulled?

Draw ▣ and ▣ to tell how likely each
color is to be pulled from the bowl.

		More Likely	**Less Likely**
1.			
2.			
3.			
4.			

Problem Solving

Visual Thinking

5. How could you change the cubes so that
   pulling a ▣ is more likely than pulling a ▣?
   Draw and color a picture to show
   your answer.

 Write About It • Draw and color a bowl from
which pulling a ▣ is more likely than pulling a ▣.
Then draw and color a bowl from which pulling a
▣ is more likely than pulling a ▣.

HOME ACTIVITY • Put 6 pennies and 3 dimes in a bowl. Ask your child if pulling a dime is more
likely or less likely than pulling a penny. Have him or her explain.

Equally Likely

Learn

Pulling yellow and pulling red are **equally likely**.

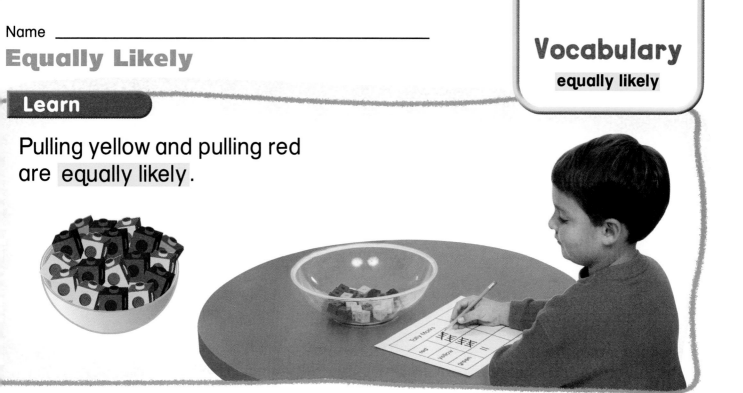

Check

Draw cubes to show which colors are equally likely to be pulled from the bowl.

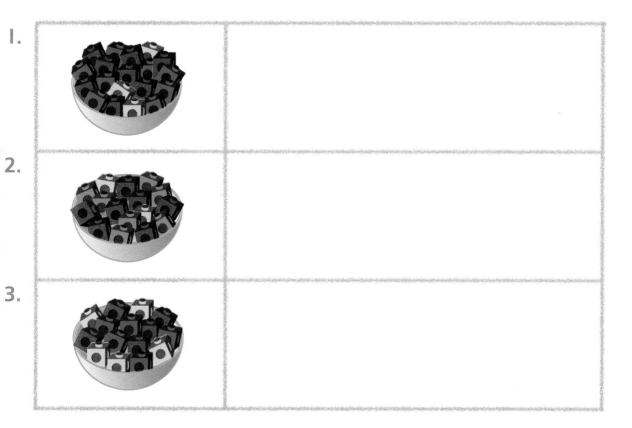

1.

2.

3.

Explain It • Daily Reasoning

What 2 cubes could you add to the last bowl so that pulling 🔲 is less likely than pulling 🔲 or 🔲 ?

Draw cubes to show which colors are equally likely to be pulled from the bowl.

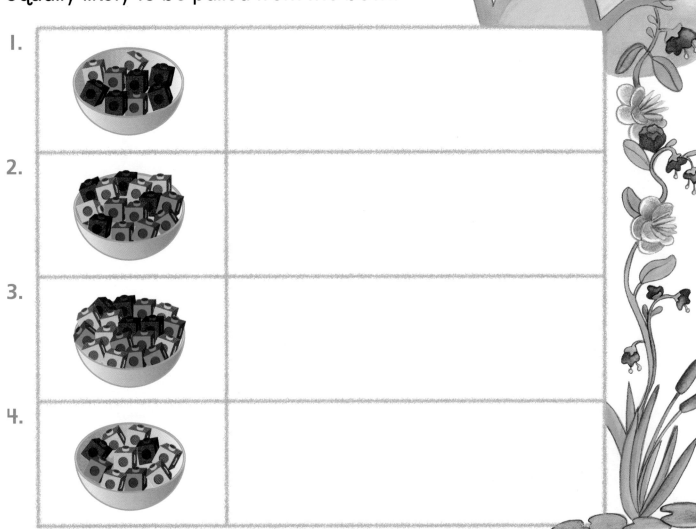

1.

2.

3.

4.

Problem Solving

Visual Thinking

5. How could you change the cubes so that pulling 🎲 and pulling 🎲 are equally likely? Draw and color a picture.

Write About It ● Draw and color a bowl from which pulling a ▬ and pulling a ▬ are equally likely. Write **equally likely** under the bowl.

🔷 **HOME ACTIVITY** • Put 6 pennies and 6 dimes in a bowl. Ask your child if a dime is more likely or less likely to be pulled or if both coins are equally likely to be pulled.

Problem Solving Skill
Make a Prediction

Use a ✏ and a 📎 to make a spinner.

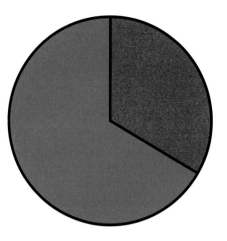

Predict. If you spin the pointer 10 times,
on which color will it stop more often?

Circle that color.

red   blue

Check. Spin 10 times.
Make a tally mark after each spin.
Write the totals.

On which color did your
pointer stop more often?

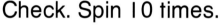

	Tally Marks	Total
red		
blue		

I. Predict. If you spin the pointer 10 more times,
on which color will it stop more often?
Circle that color.

red   blue

Then spin to check.

I. Use a ✏️ and a 📎 to make a spinner.

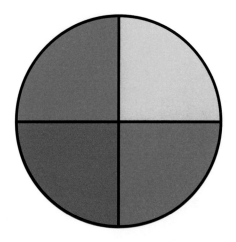

Predict. If you spin the pointer 15 times, on which color will it stop most often?

Circle that color.

green   yellow   blue

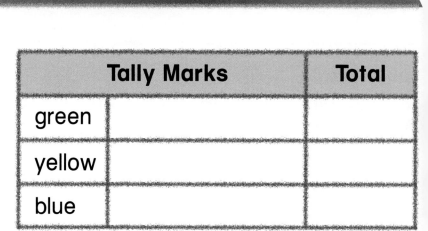

Check. Spin 15 times. Make a tally mark after each spin. Write the totals.

On which color did your pointer stop most often?

	Tally Marks	Total
green		
yellow		
blue		

2. Predict. If you spin the pointer 10 more times, on which color will it stop most often?
Circle that color.

green   yellow   blue

Then spin to check.

🏠 **HOME ACTIVITY** • Make a spinner divided into 4 equal parts. Color two parts the same color and each of the other parts a different color. Have your child predict on which color the pointer will land most often. Spin 10 times to check.

Name _____

Extra Practice

Mark an X to tell if pulling the cube
from the bowl is certain or impossible.

		Certain	Impossible
1.	blue		

Draw 🎲 and 🎲 to tell how likely each color
is to be pulled from the bowl.

	More Likely	Less Likely
2.		

Draw cubes to show which colors are
equally likely to be pulled from the bowl.

3.	

Problem Solving

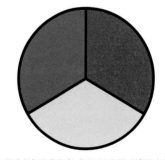

4. Use a ✏️ and a 📎 to make a spinner.
   Predict. If you spin the pointer 15 times,
   on which color will it stop most often?
   Circle that color.

   blue   red   yellow

   Check. Spin 15 times.
   Make a tally mark
   after each spin.
   Write the totals.

	Tally Marks	Total
blue		
red		
yellow		

✅ Review/Test

Concepts and Skills

Mark an X to tell if pulling the cube
from the bowl is certain or impossible.

		Certain	Impossible
1.	yellow		

Draw 🔲 and 🔲 to tell how likely each color
is to be pulled from the bowl.

		More Likely	Less Likely
2.			

Draw cubes to show which colors are
equally likely to be pulled from the bowl.

3.		

Problem Solving

4. Use a ✏️ and a 📎 to make a spinner.
Predict. If you spin the pointer 10 times,
on which color will it stop more often?
Circle that color.

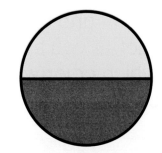

yellow   red

Check. Spin 10 times.
Make a tally mark
after each spin.
Write the totals.

	Tally Marks	Total
yellow		
red		

Getting Ready for the ★EOG Test
Chapters 1–30

Choose the answer for questions 1 – 4.

1. Amanda's mom baked some cookies. Amanda ate 2. Her friend ate 3. How many cookies did they eat altogether?

8	7	6	5
○	○	○	○

---

2. Which completes the sentence?

It is impossible to pull a _____.

○   ○   ○   ○

3. Predict. If you spin the pointer 10 times on which color will it stop more often?

red   green
○   ○

yellow   blue
○   ○

---

4. Which completes the sentence?

I am least likely to pull a _____.

○   ○   ○

Show What You Know

5.

Color the cubes to explain which cubes are equally likely and less likely to be pulled from the bowl.

I am equally likely to pull a 🎲 or a 🎲.

I am less likely to pull a 🎲 than a 🎲.

IT'S IN THE BAG
Cool Cat Hat

PROJECT You will make a hat and measure with paper clips how far it flies.

You Will Need

- Lunch-size bag
- Paper plate
- Crayons
- Scissors
- Tape
- Paper clips

Directions

1 Cut the circle out of the paper plate. Decorate the hat.

2 Decorate the bag on all sides.

3 Cut slits around the bag. Push them through the paper plate and tape them to it.

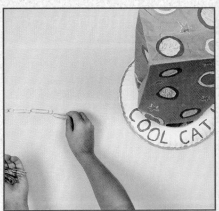

4 Throw your hat in the air. Measure with paper clips how far your hat flew.

CAT'S COOL HAT

written by Fay Robinson
illustrated by Lori Lohstoeter

🎩 This book will help me review measurement.

This book belongs to _____.

"Good morning, Turtle," said Cat.
"How do you like my cool hat?"

"It's very nice," said Turtle.
"You do look cool!"

B

The wind blew Cat's hat into the pond.
"Help!" called Cat.
"I need a long stick to reach my hat."

Turtle said, "Cat, I can get your hat."

Squirrel got a stick.

About how long is this stick?

about _____  long

D

Squirrel's stick wasn't long enough.

Turtle said, "Cat, I can get your hat."

Rabbit got a stick.
It wasn't long enough.

About how long is this stick?

about _____ ⬭ long

Cat was not cool now.
"I'll never get my hat back!" he said.

Turtle said, "Cat, I can get your hat."

"Oh, Turtle, I don't think so," said Cat.
"There aren't any sticks long enough."

But Turtle didn't need a stick.
He swam out to the hat.
Then he swam back with
the hat on his back.

"Oh, thank you, Turtle!" said Cat.
"You are the coolest one of all!"

Name _____

PROBLEM SOLVING IN NORTH CAROLINA

Morehead City, NC

On the Coast

You can see wild horses and find sea shells on the beach at Morehead City.

How many centimeters long is each shell? Use a centimeter ruler and measure.

1

_____ centimeters

2

_____ centimeters

3

_____ centimeters

CHALLENGE

Area

How many units does it take to cover this shape?

_4_ units

How many units does it take to cover
the shape? Use 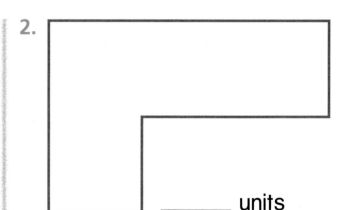. Then count.

1.

_____ units

2.

_____ units

3.

_____ units

4.

_____ units

Name _____

✅ Study Guide and Review

Vocabulary

Draw a line to the tool you use to measure with each unit.

1. **centimeter**

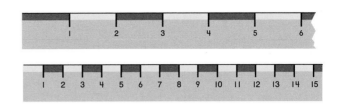

2. **inch**

Skills and Concepts

About how long is this?

3. Use an inch ruler to measure. _____ inches

4. Now use a centimeter ruler to measure. _____ centimeters

Look at each object.
Circle the better estimate.

Object	Estimate
5.	about 1 pound about 10 pounds
6.	about 1 pound about 10 pounds

Draw cubes to show which colors are equally likely to be pulled from the bowl.

7.

Read the temperature. Color the thermometer to show the temperature

8. 20°F

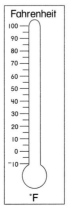

Add or subtract.

9. 20
  + 40

10. 60
   − 30

11. 50
   + 30

12. 71¢
   + 23¢

13. 87¢
   − 25¢

14. 98¢
   − 50¢

Use Workmat 3 and 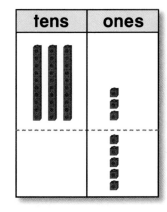 to add.

15.

tens	ones
2	6
+	3

tens	ones

16.

tens	ones
3	3
+	5

tens	ones

Use Workmat 3 and 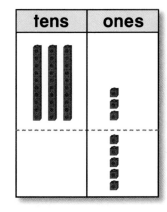 to subtract.

17.

tens	ones
2	9
−	4

tens	ones

18.

tens	ones
4	7
−	3

tens	ones

Problem Solving

Circle the best tool for finding each measurement.

19. Which shoe is heavier?

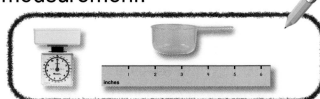

20. Which holds more?

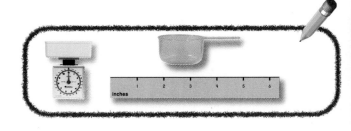

Performance Assessment

Hannah's New Lunch Box

Hannah wants to measure her new lunch box.

Here are the tools she can use.

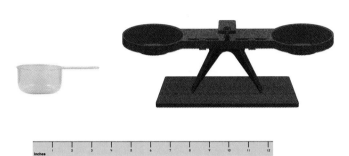

- Circle one of the tools.

- Draw a picture to show how Hannah can use the tool.

- Use this tool to measure a real lunch box.

- Estimate what you think your measurement will be.

- Then measure.

Show your work.

Estimate _____   Measurement _____

TECHNOLOGY

Calculator • Find the Greatest Sum

$$25 + 35 + 16 = \underline{\hspace{2cm}}$$
$$65 + 11 + 23 = \underline{\hspace{2cm}}$$
$$70 + 12 + 14 = \underline{\hspace{2cm}}$$

Which has the **greatest** sum?

Use a 🖩. Add.

Press ON/C [2] [5] [+] [3] [5] [+] [1] [6] [=]

Write the answer. [76]

Press ON/C [6] [5] [+] [1] [1] [+] [2] [3] [=]

Write the answer. [ ]

Press ON/C [7] [0] [+] [1] [2] [+] [1] [4] [=]

Write the answer. [ ]

Compare. _____ is the greatest sum.

Practice and Problem Solving

Use a 🖩. Find each sum. Circle the greatest sum.

1. $15 + 23 + 31 = \underline{\hspace{2cm}}$

   $44 + 11 + 13 = \underline{\hspace{2cm}}$

   $10 + 24 + 65 = \underline{\hspace{2cm}}$

   Which place value shows
   which sum is greatest?
   Underline it.

   tens   ones

2. $21 + 22 + 23 = \underline{\hspace{2cm}}$

   $51 + 10 + 15 = \underline{\hspace{2cm}}$

   $45 + 19 + 11 = \underline{\hspace{2cm}}$

   Which place value shows
   which sum is greatest?
   Underline it.

   tens   ones

PICTURE GLOSSARY

above (page 269)

add (page 5)

$$3 + 2 = 5$$

addition sentence (page 9)

$$4 + 1 = 5$$

after (page 181)

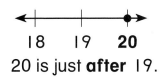

20 is just **after** 19.

afternoon (page 419)

are left (page 33)

3 **are left**.

balance (page 457)

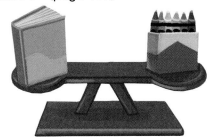

bar graph (page 145)

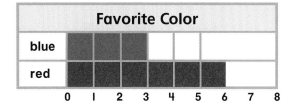

before (page 181)

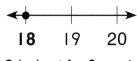

18 is just **before** 19.

below (page 269)

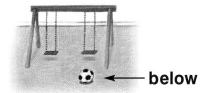

beside (page 270)

between (page 181)

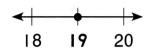

19 is **between** 18 and 20.

centimeter (page 447)

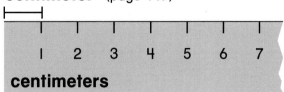

centimeters

certain (page 507)

Pulling green is **certain**.

chart (page 423)

Subject	Start	End
math		
science		

circle (page 255)

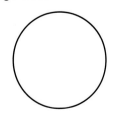

close by (page 269)

closed figure (page 267)

concrete graph (page 139)

The Fruit Bowl					
apples					
oranges					
bananas					

cone (page 251)

corner (page 253)

corner →

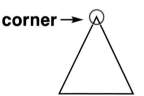

count back (page 101)

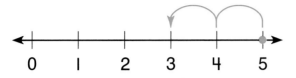

$$5 - 2 = 3$$

Start at 5. **Count back** two.

You are on 3.

count backward (page 183)

52, 51, 50

Count backward from 52.

count forward (page 183)

52, 53, 54

Count forward from 52.

count on (page 71)

$$8 + 2 = 10$$

Say 8. **Count on** two.

9, 10

cube (page 251)

cup (page 473)

cylinder (page 251)

day (page 417)

The **days** of the week are:
**Sunday, Monday, Tuesday,
Wednesday, Thursday, Friday,**
and **Saturday.**

difference (page 35)

$$9 - 3 = \mathbf{6}$$

difference

dime (page 369)

or

10¢
10 cents

dollar (page 387)

1 dollar = 100¢

doubles (page 75)

$$4 + 4 = 8$$

doubles plus one (page 213)

$$4 + 4 = 8, \text{ so } 4 + 5 = 9$$

down (page 271)

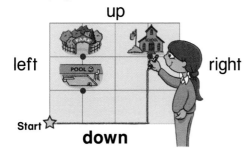

up

left   right

Start ☆

down

equal parts (page 351)

equally likely (page 511)

Pulling blue and red are
equally likely.

equals = (page 5)
            the same as

$4 + 1 = 5$

4 plus 1 **equals** 5.

estimate (page 167)

about 10 buttons

even numbers (page 199)

0, 2, 4, 6, 8, 10 . . .

evening (page 419)

face (page 253)

fact family (page 121)

$5 + 3 = 8$ $3 + 5 = 8$

$8 - 3 = 5$ $8 - 5 = 3$

far (page 269)

far

feet (page 445)

Use **feet** to measure
longer objects.

fewest (page 384)

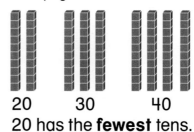

20   30   40

20 has the **fewest** tens.

foot (page 445)

12 inches = 1 **foot**

gram (page 461)

This paper clip is about 1 **gram**.

half dollar (page 387)

 or **50¢ half dollar**

half hour (page 407)

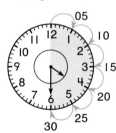

4:30

There are 30 minutes in a **half hour**.

hour (page 405)

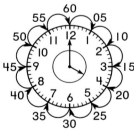

4:00

There are 60 minutes in an **hour**.

hour hand (page 401)

hour hand

hundred (page 163)

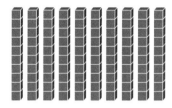

impossible (page 507)

Pulling red is **impossible.**

in all (page 3)

There are 3 **in all**.

inch (page 443)

| 1 | 2 | 3 |

inches

is equal to (page 180)

25 **is equal to** 25.

25 = 25

is greater than (page 175)

5 **is greater than** 1.

5 > 1

is less than (page 177)

3 **is less than** 5.

$3 < 5$

kilogram (page 461)

This large book is about 1 **kilogram**.

left (page 271)

up

left right

Start down

less likely (page 509)

Pulling red is **less likely** than pulling blue.

line of symmetry (page 273)

Both parts match.

liter (page 475)

longest (page 439)

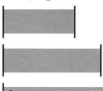

longest

make a ten (page 303)

Move 1 counter into the ten frame. **Make a ten.**

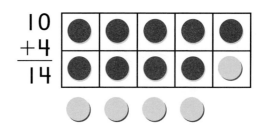

$$\begin{array}{r} 10 \\ +4 \\ \hline 14 \end{array}$$

minus (page 35)

$3 - 2 = 1$

3 **minus** 2 equals 1.

minute (page 403)

You can estimate a **minute**.

minute hand (page 401)

minute hand

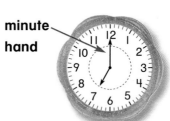

month (page 417)

December						
Sunday	Monday	Tuesday	Wednesday	Thursday	Friday	Saturday
			1	2	3	4
5	6	7	8	9	10	11
12	13	14	15	16	17	18
19	20	21	22	23	24	25
26	27	28	29	30	31	

more (page 143)

40   30

40 has **more** tens than 30.

more likely (page 509)

Pulling red is **more likely** than blue.

morning (page 419)

near (page 270)

next to (page 270)

nickel (page 367)

   or   5¢
5 cents

number line (page 101)

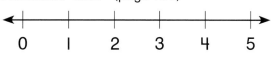

0   1   2   3   4   5

o'clock (page 401)

The clock shows 1 **o'clock**.

odd numbers (page 199)

1, 3, 5, 7, 9 . . .

$\frac{1}{4}$ **one fourth** (page 353)

$\frac{1}{2}$ **one half** (page 351)

$\frac{1}{3}$ **one third** (page 355)

ones (page 157)

There are 3 **ones**.

open figure (page 267)

Order Property (page 17)

$2 + 3 = 5$ and $3 + 2 = 5$

You can add in any **order** and still get the same sum.

ordinal numbers (page 203)

first   second   third

over (page 269)

over ⟶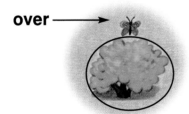

pattern (page 283)

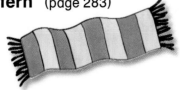

pattern unit (page 285)

penny (pennies) (page 367)

 or

I ¢
I cent

picture graph (page 141)

Our Pets			
dog	🐕	🐕	
cat	🐈	🐈	🐈
rabbit	🐇		

pint (page 473)

plus + (page 5)

$4 + 3 = 7$

4 **plus** 3 equals 7.

pound (page 459)

This weighs one **pound**.

pyramid (page 251)

quart (page 473)

quarter (page 385)

 or **25¢**
25 cents

rectangle (page 255)

rectangular prism (page 251)

related facts (page 105)

2 + 3 = 5 is **related** to

5 − 3 = 2 and 5 − 2 = 3.

right (page 271)

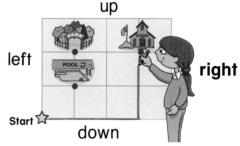

rule (page 91)

Add 2	
4	6
6	8
8	10

The **rule** is add 2.

shortest (page 439)

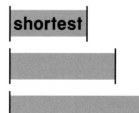

side (page 257)

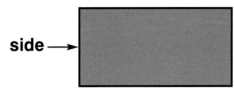

side →

slide (page 275)

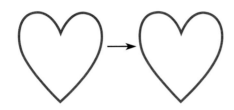

sort (page 137)

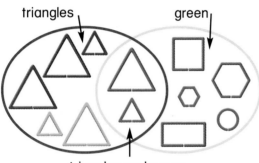

triangles

green

triangles and green

You can **sort** these shapes.

sphere (page 251)

square (page 255)

subtract (page 35)

$6 - 2 = 4$

subtraction sentence (page 37)

$8 - 2 = 6$

sum (page 5)

$5 + 1 = 6$

sum

tally mark (page 143)

~~||||~~ | ← tally mark

tally table (page 143)

Colors of Butterflies		Total
red	~~||||~~	5
blue	~~||||~~ ||	7

temperature (page 477)

The **temperature** is 65 degrees.

ten less (page 185)

25	35	45

25 is **ten less** than 35.

ten more (page 185)

25	35	**45**

45 is **ten more** than 35.

tens (page 157)

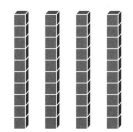

to the left of (page 270)

to the
left of

to the right of (page 270)

to the
right of

trade (page 383)

triangle (page 255)

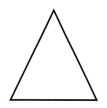

turn (page 275)

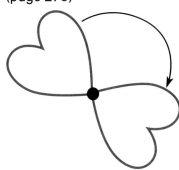

up (page 271)

up

left

right

Start

down

zero 0 (page 7)

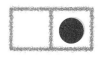

$0 + 1 = 1$